Contemporary Preschool Education:
A Program for Young Children

Contemporary Preschool Education:
A Program for Young Children

SHIRLEY G. MOORE

Professor of Child Psychology
and Director of Laboratory Nursery School
Institute of Child Development
University of Minnesota
Minneapolis, Minnesota

SALLY KILMER

Assistant Professor of Child Psychology
and Coordinator for Early Childhood
Education Planning Committee
Institute of Child Development
University of Minnesota
Minneapolis, Minnesota

Photographs by Myron Papiz

JOHN WILEY & SONS, INC.,
New York · London · Sydney · Toronto

014933

Library of Congress Cataloging in Publication Data:

Moore, Shirley G   1936–
    Contemporary preschool education.

    Bibliography: p.
    1. Education, Preschool—1965–   I. Kilmer,
Sally, joint author.   II. Title.

LB1140.2.M65   372.21'09'046   73-1922
ISBN 0-471-61463-7

Printed in the United States of America

10 9 8 7 6 5 4 3 2 1

Preface

This book is written for teaching staffs, trainers of teachers, parents, and others who work with young children or who are preparing to do so. It examines a contemporary preschool program at the Laboratory Nursery School in the Institute of Child Development, University of Minnesota. The nursery school described here integrates the educational philosophy of preacademic, school readiness programs and traditional, child-centered programs in an open and supportive classroom environment. It is a model of early childhood education that is consistent with our understanding and knowledge of early development.

The book begins with general background information about the school in which the program is being carried out and a statement of the particular educational needs of young children. The school curriculum and practices are then described in considerable detail. The book is practical with many specific suggestions for the classroom teacher. Among the curricular content areas discussed are social studies, language arts activities, prereading and premath activities, and the development of general cognitive skills. Specific school activities are given as *examples* of the kinds of things teachers might do; they are descriptive rather than prescriptive and are intended to stimulate thinking of still other curricular activities.

The educational philosophy espoused also places value on the school's contribution to the child's social development through play activities and free social interchange with adults and peers. Among the relevant topics discussed are classroom discipline and control techniques, independence training, achievement behavior, the development of a good self-image, and the management of aggression. The nature and importance of communication between home and school are carefully examined.

The final chapters of the book broaden the reader's perspective of the current issues and needs in the field of preschool education. Contemporary nursery school models, including the Montessori model, are briefly described and compared. Recent research activities are discussed and reflections on the current state of the field are presented.

Shirley G. Moore
Sally Kilmer

Minneapolis
December 1972

Acknowledgments

Throughout the preparation of this manuscript, we benefited greatly from the support and suggestions of our colleagues at the Institute of Child Development. We thank particularly Willard W. Hartup, Director of the Institute of Child Development, and Harold W. Stevenson, the former Director (now at the University of Michigan) for their encouragement and their critical reading of the manuscript in its initial stages. We are also indebted to the many truly excellent teachers in the laboratory school whose curriculum activities and helpful suggestions over the years have contributed substantially to our thinking as we have gradually defined and elaborated our educational philosophy.

We give special thanks to Dr. Ruth Updegraff whose thoughtful and sound approach to the education of young children has influenced, directly and indirectly, literally hundreds of this country's developmental psychologists and preschool educators over a period of many years. Her perceptive observations of young children and their teachers led her to insights that have stood the test of time. Ruth Updegraff's friendship and counsel were an invaluable source of inspiration to Shirley Moore while at the State University of Iowa.

We also thank Marcy Russell Hull who guided Sally Kilmer's early experiences in the nursery school during her graduate days at the Pennsylvania State University and who introduced us to each other.

The outstanding pictures accompanying the text were taken by our friend Myron Papiz. We are grateful for his patience and his willingness to become acquainted with the children and with our educational philosophy so as to provide the "right" pictures for this book. We appreciate his long hours in the nursery school and in the darkroom.

S.G.M.
S.K.

Contents

014933

1
Introduction

1 Introduction

During the past decade there has been a steadily growing interest in improving and expanding educational opportunities for young children in the United States. Group experiences away from home have become a popular and acceptable means of supplementing a child's home education and of offering alternative child care arrangements for working parents. Increasing numbers of children are participating in a whole spectrum of programs that range from half-day nursery schools to nine- to ten-hour day care centers.

Until 1965 interest in the education of young children was maintained in this country primarily by parents, a few educators, and psychologists and social workers. Although the number of private, cooperative, and community sponsored preschool programs had been increasing steadily prior to Head Start, the federally sponsored Head Start programs have been responsible for that surge of interest in early childhood education on the part of public officials, community planners, and laymen. With the funding of Head Start, the number of programs for young children mushroomed. An estimated 1,500,000 preschool children are currently enrolled in nursery schools and Head Start. The number of children enrolled in public and private nursery schools alone increased 83 percent (from 471,000 to 860,000) in the five years between 1964 and 1969. In addition to the children in nursery schools and Head Start, there are now more than 3 million children in kindergarten and, at least, 200,000 children under the age of six in group day care programs in this country. The growing awareness of the need to upgrade day care services for the children of working mothers has also added to the investment in sound educational programs for young children. The level of federal support for all-day programs that incorporate educational experiences for young children as well as the provision of good care has increased markedly.

If this rate of expansion of programs for young children continues, by 1980, approximately 90 percent of all five-year-olds, 40 percent of all four-year-olds, and 20 percent of all three-year-olds will be enrolled in some form of preschool activity.

The prevalence of preschools and day care centers in most communities has contributed to a growing curiosity about programs for young chil-

3

dren and a need for information. The purpose of this book is to help fulfill this need by offering, in pictures and in text, an example of a contemporary nursery school program. From it the reader will learn what three- and four-year-old children do in one nursery school, the materials and equipment they use, and what they learn there.

2
The Nursery School Program

2 The Nursery School Program

The primary goal of all nursery schools is to provide sound educational experiences for young children; however, programs vary widely in the specifics of their educational philosophy and the content of their curriculum. The traditional nursery school emphasizes social skills, the learning potential of play, and the value of creativity in the use of materials and equipment, placing relatively little emphasis on formal instruction. Montessori schools and many of the demonstration experimental nursery schools, on the other hand, provide highly structured learning materials to be used by the child in prescribed ways, placing relatively little emphasis on the free exploration of materials and equipment and informal social interaction. Many contemporary programs for preschoolers are someplace between these two extremes. The program described here is one example. It is an attempt to provide a balance of informal social experiences and challenging intellectual experiences. Learning opportunities are at times structured, teacher-directed activities, but at other times the children are encouraged to explore and investigate on their own without direct teacher instruction.

This program is being carried on in the Laboratory Nursery School of the Institute of Child Development at the University of Minnesota. The pictures were taken in four nursery school groups of from 18 to 20 children each. Most of the children shown are between three and five years of age. They attend the school half-days and are grouped by age, with the three- to four-year-olds together and the four- to five-year-olds together. The school's curriculum has been successfully implemented with racially and socioeconomically integrated groups of children representing both low and middle income families.

The goals of the program are:

1. To develop in each child an active curiosity about the world in which he lives and an enthusiasm for learning based on personal satisfaction and involvement.

2. To provide the child with opportunities to develop basic learning skills and to acquire new information and knowledge.

7

3. To provide the child with opportunities to be expressive and creative through the use of language, physical activity and play materials, and through the media of art and music.

4. To help each child establish satisfying and successful social relations with children and adults in the school.

5. To develop in each child a concept of himself as a worthy individual, a good friend of his classmates, a good learner, and an eager participant in school activities.

It is the rule rather than the exception for the young child to be enthusiastic about nursery school. School is a place where challenges are met in an atmosphere of nurturance and support. Teachers are friendly and attentive and have both the time and inclination to talk with children about things of importance to the children themselves.

The nursery school program is flexible and informal. During much of the school day children move about freely, talk casually with each other, and work or play alone or in small groups. The teacher is unhurried. Teaching is often carried on through individual exchanges and brief conversations between a teacher and child.

The school room is composed of activity and play centers rather than being furnished with individual student desks. Centers include a doll-play and home-making area with dress-up clothes and child-sized household equipment, a block area with plenty of floor space for building, and low shelves for toys and equipment. One section of the room is furnished with tables and chairs for use with special projects, games, puzzles, small toys, and construction materials. Relatively isolated areas of the room are used for looking at books, listening to records, and painting at easels. On most days two or three additional areas of the room house things of current interest to the group. On a given day, there may be such diverse things as a "hat store," a display of Indian relics, a cross section of a tree trunk, and a collection of common objects representing different geometric shapes.

Nursery school activities are selected for their interest to the children; the ultimate value of an activity, however, is determined by the contribution it makes to an aspect of child development. Some activities are made available because they presumably contribute to the child's *intellectual development*. Included in this catagory are social studies and science activities, prereading and premath activities, language experiences, and practice in cognitive skills such as observing, reasoning, and problem-solving. Other activities contribute primarily to the child's *social development*. Play materials, for instance, entice the children into social interactions with companions, giving them opportunities to learn constructive ways of getting along with others. Some activities contribute primarily to *motor development;* yard equipment encourages climbing, jumping, running, and balancing. Still other activities contribute primarily to the development of *aesthetic interests,* through exposure to art, music, and drama both as a participant and as a consumer.

Some nursery school materials such as blocks and clay are essentially raw materials to be used by the child in many different ways. Other materials like books, puzzles, and games are used only in prescribed ways or with teacher supervision. Whether an activity is teacher-directed, or structured by the child, the teacher will make herself available when and where she feels she can respond to the child and can enhance his learning by supplying pertinent facts or helpful suggestions. When the purpose of a nursery school activity is to develop a particular skill or to produce a particular product, the teacher is more likely to emerge as the source of direction and control. Her presentation to the children is then more formal. If the children are going to bake bread, for example, a teacher will read the recipe to them and help them to follow the directions carefully so that they combine incredients in the proper order and amounts. If they are about to play a game, she will explain a few simple rules of procedure to be followed by the participants.

Although the nursery school setting generally invites social interaction, there are times when teachers support the child's undivided attention to a cognitive activity that requires concentration and effort.

Since much of the young child's learning seems to depend on direct contact with things in the environment, there is an attempt, in planning the nursery school program, to provide an abundance of concrete firsthand experiences for the child. Field trips are taken, objects of interest are brought into the school for children to observe and study, people with interesting things to show or tell are invited in, and materials are provided that encourage the child to play at performing tasks and carrying out activities that are a part of the adult culture.

THE DAILY SCHEDULE

The daily scheduling of nursery school activities is flexible so that about one half of the child's school day is spent in free play or free activity. The school day is likely to begin and end with a free-activity time while routines (such as clean up and snack) and some of the more formal group activities occur in the middle segment of the session. During free-activity time much of the basic equipment of the nursery school is made available to the group, and children are permitted considerable freedom to come and go from activities at will. Choices available during this time include play materials and equipment, table activities, stories, and art materials. Each day one or two more formal teacher-directed activities such as a language game, or a social studies or science project is offered to several children at a time throughout the free-activity time, and each child is invited to these activities sometime during the morning. Balance and variety in the school program are accomplished in part by regulating the availability of materials and equipment. Most days include a time—possibly midsession—when all of the children come together for a group activity that may involve stories, music, or films, or for some special event such as a visit from a guest. During these times the play and activity centers are taboo.

Within this general framework of scheduled and free time, most children participate in at least four and usually five or six different activities each day. Most voluntarily balance out their day with a variety of activities—some social, intellectual, aesthetic, and teacher-directed, and some self-initiated. If a child consistently restricts his participation to a few activities, ignoring whole segments of the nursery school program, his teacher is likely to intervene, requesting him to try some of the neglected activities. She also helps in any way she can to ensure that the new experiences he tries are rewarding, so that he will choose to try new ones another time.

Although the children do participate in some full-group activities, much of their participation is with small subgroups. Play groups are typically composed of from two to five or six children. Table games that require turns, music or art activities that require supervision, and social studies or science projects that require teacher-direction are usually offered to five or six children at a time so that each child has ample opportunity to hear, see, touch, try, or comment. A ratio of three adults to twenty children makes it possible to offer activities to two or three small groups simultaneously, or to maintain an activity for an hour or two until all of the children have participated, four or five at a time. In this way, curriculum can be offered to groups of the optimum size for the activity, and individual differences in interests, skill, and attention span can be accommodated.

THE NURSERY SCHOOL STAFF

A program of the kind described here requires a generous ratio of adults to children—approximately one adult for each six or seven children— and staff leadership is necessary. While the lead teacher is a fully qualified person, generally the other adults working with the children have had minimum training or experience, if any at all. They are eager and willing to work hard on behalf of the children, and the program would not be workable without them. Fortunately, most communities are well endowed with potential center volunteers, including college or high school students, housewives, members of church groups, senior citizens, and the parents of the children attending.

The lead teacher, of course, is ultimately responsible for the overall quality of the program and for staff supervision and guidance, but *all* adults working with the children perform the strategic functions of a "teacher." All are encouraged to contribute to the curriculum of the group, and all are expected to share in the significant tasks of nurturance, care, education, and guidance. All, including the lead teacher, also share in the daily chores of housekeeping and in the management of routines. The lead teacher supports in both attitude and deed each adult's importance to the group. The group's staff plans the program and works together, and the opinions and observations of all are given full consideration.

The curriculum discussed on the following pages is geared toward all those—lead teacher, assistants and volunteers—who work in a classroom with young children. The terms teacher and adult are used interchangeably throughout to denote any adult working directly with a group of preschool children.

Although the center described in this book is a laboratory nursery school geared to training, demonstration, and research, the program of activities and the school philosophy is readily applicable to other types of centers including day care and Head Start centers. The trainees at the school (who, in many instances, will be going to low-budget centers) are encouraged to be imaginative in considering inexpensive substitutes for expensive commercial materials. Some of the most successful games and learning materials in use in the school have been made by staff members at the cost of a few cents. With a little ingenuity, a staff can supplement both large and small equipment with an impressive array of materials at very little cost.

Before describing the Laboratory School program in greater detail, we give a brief historical overview of the preschool and day care movements in this country to help the reader better understand the philosophy that characterizes them.

3
A Historical Overview
of Preschool
Education in America

3 *A Historical Overview of Preschool Education in America*

Programs for preschool children in the United States have developed in two separate movements, the nursery school movement and the day care movement. Although the differences are becoming less distinct, historically nursery school and day care centers have differed in several ways, especially in the primary emphasis of the program and in the types of children served. Day care centers have concentrated more on the care of children while nursery schools have focused on the provision of stimulating educational and social experiences for the preschool child. Many of the early day care centers, and some of those still in operation, were established for and limited to the care of children from poor families. Nursery schools, on the other hand, have been used more by families from middle class backgrounds.

The first nursery school in the United States is believed to have been opened in New Harmony, Indiana in the 1820s. A few years later, in 1838, the first day nursery was opened in Boston for the children of seamen's wives and widows who were employed. Since then, the number of day nurseries, or day care centers as they are now called, has increased to an estimated 17,500 in the United States in 1970. The growth of day care centers has been directly related to the need for women to work as a result of financial necessity, wars, or other national emergencies when men have not been available in sufficient numbers for the labor force.

After their early beginnings, nursery schools did not grow much in the United States until the early 20th century, when the McMillan sisters began their educational program for young children in London. Most of the early nursery school programs were laboratory research facilities associated with departments of child development in colleges and universities and were established specifically to contribute to our knowledge of normal child development. Five of the most prominent and illustrious of these facilities were established before 1930 with the help of the Laura Spellman Rockefeller Foundation at the University of California, Columbia University, the University of Iowa, the University of Minnesota, and the University of Toronto. Since that time dozens of other laboratory facilities for preschool children have been established for the study of children and the training of preschool teachers. Although at present most preschool programs are private operations, the laboratory facilities sponsored by colleges and universities continue to influence programs for young children through their demonstration, research, and teacher training activities.

Because of the common link with child development, nursery school teachers and day care workers have typically received their academic training in psychology, social work, or child development instead of in departments of education. Most laboratory nursery schools continue to include among their purposes the academic study of normal child development and family relations as well as the demonstration of nursery school practices and the training of nursery school teachers.

Since the advent of Head Start in 1965, many new training programs have been established for the preparation of nursery school teachers, day care workers, and teacher aids. Some of these programs are associated with departments of elementary or early childhood education and provide a promising link between the education of preschool children and the education of school-age children.

Because of their similar historical roots, nursery school teachers and day care workers in the United States hold many values in common even though the programs have typically had different emphases. Regardless of whether its primary purpose is child care or education, children are learning from the experience. It is generally accepted that good programs for young children are child-oriented, geared to the enjoyment of the children participating, and are devoid of excessive demands and stress. Children are allowed to grow and to develop at a leisurely pace. Play is seen as one of the more important avenues by which children learn about the world of people and things, and plenty of time is allowed for this activity. The staff in child-centered programs view the children as growing individuals who benefit from the care of kindly, nurturant adults. Effective teachers of young children must themselves be mature enough to accommodate to the immaturity of the children.

The importance of attending to the "whole child" has been a popular concept in the training of day care workers and nursery school teachers. Children are recognized as having physical needs, intellectual needs, needs for security and dependence, autonomy needs, and needs for companionship with peers. A well-rounded program must provide for the child's development in all of these areas.

Despite the overriding attention to the whole child, one can identify periods of time when one or another aspect of the child's development seemed prepotent in the minds of day care workers and nursery school teachers. In the late 1920s and early 1930s, for example, much attention was given to the adequate physical care of children and to routine habit training. Sleeping and eating habits, cleanliness, and health care were emphasized. In some laboratory facilities teachers were required to record specifically what each child ate for the midmorning snack and for lunch, how long he had slept at naptime, and whether or not he had had a bowel movement that day. School routines sometimes included the brushing of teeth and the combing of hair as well as the usual toileting and handwashing.

Extensive attention to routines in nursery schools and day care centers seemed to be in vogue during the period of time when child development specialists were giving much attention to early physical growth and health care; consequently, teachers and informed parents became overly conscious of "habit training" in these areas. Currently both teachers and parents are more relaxed about routine habit training for children. Reasonably stable time patterns for eating, sleeping, and toileting are still recommended for young children, but it is also recognized that children accommodate to exceptions quite easily, making up deficits in sleep and balancing food intake over a period of several days.

Health care is also approached more casually by parents and teachers. A generally healthy child is considered to be less medically fragile than was once the case. Undoubtedly, bringing preschool children together in groups exposes a child to some communicable diseases that he would not otherwise be exposed to until he reached school age, and group programs for young children were once questioned on the basis of this hazard. Improved treatment of childhood diseases and improved immunization procedures have, however, reduced the threat of disease to the child's general health. It is, nevertheless, still a common procedure in day care centers and in some nursery schools to provide a daily "health check" and to temporarily exclude children from the group who appear to be ill or insufficiently recovered from an illness.

Following the emphasis on health care and routines, nursery school educators began to pay more attention to the psychological development of the child and to the value of socialization within the peer group. Concurrently some child psychologists were studying things such as the complexity of children's play groups, the incidents of friendliness and aggression in nursery schools, childish egocentrism, and the gradual development of sympathy for others.

The theoretical formulations of Sigmund Freud published during the 1930s and 1940s made students of child behavior particularly conscious of the need for the proper management of the child's socialization. Freud and his followers viewed social behavior as motivated by very powerful natural psychological forces that caused the child to resist socialization; misbehavior was often interpreted as having hidden, symbolic meaning as well as a more obvious functional meaning within the context of a social situation. According to Freud, early development was dominated by conflicts that the child experienced in his relations with parents and, to a lesser extent, with other authority figures. Freud recognized that the young child has immense love for his parents, but he also rivals them for affection or control and fears their retaliatory power. Authority figures respond to the child's challenge of their authority by exerting control over the child, punishing misbehavior and, in the process, generating guilt and anxiety in the child. While guilt and anxiety were viewed by Freud as necessary components of self-control and the development of a conscience, they were also regarded as potential sources of later maladjustment. Excessive demands or lack of early fulfillment of psychological needs for affection and autonomy could cause the child to become bogged down at an immature stage of psychological development or even to regress to an earlier stage of emotional immaturity. Aggressive, antisocial behavior was attributed to strong psychological needs, the expression of which was necessary for good mental health. Some teachers and parents expressed their concern about these issues by becoming overly indulgent of the young child's inclination to be selfish, demanding, and aggressive—though there is some question whether Freud himself would have implemented his theory in this way. In any case, during the period from 1940 to about 1955 observers of nursery schools in this country characterized many teachers of young children as overly "permissive" in the handling of children's dependent behaviors and aggression.

Patience and reasonable permissiveness are still thought to be important characteristics of the ideal nursery school teacher, but the child is no longer considered to be so psychologically delicate that exposure to mild stress or disapproval is seriously damaging. The child's social behavior is likely to be viewed as the product of his experience; dependence, aggression, and autonomy-striving are seen as behaviors that are used by the child because they help him to overcome obstacles and solve problems. As the child matures he must learn to control the expression of these behaviors—particularly aggression—using them only within acceptable limits in order to function in society.

During the 1940s and 1950s child psychologists were paying considerable attention to principles of learning and reinforcement theory, a theory that hypothesizes that behaviors that bring the child pleasant consequences will be strengthened and will occur again and again, while those that do not pay off, or are punished, will diminish in strength and be less likely to recur. An interest in the learning antecedents of child behavior continues to occupy many child psychologists today, and the influence of reinforcement theory (and the wealth of evidence in support of it) has been felt by educators at all levels. Classroom teachers are being made aware of the powerful positive effects of "social reinforcement" in the form of approval, compliments, and sanctions on the behavior of young children. Psychologists who subscribe to the formulations of B. F. Skinner are recommending techniques for changing misbehavior that stress (1) more conscientious and consistent attention to "appropriate behavior" whenever it occurs, and (2) the calculated use of "withdrawal of attention" for misbehavior. Although formulas of this kind are always an oversimplification of the issues, the point to be made is a valid one. In the hurly-burly of routine child management, both teachers and parents are inclined to be more attentive to misbehavior than they are to good behavior. Reversing this trend is a sensible application of principles of learning. Young children are very sensitive to adult attention, and some misbehavior is undoubtedly maintained by the very fact that it draws the teacher's attention and concern. If we combine teacher attention for misbehavior with a system in which good behavior is routinely taken for granted and goes unnoticed, we are inviting the child to turn to misbehavior to get his share of attention. More is said later about the use of principles of reinforcement in the management of behavior in the nursery school.

The 1960s proved to be a period of reassessment and change in approaches to early education. Two events occurring during the first few years of that decade have had particular impact on teachers of preschool children as well as teachers at other levels of education, causing them to re-examine their educational goals and curriculum. One event was the "sputnik crisis." When it appeared that our technological skill was not keeping up with that of Iron Curtain countries, politicians and educators began questioning the scientific and technical competence of the products of our American schools compared with the graduates of European schools. Scientists were asking educators if they were, in fact, producing students who were academically informed and intellectually disciplined enough to cope with scientific subject matter and to make significant contributions to our knowledge. Although colleges and universities bore the brunt of this questioning, educators of children were also being asked to give an accounting of their products. Teachers of younger children were asked if they were not unnecessarily postponing reading and the child's introduction to mathematics and science, losing valuable learning years and missing the optimum time to indoctrinate children with the importance of rigorous study. Nursery school teachers were urged to pay less attention to the child's psyche and social adjustment and more attention to his intellectual development; to rely less on play as an avenue for learning and more on teacher-directed instruction.

A second influence during the 1960s that affected the nature of preschool education in America was the previously mentioned advent of the Head Start program in 1965 as part of the War on Poverty. Head Start is a compensatory preschool program, locally operated but subsidized by the federal government. The target subjects are children from three to five or six years old who lack the language and conceptual skills, vocabulary, and motivation to do well in school. Since failure and high dropout rates are far more frequent in low income neighborhoods than in middle-class neighborhoods, Head Start has existed primarily in communities of economically poor families.

In practice there is no such thing as "the Head Start program." Head Start groups vary one from another almost as widely as do other nursery schools and kindergartens. Some programs are indistinguishable from the local day care centers, middle-class nursery schools, or public kindergartens; others are more didactic and slanted toward the acquisition of specific school readiness skills. Some programs are operated by fully certified nursery school or kindergarten teachers. Other groups are taught by elementary or secondary school teachers with no experience or training for work with younger children, while still others are operated by adults with little or no teacher training of any kind. Some Head start programs have been judged by competent observers to be excellent educational programs for young children; others seem to be providing no more than minimal custodial care.

One very striking effect of the Head Start movement in America is the extent to which it has motivated preschool educators everywhere to pay more attention to the intellectual and cognitive aspects of their programs than they had paid previously. The new "cognitive look" in nursery schools today is not, however, without its controversial aspects. Nursery school teachers and many parents, too, are very concerned about the possible negative effects of highly didactic lesson-type instruction in which the child must sit still for extended periods of time and in which he has very little choice about whether or not he participates.

Some teachers feel that the "natural" way for the young child to learn is incidentally, as he moves about at will in an environment in which there are many things for him to do and different kinds of materials with which to work. The instructional role of the teachers and assistants in this setting is an informal one, much like that of an interested parent as the adults and the children talk together about things related to the books, the toys, the construction materials and games, the climbing equipment, and the creative materials that the child may be using at any given time.

Preschool children undoubtedly do have the capacity to sit quietly and attend to didactic presentations for surprisingly long periods of time, but they do this best when the materials are highly interesting to them and their attending is of their own choosing. Young children do not discipline their attention nor do they concentrate on things that are not of immediate interest to them, without considerable pressure or coersion from adults. Adults who have observed young children are well aware of the need for an increase in discipline during times when children must attend activities in which they do not care to participate. Some children daydream or withdraw from any real involvement in the situation, others fidget or tease, and some rebel openly and refuse to cooperate.

Teachers in some of today's more didactic preschool programs undoubtedly do put pressure on children to sit still and attend lesson presentations for longer periods of time than most preschoolers would otherwise choose to stay. Children who are restless and immature may find the experience a trying one. In contrast to forced participation, a teacher who allows the child considerable latitude in the choice of activities puts the burden of success on the curriculum, not on the patience of the children. If the children do not choose to participate in structured lesson-type activities, or if they come to an activity but quickly become bored and restless, teachers first examine the materials or the method of presentation for the source of the difficulty. It is not automatically assumed that the fault lies with the children.

Ironically, coincident with the more formal, didactic preacademic movement in preschool education, there is a movement afoot among elementary educators away from traditional didactic education for school-age children. Proponents of the "open school" movement are attempting to increase the meaningfulness of learning experience in the elementary school by allowing children to plan their school day in a way that is more in keeping with their individual interests. With no more than minimal restrictions having to do with the mastery of basic skills in reading, writing, and arithmetic, children in many schools are being allowed to move about the school environment freely. They may work for many school hours at a time in small homogeneous interest groups on projects of their own choosing. Traditional preschool programs have always offered this style of education. Preschool children have typically been allowed to move about in the school environment, planning their own school day from among the many options available to them.

Predicting the long-term educational effects of didactic lesson-oriented preschool programs is almost impossible in our present state of limited knowledge of children's cognitive styles and the sources of their motivation to learn. The proponents of programmed, lesson-type instruction contend that the young child takes great satisfaction in a learning environment in which the learning task of the moment is clearly deliniated —that is, the child has a letter to learn, a number symbol to understand, or a concept to master—and feedback is immediate when he offers a correct answer or makes a correct response. If the material is programmed so that the child makes many more correct than incorrect responses, his motivation to participate should remain high. Our observations of children's participation in well planned, appropriate "lessons" support this analysis. The extent to which young children eagerly attend "Sesame Street" and appear to understand and assimilate its content is testimony to the appropriateness of well conceived didactic material. Observation does not, however, answer important questions such as how much of the young child's education should be carried out in this way and what, specifically, should be taught in this way instead of through informal incidental learning. If the child can learn to count to ten either through informal counting opportunities with adults around to help, or through formal lessons in counting, which style of education should be used? Will the freedom to learn incidentally and informally during the preschool years cause the child to resent didactic school lessons later? On the other hand, will demands for the early disciplining of learning efforts for the active preschooler who has a short attention span cause frustration that will interfere with the child's motivation to participate in school later?

Educators clearly do not agree on this issue and both educators and psychologists are constantly seeking new evidence to answer these important questions. In any case, there does seem to be a danger of "turning children off" to education when pressure is exerted to get them to participate in learning experiences that are uninteresting to them. It behooves the preschool educator to hold fast to the premise that preschool education should be interesting and enjoyable to the children participating as well as being academically useful.

A related issue that concerns contemporary preschool educators and about which we know very little is the cumulative effect of any one style of education, whether it is learning incidentally through exploration and discovery or didactically through instruction and lessons. One usually thinks of the mature "student" as a person who is able to make good use of both styles of education; that is, he is able to take instruction and assimilate information taught formally through lectures, books, or demonstrations, but he is also able to identify a problem and attack its solution on his own without having the steps to a solution explicitly laid out for him. Does the early indoctrination in *either* style of learning, to the exclusion of the other, restrict a child's flexibility as a learner? One concern that some educators have about the teacher-dominated programs of education for young children is the extent to which learning depends upon the child proceeding strictly as directed by his teachers. Though we do not know this, there may be detrimental cumulative effects of educational procedures in which very little initiative for learning and problem solving is left to the child. Many educators of older children and adults in our society are genuinely concerned about the extent to which our educational systems reduce the learner to a passive recipient of information or instruction until, finally, even as a college student, he writhes over any situation in which a problem, and the steps toward its solution, are not explicitly laid out for him.

Some of the decisions faced by preschool educators are peculiar to that setting because the children involved are so very young. Even if, for example, it is deemed desirable that a "mix" in style of education is appropriate for the school-age child, some of his learning being didactic and some self-directed, it is still possible that, for the younger child, one style should predominate. We know that as an infant and toddler, much of the child's learning will be incidental and independent of formal instruction. When should other more formal styles of education be used? Should formal instruction begin when the child is sufficiently verbal to converse with his teacher, say at three or three and one half, or should it be postponed until he is of elementary school age? Would some children benefit from earlier didactic instruction while for others, formal instruction should be postponed for a year or two? If the child seems tempermentally suited to one or the other style of education (for example, self-directed activity for the active child and didactic instruction for the quiet, docile child) should the educator use that style, or should he attempt to help the child learn to benefit from both styles, on the assumption that as a mature learner he will need the respective advantages of both?

A look at contemporary demonstration and research programs of education throughout the United States in the late 1960s and early 1970s leads one to believe that while there is still some mix in preschool education, the movement is toward more didactic experiences and fewer self-initiated, play-oriented experiences for children from three to five, whether culturally deprived or advantaged. Most experimental preschool programs give, at least, lip service to the importance of free exploration of the environment as a vehicle for learning, but this is an explicit program goal of only a few programs.

Though social play is tangential to the educational philosophy of most experimental programs, nursery school play materials are often available, including doll corner equipment, toy cars, trains, and airplanes, blocks, put-together materials, art and craft supplies, puzzles, outside climbing equipment, and wheel toys. Field trips are planned and language activities are stressed. In addition, however, more structured learning materials have been introduced to help the child learn to observe and listen carefully, to identify letters, numbers, shapes, and colors, to learn the names of common objects or animals, and to organize these things into appropriate classes or groupings. Attention is given to the development of materials that are attractive to the children and will capture their interests. The curriculum of some of the contemporary demonstration and research programs is discussed in Chapter 16.

4
Providing for the Needs of Children

4 Providing for the Needs of Children

Respect for individuality among children is one of the most persistent tenets of traditional nursery school philosophy. Teachers of young children are particularly sensitive to indicators of unhappiness, distress, or disinterest in their groups and attempts are made to accommodate the needs of individuals. Activities are often planned with individual children in mind, and the adults do not assume that all children will be equally interested in participating in a given school activity or project. The child who is reticent to participate in school activities is permitted to stay on the fringes of things and watch others for long periods of time without being made to feel uncooperative or ungrateful for his lack of eager participation.

A feeling of security seems to be one of the prerequisites of the young child's enthusiastic participation in experiences away from home. Children coming to nursery school are without the direct support of their families often for the first time in their lives, and they can easily be made to feel threatened by the strangeness of their surroundings. The young child's relationship with members of his family is usually a very close one involving much affection, care, and help. To bridge the gap between home and school, teachers fulfill this need while the child is in school by being especially nurturant and attentive. They express their friendliness freely and may occasionally pick children up or hug them; they console them when they get hurt, offer support and protection if a child seems fearful, and help them with tedious tasks like dressing or putting away toys.

Nursery school teachers are sometimes accused of being too solicitous of children, and there is undoubtedly some risk of encouraging dependency; however, laboratory research and observation suggests that when children learn that help and support are available when sought, they are even more inclined than otherwise to move toward independence. This is especially true if the adults responsible for them take great satisfaction in the accomplishments of the children and convey this to them through social approval.

Adjustment periods for children new to school vary from child to child. Though some children adapt quickly and can separate from their parents the first day of school, plans for others may involve several days when a mother, father, or another familiar person stays at school or comes and goes freely, gradually increasing the amount of time the child attends while he becomes accustomed to the group. During this time teachers convey their willingness to accommodate the idiosyncracies of a child. While a child is getting used to school the teacher will permit him to spend most of his time on a few favored activities. A special effort is made to befriend the child and to find things that he will enjoy doing at school. Few demands are made.

Communication between a child's parents and teachers is established before the child enters the school program or during the initial days of school. Teachers encourage parents to let them know how their child feels about school—especially if there is anything that makes the child reluctant to come each day. In turn, teachers let the parents know how things are going at school through informal conversations, phone calls, and conferences. Parents are made to feel at home in school and frequently linger to watch their child at play, have coffee, or chat with other parents. The atmosphere between teachers and parents is one of mutual concern and planning on behalf of the child enrolled.

Developmental goals for children change as the year progresses. When the children are more comfortable and secure in school, more is expected of them. Nevertheless, teachers continue to take into account children's idiosyncracies and attempt to match expectations to each child's capabilities and interests. Through much of the school day children are allowed considerable latitude in selecting what they wish to participate in and in deciding how long to stay at an activity. Teachers do not expect that every child will participate in every school activity.

Strife and conflict are kept to a minimum in the nursery school, in part, by providing enough materials, space, and time for children to pursue their individual goals. While misbehavior does occur, it is surprisingly infrequent. Rules and restrictions that are deemed necessary for the comfortable and safe management of the group are made clear to the children and are applied with consistency so that children can learn what is expected of them. Good behavior is rewarded with warm approval. Punishment for misbehavior is used sparingly.

Although the nursery school environment is designed for the comfort and satisfaction of the children, it is by no means devoid of failure and frustration. Occasional failure is a necessary part of any challenging learning environment. Rather than protect the children from the frustration of failure, they are helped to cope with it by setting reasonable goals for themselves and by gradually learning that difficult tasks are worth trying even if success is not a certainty. To prevent excessive discouragement,

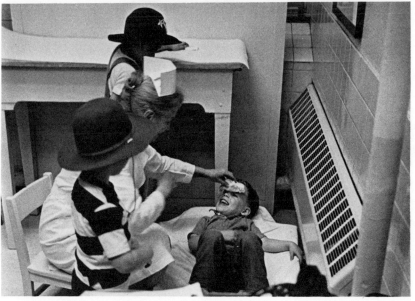

the school (1) provides many more opportunities for success than failure, and (2) helps children to appreciate their partial successes as they gradually improve in the mastery of tasks or the development of skills.

It is the teacher's job to help children attain academic and social goals that do full justice to their abilities without having more than an occasional incident that arouses unmanageable fear or reduces a child to tears, rebellion, or boredom.

There are a number of things that nursery school teachers must take into consideration in planning a school program for young children. Some of the more important considerations have to do with the nature of the learner. It is a common observation of teachers and parents, for example, that the young child has a *short attention span*. His tolerance is especially low for activities that require him to sit quietly for long periods of time and attend to details. He will occasionally stay at something for hours, but parents and teachers remark about this partly because it is recognized as remarkable! It does not ordinarily happen. To accommodate the young child, school activities that require the inhibition of motor activity should be kept short and should be spaced throughout the school day.

Another characteristic of the preschooler is that he is a *superficial learner*. He is more interested in learning a little about a lot than a lot about a little! He explores everything in sight—but in bits and pieces instead of in depth. He attends to what catches his eye at the moment and then readily becomes distracted by something else. He notices details, but not systematically or exhaustively as a mature learner does when he attempts to learn all there is to know about a subject. Some of what he learns will be trivial (like the fact that the zoo is the place where they sell pink cotton candy). Each time the child reencounters an experience, object, or event he asks new questions and learns a few more bits and pieces. As he matures, he will gradually fit the pieces together and will separate the significant from the trivial. During the preschool years, however, the child seems to need many opportunities to make new observations and to learn new facts without excessive demands being placed on him for the disciplined, exhaustive mastery of subject matter.

A third characteristic of the preschooler is that he does much of his learning through *direct sensory-motor involvement*. He seems to maintain interest and to learn best when he can see and touch objects in the environment as well as hear someone tell about them. When he cannot confront things directly he makes good use of visual material such as well-illustrated books, photographs, movies, television, accurate miniature replicas, or anything else that helps him to "picture" something. The nursery school curriculum should therefore include many first-hand learning experiences and an abundance of supplementary visual materials.

A fourth characteristic of the young child is that he revels in the *familiar and the accomplished*. He repeats again and again, the things he already knows how to do that give him a feeling of mastery. He enjoys demonstrating his competence—sometimes to others, but often just to himself. If he builds a particularly good block structure one day, he may repeat it again with slight variations, for several days in a row. Once he learns to do a puzzle he may dump it out just to do it again. When he learns to zip his jacket or tie his shoes, he may undo them just to do them again. He does the same trick over and over on the jungle gym before trying new ones and asks for the same story again and again after he knows every word of it by heart.

Repeated experiences probably have, at least, three advantages for the child. First, the child misses much of what can be learned from a single exposure to new facts and information; second, he forgets easily and overlearning may help him to retain more of what he has learned; and third, the child seems to enjoy the feeling of accomplishment that comes from putting into use a skill that he has already mastered or confirming a bit of knowledge he already knows.

Because of the child's tolerance for overlearning and repetition, many projects and activities in the nursery school can be repeated to the profit of the children and without risk of boring them. The same questions can be asked and answered two or three times, the same bits of information can be repeated, the same riddles can be enjoyed even after the child knows all of the answers, and the same storybooks can be read over and over.

A fifth characteristic of the young child is that he is *motivated to learn about very ordinary things*. Compared with the schoolage child, he is less interested in studying things that are remote from him in time and space. While the older child reads "Interesting Facts About the Empire State Building" or "How to Train Race Horses," the preschooler watches a man repair the chimney of his house and befriends a retired nag roaming in a field near his home.

This, of course, does not mean that the child is never told about things that are remote in time and space. The young child's exposure to television, toys, and books makes him very curious about some things with which he has had no direct experience—like prehistoric animals, spacemen, and ballerinas. The point, however, is that one should not underestimate the appeal that common, everyday things have for the child. Dozens of interesting places or objects for study can be found within two or three blocks of almost any school one could name. In fact, teachers often are surprised at how much they themselves find to notice about some very ordinary things when they look at them with young children.

5
Developing
Intellectual Competence

5 Developing Intellectual Competence

Young children are remarkably eager learners. They ask question after question about the people and animals they see and about man-made objects such as houses, stores, tools, roads, and vehicles. They are curious about events of nature involving rain, ice and snow, clouds, air, and earth. Nursery school can widen the child's perspective by showing him things he ordinarily does not get to see—like the kitchen in a restaurant, a magnified view of an ant, x-rays of bones, a close look at a football player's gear, the inside of a peach stone, or a film that condenses the development of a butterfly into minutes.

Nursery school activities contribute to the child's intellectual development in two general ways. One is by presenting new information, and the other is by fostering the cognitive skills necessary for the efficient acquisition, organization, and use of information. These two types of activities are closely related, of course, and many curriculum projects make a contribution to both of these aspects of the child's cognitive development. A field trip to a zoo, for instance, provides the child with an opportunity to learn new facts and a new vocabulary and also provides the impetus to recall previous experiences, and to think and to reason about what he has seen.

Some nursery school activities contribute more to one aspect of intellectual development than another. Many social studies and science projects, for example, have as their main purpose an increase of the child's knowledge about the world.

Other experiences are presented that help children to develop their abilities to observe, to listen, to remember, to use language effectively, and to reason. While the young child will not attain a high degree of skill in thinking and reasoning, he is clearly beginning to use important cognitive operations in his daily life. Although surprisingly little is known about the thought processes and the intellectual potential of young children, some of the skills and operations needed for effective learning have been identified. The following are some of these skills which, in all probability, can be fostered by appropriate curriculum activities.

To learn the child must be able to:

OBSERVE
Focus attention for extended periods of time.

Pay attention to the right thing at the right time.

Notice details.

REMEMBER
Retain information over a period of time.

ORGANIZE INFORMATION
Group familiar objects, people, and events into appropriate categories, using both broad general classes (such as "animals") and smaller sub-classes (such as "dogs").

Notice how things are alike or different.

Notice the separate parts of objects; combine parts into wholes.

Associate one experience with another.

COMMUNICATE EFFECTIVELY
Explain ideas and convey information to others.

Master the role of a listener; attend to others and interpret what others say.

Ask and answer questions.

UNDERSTAND BASIC RELATIONAL CONCEPTS
Concepts of space (such as in, on, under, over, in front of, etc).

Concepts of time (such as before, after, earlier, later, yesterday, and to-morrow).

Concepts of size (such as big, little, smaller, smallest, tall, and wide).

REASON
Draw sensible conclusions from information available.

Formulate and informally "test" hypotheses or hunches.

Notice what things "cause" other things.

QUANTIFY AND ORDER OBJECTS AND EVENTS
Rank things from smallest to largest, first to last, lightest to heaviest.

Measure, count, match sets, add, and subtract small quantities.

FOLLOW DIRECTIONS
Attend to demonstrations.

Use simple diagrams, plans, or recipes.

Remember sequences.

TAKE INITIATIVE IN PROBLEM SOLVING
Strive toward solutions without help.

Try new approaches.

EVALUATE
Judge, express an opinion.

Distinguish between reality and make believe.

There are many opportunities during the day for children in the nursery school to cope with problems and their solutions as they play with the toys, use the materials, and interact with the people. To give children additional practice in thinking, reasoning, and problem solving, some activities are presented in the form of simple games played by the entire group during group times or played by a small group of children during free activity time. The format of games in the nursery school is reminiscent of the table games of older children and the parlor games of adults. They require the child to do things such as identify an object from clues given him, think of ways in which objects are alike or different, group objects that go together in some way, solve verbal riddles (for example, "What has legs but does not walk?"), or think of all the things they can that have a given characteristic (such as a "trunk"). Other games require the child to find a hidden object in the room, or to recall a missing object from an array before him, or to identify an object by touch or sound alone. The rules of some games require children to follow directions or to perform simple counting or matching operations. Some of the games are played at tables with attractive materials and equipment such as picture cards, blocks of different shapes, colors, or sizes, or minature toy objects. Others are played as children sit together on the floor or in the yard and require only the child's attention and involvement. New games or variations on old ones are sometimes made up on the spot by a teacher or even suggested by the children themselves.

Care is taken to keep the games interesting and enjoyable to the children. Long waits for turns are avoided by having children play in small groups, and only games that move quickly or that easily maintain high interest are played in a large group. Children are free to come and go from games as they wish. Almost without exception games in the nursery school are played noncompetitively. There are no winners and losers. Though young children like winning, they are notoriously poor losers; consequently, game-type situations in the nursery school are more successful when each child's own success is the critical issue instead of winning or losing relative to the others. Game tasks are selected to be well within the children's ability so that there will be relatively few failures compared with the successes. Teachers see to it that each child ends his turn with a success experience by helping a floundering child to understand the task and to make a correct or reasonable game response.

FAVORITE "THINK GAMES" IN THE NURSERY SCHOOL

Some examples of the think games children play in the nursery school provide a greater understanding of the multiple purposes of these activities.

Pretzel

One favorite game called "pretzel" requires a grid of from 8 to 12 squares marked out in chalk on the sidewalk outdoors or on the floor indoors. In each square of the grid, the outline of a familiar shape is drawn such as a circle, rectangle, triangle or square using bright colored chalks. Colors and shapes are repeated in various combinations. A child is then given an instruction by his teacher indicating that he must put each of his feet in a particular square and, at the same time, touch other specified squares with his hands. For example, the child may be instructed to "put one foot on the red triangle, the other foot on the blue circle, and both hands on the red square" or, if the child knows his left and right hands and feet, he may be given instructions that specify which hand or foot to put where. The adult presenting this game varies the instruction according to the child's ability to follow it. A child who is just learning to identify the shapes or colors, or one who is just learning to follow instructions of this kind may be given a very easy instruction involving, for example, only two squares, one for his feet and one for his hands. On the other hand, a child who is experienced at the game may be given an instruction that literally "ties him in knots" in an attempt to make the various connections with his hands and feet to the mutual delight of the performer and the children watching. If a child has trouble identifying a figure, the teacher simply points it out to him, repeating the identifying characteristics.

At first the adult may give instructions one at a time so that a child can concentrate on one before receiving the next instruction. Later, to make the game more challenging, she may give the child instructions in pairs, or ones that involve as many as three or four squares in one statement and the child must keep them in mind as he follows them in sequence. One can sometimes see a child watching the grid intently as he receives the instructions, seemingly "rehearsing" where he is to put what!

A game such as this gives children a chance to listen intently, follow instructions, and identify common shapes and colors. When children have some knowledge of less common shapes (such as cones, cylinders, or hexigons), these too can be used. This game can readily be adapted to help children to identify number symbols or other classes of objects such as birds, flowers, or animals by using taped-down laminated photographs or prints of these things. The children thoroughly enjoy the game, and it gives them a chance for active physical participation. The game is usually played by no more than five or six children at a time, since waiting longer for a turn can become tedious. It is possible, of course, to construct a larger grid that could accommodate two or three children at a time.

Shapes and Colors

Another popular think game requires an extensive set of *attribute blocks* which are small table blocks cut into different geometric shapes and painted different colors. Children may sit at a table or around a space on the floor for this game. An array of seven or eight blocks representing different shapes and colors is spread out in the center of the circle of children. Each child playing the game has a pile of six or seven additional blocks before him (or a common box of all of the remaining blocks can be passed from child to child). Each child in turn is given an instruction to put a specific shape and color block in some specific relation to one of the blocks in the middle. For example, a child may be asked to "put a red square (from his pile or from the box) *on top* of a blue circle. In the course of the game the adult will be sure to include a variety of relational directions, including *under, beside,* and *next to,* so that the children become familiar with these important terms. If she elects to use this as a brief diagnostic tool, she may be sure that each child gets one or two tries at each relational direction, noting any that he has trouble with. When the children show evidence of having caught on to the kind of instructions to give, they may take turns in the role of instructor, giving instructions to each other.

A teacher may occasionally "throw a child a curve" by asking him to place a block "under the green triangle" when there is no green triangle in the center of the table. Instructions can also be made more challenging by combining two actions. For example, a child may be asked to "place an orange square under the red triangle, and take a blue circle for the box." When a child cannot follow an instruction, the adult usually indicates that it *is* a hard one and follows it through herself, or helps him to follow it through repeating it as she does. The adult makes certain that no child continually gets instructions that he cannot follow. The number of instructions he can do readily should far outweigh the number that he has difficulty following.

If, in fact, the children are having their very first experience in identifying the shapes and colors of attribute blocks, this game may begin by simply selecting blocks one by one in turn and identifying each one's shape and color after which the information can be incorporated into a game like that described above.

Nesting Barrels

Another game to help children practice using size and relational concepts is played with sets of five nesting barrels or boxes (in which each successive barrel or box is a little smaller than the last and incidentally, of a different color). The barrels can be set out in a row on the table, and children can take turns in pointing out a specific barrel identified by the adult. Instructions can be very easy, like "find the *biggest* barrel," or "which is the *red* one?"; or they can be more complicated, like "which barrel is *between* the *red* one and the *blue* one?" or "which barrel is the *middle-sized* one?" or "which barrel is just a *little smaller* than the *biggest* one?" If more than one set of the barrels are being used, a child may be asked to "find a *red one* that is *next to a green one*," or harder yet, "find a *red one* that is *not next to a green one*." If each child has his own set of barrels, the child may be asked to "put your *red* barrel *between* a *blue* and a *green* barrel," or "put your *smallest* barrel on top of the *largest* barrel on the table.

Games of this kind have the advantage of accommodating very wide ranges of ability and sophistication in the children playing at any one time, since the adult can give an easy item to a younger, less capable or less confident child and a hard item to a child who will enjoy the challenge. Children rarely seem to notice this discrepancy in difficulty from child to child and almost never make any comment about it.

A Balloon Game

One improvised game that helps children learn to count involves keeping a large balloon in the air. Five or six children can take turns hitting the balloon while the number of hits before the balloon touches the ground is counted. Children can be shown how to keep the balloon up—by hitting it gently from the bottom upward, and the adult can take an occasional turn when it goes too far astray. If children get good enough at this game to maintain the balloon beyond where they can count, the teacher continues to count for them, and they can repeat the unfamiliar numbers if they wish. Children love this game and two or three may elect to keep playing it on their own after the group has dispersed. If they have trouble counting far enough, they may count to 10 or, perhaps, 20 and then start over again.

What Is It?

One game that has been particularly successful with the children requires them to attend carefully and to make judgements. For this game two shoe boxes are needed plus an array of pairs of items that represent very different textures, weights, and sizes but that are each small enough to fit into a shoe box. Sample items that can easily be obtained in pairs are flashlight batteries, golf balls, buttons, cotton balls, small baggies filled with rice, noodles, or rocks, plastic coffee cups, sets of car keys, and kitchen pot holders. For this game the adult has access to one member of each pair of items, and the other member of each pair is set out on the table before the children. The adult then selects an item from her set (hidden from view of the children) and places it in one of the shoe boxes, closing the box tightly with a rubber band or two. The children are told that an item just like *one* of the things on the table is now in the box, and they will have to decide which item it is. The children are allowed to lift the box, shake it, tilt it, or rattle the object inside in an attempt to guess its contents. They are given the second shoe box so that they can also try out items on the table until they find one that sounds and feels like the first box. Children playing this game typically begin selecting items by trial and error but soon learn to select only sensible items considering the noise and weight of the object in the box. The adult may talk with the children about why they think it is (or is *not*) some specific item on the table. In one variation of this game a teacher cut some slits in the side of her box and allowed the children to poke tongue depressors into the box in an effort to make judgements about the composition and size of the item inside. Children can easily share the leadership role in this game, selecting the item to be placed in the box.

Alike and Different

Some of the games played in the nursery school require a verbal response from the children. Riddles and brainteasers are examples. In one such game the child is confronted with a pair of items or pictures of items that are *alike* in some obvious way, and *different* in some obvious way. For example, a picture of a car and a picture of a bus may be paired. The child is asked to "think of some way that they are *alike*" (for example, the fact that they are both vehicles, have wheels, horns, and motors, and carry passengers) and "think of some way that they are different" (for example, the fact that the bus is longer, collects money from its passengers, and has a schedule to keep). The number of items or pictures of items that can be used for this game is infinite. In preparation for the game, teachers select items that are familiar to the children and whose class and subclass names they are likely to know. (Some of the more common classes of objects that have been used are animals, people, furniture, and foods.) The purpose of the game is not to teach the children to identify the items but is, instead, to help them become attentive to the characteristics of objects that are important to notice in comparing, contrasting, and classifying objects. This type of game can also be played with carefully prepared materials (such as the attribute blocks mentioned previously) in which the number of likenesses and differences involved are well controlled.

Here's What I Did With It

One popular riddle guessing game is called "Here's what I did with it!" For this game the adult, or one of the children, describes the use of a familiar object while he deliberately mislabels it. For example, the leader might say "I picked up my bed this morning, squeezed my toothpaste all over my bed, and then I put my bed in my mouth and brushed my teeth with it," or "I ate my boots for breakfast this morning. First I poured my boots into a bowl and put some sugar and milk on them, and then I ate my boots with a spoon." In playing this game the children must guess the object from the clues given. A child may just identify the object involved and go on to the next riddle, or he may volunteer to tell something he did with his "bed" or his "boots." Asking the child to tell what else could be done with the bed or boots helps the adults to assess the child's understanding of the substitution. In the case of the bed, for example, the child must say something that is reasonably done with a toothbrush like "I hung my bed up in the holder."

Find the Letter

This game can be played once the children have a little familiarity with letters. The teacher presenting the game must compose some common words, names, or a brief sentence to be matched by the children. The words selected should be ones with some meaning to the children. They may be their own names, the names of common household objects or foods that can be seen on packages, names of automobiles, or the names of some of their favorite books. Short sentences can also be used that have meaning for the children, such as "Beth is back from her vacation." The words or sentences are presented in front of the children (or on a turntable if the children are sitting around a table). The adult reads the words to the children, then each child in turn draws a letter on the table. The child must find a place to match the letter he has drawn, placing his letter just below its match. Each time a letter is added to a word, the teacher or the children identify both the letter and the word it is in. When the last letter is added, the game is over or begins again with new words or sentences. The children sometimes suggest what they would like the center words to say. Needless to say, a large supply of well organized letter cutouts is required for this game so that the adults can compose words and their matches quickly.

Games using words and letters that are well within the children's abilities help to familiarize the children with the letters of the alphabet of which words are composed. They also help the children to develop sight vocabularies of a few particularly meaningful words and, hopefully, contribute to their curiosity about reading materials in general.

What's Missing

One game that is popular in school requires the children to observe carefully and to remember what they have seen. For this game the adult provides an array of small familiar objects that can be placed out on a tray or lined up on a table before the children. A child takes his turn by looking very carefully at all of the items, closing his eyes while one item is removed (either by the adult or by one of the other children) and then looking and naming the missing object. This game can be made very easy for the children by using only three or four items and repeating the same array as children take turns around the table, or it can be made more difficult by using seven or eight items and changing the array oftener. The task can also be made easier if the array is left in a line with a space open where an object has been removed, and harder if the array is shuffled around after removing an object. Also more than one object can be removed at a time.

Children enjoy this game and can function as the leader as well as the guesser. Ironically, when children have trouble with the game is usually because they can't resist "peeking" while an object is being removed and not that they can't remember it. Even when children are thoroughly enjoying the guessing aspects of the game, the temptation to look while the object is being removed is overwhelming. Teachers have found it more successful if they ask a child to turn around in his chair or to put his head in his lap rather than to just close his eyes, when peeking is taboo!

Of course, another technique that children must learn as part of their "game playing" behavior is to resist the temptation to blurt out answers when it is another person's turn. Even young children are willing to abide by this protocol—with occasional reminders—if they do not have to wait too long for their own turn. Often, the children attending the turns of others seem to be silently making the same judgements to be made by the person whose turn it is. They then watch to see if their judgement is confirmed.

LANGUAGE EXPERIENCES
IN THE NURSERY SCHOOL

From the moment children arrive in school each day there are exchanges of greetings, communications about events at home or on the way to school, observations of new things in the room, or comments about the activities planned for the day. Children are encouraged to talk freely with their companions and with the adults in the school.

The comments of the younger preschoolers are often no more than one-sentence pronouncements from a child about something he has received as a gift, something new in his home, or some recent event of significance to his family such as a visit from a grandmother or an accident involving an older brother or sister. Some comments are simple bids for recognition for what the child is doing at the moment or what he plans to do next.

The social speech of the three-year-olds is often quite egocentric in that their comments are likely to be about their own affairs rather than events of mutual interest to them and their companions. Two children may be talking together each commenting about things of personal interest, neither seeming to respond directly or relevantly to the comments of the other. A brief three-way conversation recorded by a student observer will illustrate the point. One four-year-old said, "I have to get a shot today." A three-year-old companion said, "My dad is going to buy me new shoes," while a second four-year-old said, "Will it hurt?"

Older nursery school children work harder at keeping the attention of their listeners by being interesting, amusing, or informative. Discussions resemble adult conversations in which there is a volley of communication back and forth with each child making related comments that are attended and responded to by the other children. The relating of one incident may remind a listener of a similar incident which he then tells. The children may become absorbed in hearing a companion tell about such things as the aftermath of a recent storm or the birth of a litter of pups. Funny events or fantasies about the horrible things one might do to one's enemies are likely to spring up as topics of conversation among the children, and each may try to outdo the others in verbal absurdities.

During times when children are working or playing together toward a common goal, conversations serve a more functional purpose. Questions, requests to others, protests over procedures or property rights, and attempts to persuade another are all part of the communications that occur between children.

Teachers in the nursery school take advantage of numerous opportunities during the school day to talk informally with small groups of children. Snacktimes, going for walks, working on things that do not require undivided attention, or waiting briefly for some event to begin, are good times for informal conversation.

Conversations with adults in the school have a number of educational advantages for the child. Adults are good models for correct grammar and acceptable language usage. Also the adults in the school are interested, nonegocentric listeners. They are inclined to encourage extensions of the child's conversation by asking questions, seeking clarification when the child's meaning is not clear, and by generally contributing relevant comments of their own. The child who is self-conscious about talking before a group of his companions can often be encouraged to talk informally with a teacher under conditions that are casual and nonthreatening before he feels inclined to contribute in the more challenging group situation.

There are times during the nursery school day when the children are brought together more formally to talk about a particular issue, a plan, or their reactions to an event—perhaps a holiday celebration or a special school project. During these times teachers help the children manage their group conversation constructively, making certain that each child who wishes to contribute gets his chance and that the more talkative children do not take undue advantage of the group. Some discussions of this kind are to inform the children of coming curricular events that require planning. The children may be asked to consider what preparations are necessary and how they should be accomplished. Although the teacher does not rely on the children's foresight or their skill in planning, she may expect them to think through at least two or three of the jobs to be done if an event is to be a success.

The importance of communication through language may be emphasized at times in school by helping the child to preserve his comments for use on some later occasion. A child may be invited to come to a quiet part of the room to dictate material into a tape recorder or to a teacher for typing. He may wish to tell about a significant event in his life or he may reiterate a favorite storybook, complete with inflections, perhaps using the illustrated book as a prop for remembering details and sequences. His personal version of the story may then be read or played back to the group during a story time and shared with classmates. At other times, he may wish to make up his own story to be presented to the other children. Interesting pictures, hand puppets, or cutout figures of people and animals are sometimes used to elicit stories from the children.

The goal of the child's early attempts at event-telling or storytelling may be simply to get the child to talk freely and to enjoy listening to what he says. As children approach four and become more experienced in this activity, however, the teacher is more active in helping them to improve the product, searching their memories or imaginations for details that enhance the experience for the storyteller as well as for the listener. Transcribed comments or stories may be saved for many days or weeks and then reread to the child, or they may be sent home to be read by other members of the family.

Some of the most valuable language experiences in the nursery school are incidental to social studies or other curricular activities. For example, a project about pets may involve several children's contributions to a "book" about what kinds of things they, or the other members of their families, must do to care for family pets. For another project, the children may be asked to compose a note to a guest inviting him to come to school, or a thank-you note may be written to someone who helped out on a field trip. Notes may be composed that will go to children who are at home ill or on vacation, or to parents at Christmastime or Valentine's Day.

The small-group games children play in the nursery school also give them special language experiences. For example, once the children begin to recognize that some words rhyme, word games can be played in which they must think of "the name of an animal that sounds like 'hat,' " or "something to ride in that sounds like 'rain.' " Other games involve such tasks as describing a location in detail so that a companion can find a hidden object in the room. Through these experiences the child is encouraged to translate his observations into language that supplies another person with comprehensible, useful information.

Fun with Sounds and Words

A deliberate attempt is made to convey to nursery school children that listening to sounds and to language is fun as well as functional. When children are at play, the nursery school room is full of simulated sounds of roaring motors, meowing kittens, and crying babies that are surprisingly accurate reproductions of those sounds in the environment. Game activities such as guessing each other's voices or identifying animal, street, or school sounds from a tape recorder are particularly popular with the children. Common household objects such as an egg beater, scissors, a stapler, a hammer, a steam iron, or a coffee pot can be put to use behind a screen while the children try to guess what object makes each sound.

Some of the most enjoyable times children have with sound occur when they are experimenting with language, spontaneously making up nonsense words or exploring sounds or words for shock value. Though preschoolers do not create poetry consciously, they do at times improvise word combinations that they take great delight in and recognize as having a special rhythmic quality that is enhanced by repetition. By exposing children to simple poetry, ditties, and limericks as a regular part of the school program, they begin to get a feel for the expressive potential of words and sounds. If these early language experiences are a source of pleasure for the child and for the adults around him, it seems likely that he will, in time, be more deliberate and planful in his attempts to be creative with language and sound.

The older preschoolers particularly enjoy word games that involve playful mislabeling—like calling the crackers "milk" and the milk "crackers"—during snack time so that a child who wants more milk must ask to have the crackers passed. Word distortions, subversive-sounding chants, and a play on children's names are all likely to be successful attention-getters in the group.

Books

Books are one of the more obvious sources of interest in language for young children, and they are available in abundance in the nursery school. Though some favorites are read over and over again, children in the nursery school are exposed to literally hundreds of different books each year. Some books are selected for their informational content. They may tell about families and community life, people from other lands, animals, or festive occasions. Storybooks often depict racially integrated social scenes with white and minority group children of black, Mexican-American, Indian, or Oriental heritage. Many of the children' storybooks are akin to popular fiction complete with heroes, suspense, and happy endings.

An interest in books is nurtured throughout the nursery school day. In addition to a regular story time each day, a teacher will, whenever possible, sit down during the free activity time and read to a child on request. The reading may continue for as long as any child remains interested.

While stories are occasionally read to the entire group of children, more often the class is divided into smaller groups of seven or eight children so that each child has an ample opportunity to see, hear, and comment without destroying the continuity of the story. Being able to see the illustrations and to respond to the content of the story with relevant comments of their own increases the storytime enjoyment of young children.

The young child's earliest interest in books and stories is undoubtedly due, in part, to the cozy association it gives him with an adult. A small group of children gathering around for a story often sit very close to the teacher, who sits on the floor with them. One can observe a vying for a favored position among the children gathered. As children gain experience with story groups, stories seem to take on greater significance for their own sake. Among older preschoolers it is not unusual for a group of children to be so thoroughly engrossed in a story that they completely ignore noisy, distracting activities going on around them. Minor adjustments in position to see or hear are made with no more than a fleeting interruption in their attention to the story.

Poetry reading, story records, and storytelling (sometimes with flannel board pictures or drawings) add to the variety of activities that are offered during story times. Unfortunately, the availability of so many excellent books for young children has reduced the incidence of storytelling in nursery schools. Teachers with a knack for this activity can keep a group completely spellbound with a good (and one usually suspects, well-rehearsed) story. Storytelling has the advantage over illustrated storybooks of allowing the child to develop his own imagery as the story proceeds. Creative teachers sometimes make up stories that are particularly timely or appropriate for their group of children.

PREREADING EXPERIENCES

Although children in the nursery school are not taught to read, there is considerable support from teachers for the child's growing awareness of letters and words, and prereading materials are supplied as a regular part of the school environment. Children have opportunities to see, identify, and work directly with the letters of the alphabet and with selected words that have particular meaning for them.

Letters are presented in various ways. Some are printed on cards or are cut out of heavy cardboard. Some are displayed on the surfaces of cubes or wedge-shaped blocks so that they can be lined up by the child. Magnetic-backed plastic letters are available that can be mounted on a display board and can be rearranged by the teacher or child. Cutout felt letters can be mounted on a felt-board and combined in various ways with felt-backed pictures of objects and people.

Though children are not systematically "schooled" in the identification of printed symbols, letters and words are named for the child as he asks about them or as the opportunity presents itself, just as other objects in the environment such as shapes, animals, or flowers are named. When letters are out on a table, children can be seen picking them up one by one, turning them around, tracing the edge with a finger, looking through an opening in a letter, placing letters side by side or on top of one another to see if they match, or hunting through an array of letters for all of one kind. The child may be able to name the letter he is looking for, or he may simply be matching by shape. A teacher stopping by as he works or plays with the letters may comment on their names or on the fact that some of them are the letters in his name or the letters in some word that can be seen nearby in the room.

Although preschoolers are not very precise in their attempts to print letters, they do become interested in copying them—particularly the letters in their names. The child's gross errors in forming letters are sometimes corrected by the teacher, but there is no effort made to guide a child toward a neat, perfect reproduction of the letters he wishes to approximate. Perfection in forming letters requires tedious practice for the young child that seems uneconomical for him at this point in his schooling.

Children gradually become aware of the fact that letters can be combined to form words, many of which have meaning for him. The child may go through a phase during which he thinks any combination of letters will spell a word. For example, he may combine the letters *fgel* and ask his teacher "What does this say?" In time, he comes to realize that only certain combinations of letters spell meaningful words and that one must learn what these combinations are. He learns to take his cues from two sources: people who can "read," or printed words available in the environment. He may ask his teacher to write words for him to look at, or he may check with his teacher to be sure that the letters he put together really do spell a word. He may look around in the school for what is obviously a word and copy it or ask what it says. The letters and words available to the child in school are always printed in the style that the child will use during the early primary years so that continuity between his prereading activities and early reading is maintained.

Among the most meaningful words the child is likely to encounter is his own name and perhaps the names of some of his companions. Early in

the school year he will be helped to recognize his name and will find it printed in various places around the schoolroom. It may be at his locker or in his boots. It will probably be used many times to identify a painting, clay product, or story of his. Name cards may be used in discussions of who is present or absent from school today or in a game of "Who is it?" The child's name may appear on a list of "helpers" for getting a midday snack ready, and the older children may be expected to check to see if they are helpers on a given day. A child's name may be used from time to time as a place card at tables for special occasions.

As the children become more aware of the fact that words are made up of letters, additional materials are provided as patterns and as sources of encouragement for early reading activities. Pictures of familiar objects like a cat, dog, house, boy, or baby will be made available with the name of the object printed below the picture. The child may simply look through the pictures and name the objects, or he may wish to reconstruct the name of the object from cardboard or plastic letters available to him. Some labeled pictures are constructed like puzzles, and when the child completes the picture, he can see the name of the object. Teachers sometimes label objects in the room such as tables, chairs, windows, doors, the sink, or lights. They are alert to opportunities to help the child make the connection between an object or picture and the written word so that the child understands that he can learn to recognize printed words from these materials.

As children turn four and approach five, there is a special effort to help them become more aware of the message value of written words. Attention is called to simple one- or two-word signs that convey important information. The older children may be taken for walks and alerted to look for certain words or phrases that the teacher knows will be seen along the route. For example, they can be alerted to watch for signs like STOP or EXIT, UP and DOWN on escalators and elevators, HOT and COLD on faucets, and PUSH and PULL, or IN and OUT on doors. Words like NO PARKING, BUS STOP, DRUG STORE, and TELEPHONE or requests such as "Please Keep Off the Grass" can be identified. Learning to recognize book titles, local store names, names of automobiles, household objects, or food products also gives the child a chance to associate a spoken word with a written one and helps him to realize the communication value of words. Catchy phrases or repetitive themes in poetry or books can be pointed out on a page of print. Many are readily recognized by the third or fourth time they are encountered (for example, the words "I think I can—I think I can—I think I can—I think I can . . ." in *The Little Engine That Could*).

Though not much attention is given specifically to the phonetic breakdown of words and the sounding out of new or familiar words, the children do begin to realize that words that begin with the same letters have beginning sounds that are alike as well. Here, too, as the child shows evidence of recognizing that certain sounds go with certain letters or combinations of letters, his teacher will take an interest in his "phonetic guessing." She may, for example, show him three or four words that all begin with the same letter and all sound alike at the beginning—like, boy, ball, bed, and baby. Another time she may show him a word like "cat" and then replace the first letter to form other words like sat, rat, mat, and bat.

While the child's interest in letters and words is definitely encouraged and reinforced by the teachers in the nursery school, there is little pressure exerted on the child to systematically learn the identification of letters or words and their phonetic components. Tedious drill is avoided, since our experience has shown that children absorb a considerable amount of learning if exposed to these materials over a period of many months during the time that they are three and four, under conditions that are reinforcing but casual and permissive. What the child does not learn in this way, he can learn at a later time with less investment of time and energy—when he is more cognitively mature, better able to discipline his attention and effort, and more highly motivated to learn to read for himself.

The goals of prereading activities in the nursery school are:

1. To provide the child with many opportunities to identify letters and recognize words under conditions that are pleasant and natural.

2. To reinforce the child's interest in these materials.

3. To help the child learn that printed words have meaning and communicate interesting and useful messages.

PREMATH EXPERIENCES

Most young children show an interest in numbers by the time they are three years old, especially now that many of the children's television programs include such activities. Teachers and parents observe instances of counting, specification of small quantities by numbers, and pairing or other attempts at one-to-one correspondence. A child may learn to hold up three fingers to indicate how old he is, and sometime before his fourth birthday he probably knows that he will be four fingers old when that important day comes. He may have to concentrate on isolating four fingers and will make errors, but the interest is there.

Even before the child can name numbers or count he seems to use primitive number concepts intuitively to cope with everyday problems. A three-year-old may watch carefully, for example, to make sure that he is given as many cookies or pieces of candy as his companions have. From time to time the child may need to assess the boot or mitten situation and decide if one is enough, and if not, how many more are needed. Or he may find that he has two pennies in his pocket and, knowing he had three, hunt for the missing one. The child may not even be able to tell his parent or teacher how many of something he had, yet he knows that one is missing and seeks it out. Three- and four-year-olds in the nursery school frequently make spontaneous comments about small quantities of things indicating that they have "three" of something or that they need "two more." In the course of their play they may comment on how many red or blue blocks they have or how many round and square beads there are. They pair things, distribute them evenly into containers or among people, match them, or touch each in turn as if to count them.

Conversations include references to concepts of number and quantity, such as "more than," or "as many as," or concepts of size and measurement, such as "bigger than," "as big as," "littlest," "longest," "shorter," and "taller." Adults make a special effort to use words and expressions of these kinds at appropriate times so that children refine their understanding of them and gradually include them in their own vocabularies.

As the child becomes familiar with the technique of counting as it is used by other members of the family or school group, he is likely to parrot number sequences and attempt to count objects. At first he may not use the proper sequence of numbers with the exception of the first two or three; he is likely to count "one, two, three, five, sixteen, nine" . . . etc. Neither will he properly match one number with each item being counted. He may start out with a degree of accuracy, but soon his finger is moving randomly among items, out of phase with his count. He attempts the process seemingly for no other reason than to imitate what others sometimes do with objects of this kind.

In time the child will probably develop some degree of skill in these techniques even if his family does no more than just respond to him when he attempts to count, saying the numbers in the right order for him to hear and helping him to match one number to each object. Even if one thought it wise to discourage the preschooler's growing interest in numbers, it would be hard to keep an alert four-year-old from picking up significant bits of information and practical skill with number concepts. By the time the child gets to school he will probably have learned the correct sequence of numbers up to ten and will be showing some skill in counting small numbers of objects and carrying out very simple number manipulations to get an amount of something he wants or needs. Adults can either ignore his attempts to develop facility with numbers or they can respond as they do to the child's attempts to understand any subject matter—by being interested and helping when they can. Parents and teachers of young children have had reservations about nurturing the child's interest in numbers for fear of negative effects that will interfere with the child's later learning. The evidence for negative effects is minimal. The likelihood that learning something about numbers at three or four will interfere with the child's later school progress in this area is not very great unless a child's early experiences have been so negative as to make him reluctant and avoidant of future learning. This, of course, can happen and is thought to be linked with an overly concerned, "pushy" attitude on the part of parents or teachers toward the child's early mastery of number concepts and related skills. Actually, the best guess according to the available evidence is that positive effects of early learning experiences are more common than negative outcomes. The risk of negative effects is probably minimal if adults take their cues from the child concerning his readiness and his interest, and see to it that the experiences provided the child are rewarding, not failure-ridden or stressful to him.

In the nursery school, experiences with number concepts are a part of both the informal exchanges between teachers and children and a part of the more formal teacher-directed activities. There are many informal conversations during the nursery school day when children and teachers talk about numbers and number concepts. When a good opportunity arises to count, counting is likely to be done. If paint brushes are needed, a teacher helps a child first decide from looking at the number of paint cups, how many brushes are needed if one is needed for each cup, and then helps him count out that many and put them in the cups. If snack is being prepared, the child may have to count the number of chairs at a table and bring enough juice cups so there will be one for each chair, or decide how many napkins are missing and get them. Another time a child may need to hunt among the supplies for two more wheels to complete a four-wheel construction toy on which he is working. With the older preschoolers the teacher can almost assume that they can identify at sight or count small quantities of things. She can ask a child to bring "two paper towels" or "three red crayons" without even checking to see if he knows that quantity. If the child's task is harder, the teacher may show him on her fingers, or on his, how many he must get, or ask him if he can show her how many five or six is. If he has trouble with the task, she goes with him and helps him to count them out correctly, perhaps reassuring him that six is a lot to count without help. The child is not made to feel that he has failed to live up to his teacher's expectations. The attitude the teacher conveys is that the children will find it helpful to know about numbers and counting, that they already have some skill with small quantities, and that learning to handle larger quantities will be useful and interesting for them.

Many of the children initiate number activities spontaneously by dividing supplies, composing matching sets of items, counting arrays of things before them, or by comparing amounts of things that each possesses. Even the children who do not initiate these activities are usually receptive and interested when a teacher initiates them. Sometimes the children count together. For example, at group time they may count the number of people present, the number of days on the calendar before some important event, or the number of children wearing blue socks or brown shoes. Counting together gives the child a chance to practice the counting operation and helps him to correct any errors in the sequence of numbers as he has learned them. Some songs and stories also involve counting and help the child to learn the correct sequence of numbers.

Gradually, through both planned and informal experiences the child gains some important insights about numbers. Eventually he will come to realize that three objects remain three objects even if you move them around and rearrange them. You can string them out in a line, hide them under a box, or bunch them up, but if you don't add to them or subtract from them, you still have three. He learns that you can get more by adding objects and will have less if you subtract some and that, if you put two groups of things together, you will have one bigger group (or "set" as the child may later come to call it). He learns that you have the same number of "things" in each of two groups if you have a toy dog, a pencil, and a block in one group and a bead, a crayon, and a car in another group.

Although preschoolers are beginning to use symbols, the manipulation of concrete objects facilitates their understanding of mathematical concepts. Older preschoolers are quite accurate in manipulating small quantities of objects. For example, if a child has a supply of one-inch cube blocks to work with, he will probably give correct answers to questions such as "If you have three and add two more, how many will you have?" or "How many will you have to add to two to have four?" Some children will arrive at these answers by manipulating the blocks before them while others will calculate without actually moving the blocks.

Some children facilitate their counting by lining objects up so that they can keep better track of which ones they have counted and which they have not. Some put each item aside as they count while others use less obvious grouping techniques, such as counting a group of objects from left to right or top to bottom, being careful not to miss any. Most of the children make use of some kind of organizational aid for counting more than five or six items in a group. If the child wants to count but is having difficulty, the teacher will suggest one of these techniques to help him keep track as he counts.

Though the child's casual experience with fractions is less extensive than his experience with whole numbers, simple problems do arise from time to time that necessitate dividing objects into equal parts for distribution among the children. The older children are able to recognize the need to carefully divide an apple into four approximately equal parts if they are to share it; however, the technique of dividing it first into two equal parts and then each half into two more equal parts to get fourths is not a part of their skill or experience, nor would they identify their share as "one fourth of an apple." Although the language of fractions is not a part of the child's everyday vocabulary, many four-year-olds seem to have a working notion of the meaning of "one half" and know that to get one half, one must divide something into two parts. The child's investment in the equality of the two halves, however, seems to involve his sense of fairness and justice more than any understanding of the precise mathematical definition.

Some of the teacher-directed small-group games played in the nursery school give the children practice with number concepts. For example, a game may involve matching domino-type blocks by the number of dots on the block surface, or ordering them side by side so that each domino has one more dot on it than the one before. For some games the child may have to count out numbers of beads or blocks or pegs, or compose matching groups of items for each child present, or add to various groups until each has the same number of items. The child may have to indicate as part of the game, which he has the most of, red or blue blocks, or which he needs one more of, a red or a blue block. He may have to divide some blocks, chips, or beads equally among several children, giving each child two or three. The teacher may tell him how many each should have or help him distribute them around the table one by one until they are gone.

Some games (like the popular "Chutes and Ladders" game) involve moving a marker along a path to a "goal" and require the use of a spinner or dial that indicates the correct number of spaces to move. The child then must recognize the numbers (or have them read to him) and move his marker the correct number of spaces along the path. Most nursery school games involving number concepts require the children to work with small numbers or small quantities of blocks, beads, or pegs— usually between two and six and seldom more than ten. Even if the child can accurately count more than ten, performing such an operation is tedious for others who are watching or waiting turns. If a child does wish to display his rote counting skill by pushing on to 20, 25, or 30, he can usually find a teacher in the nursery school who will be his audience at a time when other children are not involved and waiting a turn to participate.

It is the impression of many experienced nursery school teachers that young children benefit more from becoming facile and accurate at recognizing, counting, and manipulating small quantities (perhaps under 10) than from mastering the management of larger quantities which require more formal procedures and which may be more easily managed by older school-age children. When a child actually manipulates a small group of objects before him—beginning with six blocks, for example, adding two so that he will have eight or taking two away so he will have only four or dividing them equally among three children, one gets the feeling that the child is understanding intuitively what he is doing when he adds, subtracts, or divides. No doubt the child is capable of learning by rote how many of something you have if you begin with six and take two away, but without the physical manipulation of the objects he may not understand what effect the operation has on the constellation of objects.

As the children's facility with number concepts increases, they become interested in identifying written numbers. Materials are routinely available to the children in the nursery school to help them to learn the printed symbols for each number and to match the symbol with the amount it represents. Cutout boards are available in which the child can insert the numbers in order from one to nine. Peg- or blackboards are available in which a number is printed at the top of the board and the number of pegs or blocks to be inserted in the board matches the printed number. Number puzzles are provided which, when completed, match quantities with a printed number. Magnetized plastic numbers and a magnetic board are used by the children to mount numbers in order or to match them as they are printed in order at the top of the board. Although these materials may be used in game-type presentations by the teachers from time to time, they are also available on open shelves for the children to use during free activity time as they wish. Even if a child is using these materials on his own initiative and according to some plan of his own, a teacher is likely to come by, watch his activity, volunteer information such as labeling the numbers or checking his identification of them if he seems receptive to this intrusion and, generally, encourage his interest in the materials. If he is working with materials that match printed numbers with quantities (in which, for example, the printed number "3" is paired with three dots), an adult will probably check to be sure that he understands he can tell what the printed number is by looking at how many dots there are. Here, too, only the numbers from one to ten are likely to be used.

Some of the older preschoolers become quite interested in writing numbers just as they do letters and simple words. The child is allowed to do so if he wishes and is encouraged without implied demands for excellence. The children, however, are not specifically taught to write numbers, and less impetus is given to this activity than to some of the other number activities such as recognizing numbers, using them for counting, and performing simple manipulations of adding, subtracting, and dividing.

Measurement activities

Conversations of children in the nursery school include frequent references to how tall a child is compared with someone else or compared with his own height at some earlier time, how many pounds heavier he is this year than he was last year, or how much of something he possesses compared with a standard. Measuring by comparing an object with a standard or comparing one object with another clearly interests many preschoolers. The first measurement concepts used by the children in the nursery school are likely to be simple judgements that one person or object is bigger, heavier, taller, or longer than another. The child may use crude measurement techniques like placing objects side by side to compare their size, or placing people back to back to compare their heights.

The child's main interest in measurement seems to involve his egocentric investment in his own characteristics or possessions compared with those of others. If he asks how tall he is and is told the number of inches representing his height, he is likely to ask next: "Am I taller than Billy?"

Our preschoolers do not seem to show a spontaneous interest in using units of measurement such as inches, feet, ounces, or pounds for measuring objects or people. In one project conducted with the older children in the nursery school the children were able to learn how to use a standard marked off by inches to measure various objects. The objects, in this case, were carefully selected or constructed to measure no more than 10 inches (so the children could recognize the numbers involved) and to measure an exact number of inches long (so the children would not have to cope with fractions of inches). While the mechanics of measuring an object against a standard were intriguing to some of the children, most had trouble comprehending the necessity of lining up the left side of the ruler with the edge of the object to be measured. They could learn to do this as part of the "correct" procedure for measuring the objects, but they did not understand the necessity or reasonableness of the procedure. They did not feel something was wrong if, through carelessness, an object mea-

sured a different length each time they measured it; nor did they see anything wrong in having an object measure longer simply by sliding it along the ruler until it extended to a higher number. In general, the children did not seem as ready for these measurement experiences as they are for some of the other number experiences presented to them.

Some nursery school materials would seem to be particularly good forerunners to the child's understanding of measurement concepts. For example, the children use cuisinare-type measuring rods which are marked off into standard segments and are varying segments long. Children sometimes line the rods up to see which are longer and which are shorter, count the segments of the longer and shorter rods, supplement the shorter rods with a small rod that is just the correct number of segments to equal the longer one, and order the rods so that each successive one is one segment longer than the last. These activities may help the child to finally understand length as a dimension of objects that can be reduced to standard-sized segments using the segment as the unit of measurement.

The dimension of weight is brought to the children's attention through the use of a balance scale. The adults occasionally explain how the scale works so that the children understand what is required to balance the instrument. Most of the time, however, the children are free to experiment with the scale on their own, balancing it with small blocks, beads, or miniature figures, or filling one tray with blocks and then adding to the other tray until the scale is balanced.

In summary, the goals of the premath and measurement experiences in the nursery school are these:

1. To reinforce the child's growing interest in numbers, number manipulations, and measurement activities.

2. To help the child understand that facility with numbers and number concepts aids in the solution of everyday practical problems.

3. To provide the child with both informal and structered opportunities to identify and count small quantities of items, to recognize at least some of the numbers from one to ten, and to solve simple, practical problems involving addition, subtraction and division.

6
Social Studies

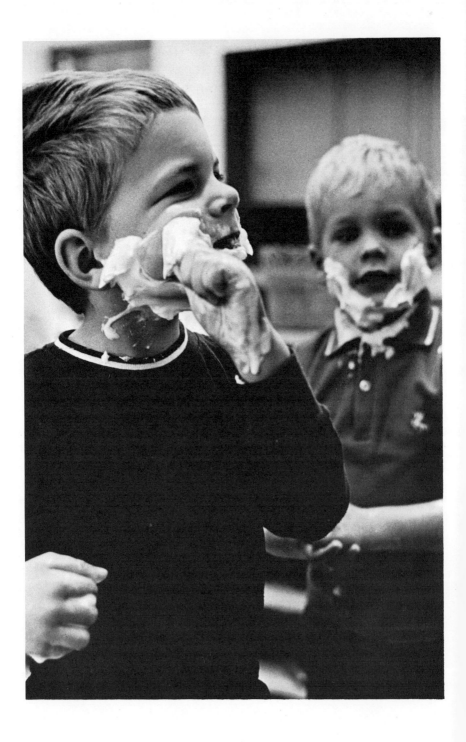

6 Social Studies

Some nursery school activities have as their goal helping the child to establish his own identity as a member of society and teaching him things about the other people with whom he shares the environment. Curricular projects of this kind come under the heading of social studies and usually are concerned with one of four general topics:

1. Self-awareness and personal identity.
2. The interdependence of members of a family, classroom, or community.
3. Material products of the culture and jobs people have: dwellings, vehicles, and work tools.
4. Community customs, differences among people within the community, and people from other lands.

SELF-AWARENESS AND IDENTITY

Some social studies projects help the children become aware of their own physical characteristics. For the youngest preschoolers, activities may be as easy as having them locate various parts of their bodies in a "Simple Simon Says" game in which Simon says, "Place your hands on your head . . . feet . . . shoulders . . . ears . . . ," and so forth. For the older children, awareness of each child's unique characteristics may be heightened by such projects as inviting the children to do "self-portraits." With the help of an adult, the child's physical outline is traced while he is lying on a large sheet of paper that is as long as he is tall. The child then decides —perhaps with the aid of a full-length mirror—what color to paint his hair, skin, eyes, shirt, pants or dress, and socks and shoes. The child may decide to draw himself in his outdoor clothes in which case he will need to find the colors for his snowsuit or jacket, hat, and boots or rubbers. The portraits are likely to be the focal point of comments and comparisons as children identify their own and find their companions'.

Some projects help the children reflect about their personal identity. The adult may, for example, record "Who am I and what am I like?"

statements in which each child is asked to supply important information about himself such as his first and last name, the names of his brothers and sisters, the names of his best friends, his favorite toys, his favorite place to visit, what he likes best on television, and his favorite foods. Each child's story can be recorded under his picture.

Game variations of the "Guess Who" type are popular with the nursery school children. The group must guess who a teacher or another child has in mind, and the clues given may be a combination of physical features like blond hair, or brown skin—and clothing like blue pants or a red sweater. Racial distinctions are included just as are other characteristics, so that children begin to accept them as casually as they do differences in hair color, eye color, or size. A child may be identified as "someone who is black and has a brother named John," or as "someone who knows how to speak Spanish," or as "someone who is an American Indian."

As children get to know each other better, Guess Who games may involve distinctive bits of information like "Who has a cat named Spider?" or "Who got a trike for his birthday?" or "Who fell out of a tree last week?" Games of this kind give each child a brief moment to be the center of the group's attention and helps each of the children to become aware of the other members of the group.

Early in the school year the adults may make a point of playing games that specifically identify children and adults by name. In this way the children become conscious of the members of their group even if they do not often play with some of the children or are not yet fully aquainted with all of the teachers.

The older children may try more difficult tasks like identifying each other from a shadow cast on a wall. If the children have trouble identifying one of their companions from a standstill shadow, the child may be asked to walk across the lighted area, giving the group additional clues from body movements. The children may also try to identify their companions just from their voices repeating a sentence like, "Guess who I am?"

Some self-awareness projects are designed to increase the child's pride in his own growth and development. For example, a group of five or six children may be asked to dictate a group story about all of the things that various ones of them have learned to do recently—like put on their boots, wash their faces, do a hard trick on the monkey bars, eat a new food, or duck their faces under water. Over a period of several days each child in the group may contribute to the story. In preparation for a project of this kind, mothers may be asked to jot down one or two memorable things that their child has learned to do during the past few months.

The children can be reminded of these things as they contribute to the story. Children may also be encouraged to talk about the things that they are not able to do yet—like tying their own shoes, stopping sucking their thumbs, staying in the dark without being afraid, and the like. Care is taken not to preach or moralize about issues of this kind; the teacher's purpose is to support the child's efforts to cope with difficult problems and to convey confidence in his ability to master the situation in due time.

About the time that the oldest children are ready to go on to kindergarten, teachers will focus some attention on this event as a new venture and an indication of their maturity. They will help the children to be prepared for what will be expected of them in kindergarten. Teachers may talk about the things the children will do there and how it will differ from nursery school: particularly the fact that there may be only one teacher and many times she will want them to do work that will help them to learn to read when they are a little older. In kindergarten they may be asked to line up to go in and out of school, raise their hands if they want to ask the teacher something, and do their work without help if they can! The group may even practice these things a few times. Some years, a kindergarten teacher has been invited to visit the nursery school or arrangements have been made for the nursery school children to visit a kindergarten a few at a time for 10 to 15 minutes.

Children generally accept the new expectations of the kindergarten as indicators of their own ability to function more independently and are not made anxious by discussing them. If a child does seem apprehensive, the adults will put more stress on the reassurance that when the time comes, his teacher will tell him all he needs to know—like what room to go to, and so forth.

Occasionally a child in the group knows that he is old enough to go to kindergarten but for some reason his parents and teachers feel he should remain in the nursery school for another year. Care is taken that this child not be a part of any discussion that would embarrass him or make him feel that he is not as capable as the other children.

INTERDEPENDENCE OF MEMBERS
OF THE FAMILY, SCHOOL
AND COMMUNITY

Some social studies projects call the child's attention to the responsibilities of various members of the family. The children talk about all of the things that mothers and fathers do to care for their families. From time to time a willing mother is asked to bring her infant in and care for him right at the school for a morning. She may mix the baby's formula, give him his bath, breakfast, playtime and, perhaps, even his nap at school so that the children can see some of what mothers do each day in taking care of their babies.

For one project a visiting toddler named Cindy was invited to spend part of one day in the group, and children were charged with the responsibility of making certain that she had plenty of things to play with, was helped on climbing equipment, got juice and crackers at snack time, and did not get lost during transition times in the program. Before the visit they discussed the fact that she probably would not know about sharing and things of that kind, so they would have to be patient with her and find her something else if she wanted a toy one of them was using. When the time came the children rose to the occasion, and Cindy had more than enough attention, care, and solicitude for one day. The point of this project was not so much to give the children a new experience (though it may have been a new one for some of them without younger brothers and sisters) but, instead, to direct their attention to the contributions that they can make to everyday family management because of their maturity and willingness to be helpful.

From time to time the children talk about the distribution of household chores among members of their own families and try to think of all of the ways that they can help. They may recall doing an errand for their mother, briefly watching a baby or younger child, putting away their own toys, or hanging up their own clothes. The preschooler should begin to think of himself as a part of a team of individuals who work together in the family and in the school.

Children particularly enjoy opportunities to perform real tasks that are ordinarily seen as part of the everyday work responsibility of adults or older members of the family. In school they frequently prepare their own special snack, which may involve cooking soup, making pudding, pancakes or waffles, or baking apples, cookies, or cupcakes. From time to time the groups embark on cleaning projects in which they wash all of the toys and equipment in their rooms. To give children a particularly gratifying work experience, teachers capitalize on the novelty of some tasks. For example, one group had a delightful time washing a Volkswagen family car from bumper to bumper as a group project. Tasks are often selected because they involve things that children particularly like to do—like scrubbing furniture with lavish amounts of soap and water, shoveling snow, sweeping sidewalks, raking leaves, planting gardens, mopping floors, and washing dolls, doll clothes, or dress-up clothes.

The children also routinely share the responsibility for keeping their playroom in order. They hang their clothes in their lockers, keep track of their belongings, help pick things up that are accidentally (or otherwise) spilled on the floor, lend a hand in getting materials or equipment moved from place to place, and help put toys away.

They are not generally asked to return toys, blocks, or equipment to the shelves directly after using them. Children tend to come and go from the play areas of the room, and a leftover block building or a "set table" in the doll corner may actually attract some children to these areas as others leave. A policy that holds a child responsible for putting away just what he uses tends to make children very conscious of the cleanup task per se; they may end up bickering over who did or did not touch something. Children are expected to be reasonable in their use of materials. If a child is building with blocks, for example, he takes them from the shelf, or from the floor, as he needs them. He does not pull them all down and then begin to build. If a child dumps the pieces of a puzzle out, he is expected to work at it, though he will not necessarily be expected to complete it.

There is usually one time in the school day that is set aside for straightening up the room. On most days that time will be directly after the free activity period and before the snack. Care is taken to keep regular cleanup responsibilities or special work projects from becoming noxious to the children. Young children can quickly become predisposed to resist work and responsibility if tasks are tedious or overly demanding of time and patience. Putting away toys, blocks, and table materials is an unglamorous job. To keep cleanup from being a painstaking process, the adults usually do the lion's share of the work, although this need not be immediately evident to the children who are working with them. The adults provide a model of fast, efficient cleanup and offer generous praise to the children for their efforts as they work along. A child who is reticent and hangs back may be handed one toy sometime during the cleanup process with the request that he find a place on the shelf for it. The rest of the time he will be ignored by the adults and usually by the children who are helping as well. The atmosphere is such that a child who does not participate has a feeling of having been left out rather than of having been favored. Hopefully, in this way, the child learns that people work together on chores and try to complete them with a minimum of procrastination and fussing. Routine tasks should take no more time than is necessary to get the job done, and the adults do not spend all of their time checking to see that a child does his share.

JOBS AND PRODUCTS

There are a number of avenues through which teachers inform children about the work and responsibilities of people in the community. Pictures are displayed showing people at their jobs, stories are read that tell about

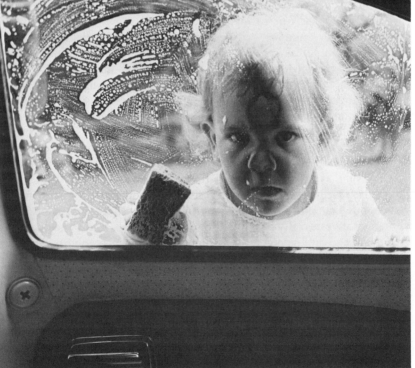

various occupations, and children talk about the services that they observe people performing in the community. Play props are introduced into the block area or doll corner to facilitate informal occupational play among the children. For example, a collection of 10 or 12 stuffed animals with a supply of bandages and splints can be the makings of an animal hospital to be introduced soon after the children have heard a story about a veterinarian. Groceries for a grocery store, hats for a hat shop, shoes for a shoe store, and clothes for a clothing store are all excellent props for stimulating the imaginative play of young children. A car made of large building blocks with a "motor" mounted on a wooden slab constructed from an array of spools, pegs, nails, removable nuts and bolts, and rubber bands provides hours of imaginative play exchanging parts and making repairs. An office corner with interesting props like a pigeonhole desk, a typewriter, paper, outdated forms with carbon inserts, a stapler, a date stamp, a telephone, and play money can involve the children in office play.

Field trips are an important source of information about work activities. Several times each year the children of a class are taken from the school as a group or in two or three smaller groups to visit places in the community where people are performing their jobs.

There are any number of interesting work sites for field trips. Some sites offer community services such as a post office, fire station, train or bus depot, air terminal, gas station, car wash, body and paint shop, bicycle repair shop, upholstery shop, a road repair or building site, and a harbor or a dock. Some sites produce or sell food products, such as a bakery, doughnut shop, sausage company, pizza parlor, grocery store, fishery, a dairy, or chicken farm. Factories that produce favorites such as peanut butter, potato chips, ice cream, cereal, soft drinks, or gum are especially attractive to the children. Some sites manufacture household objects or vehicles such as cars, boats, dishes, toys, cans, boxes, tires, shoes, candles, or children's clothing. Recreational sites are good places to visit, for instance, bowling alleys, roller-skating rinks, hobby shops, and gyms. Some craftsmen are especially interesting to watch at work, like crane operators, tree trimmers, sign painters, candy dippers, piano tuners, photographers, a shoe repairman, or a watch repairman.

The selection of sites to visit is usually determined by their potential interest to the children rather than the significance of the performance to be seen. For example, given a choice of visiting the city manager or a neighborhood mechanized car wash, the teacher of three- and four-year-olds may very well select the car wash, knowing that there will be fascinating things to watch and that the children will more fully understand what is going on.

Sites are selected on the basis of several criteria. First, there should be something of interest to see. Second, the facilities should be such that the children can get close to what there is to see without danger to themselves or excessive interference with the ongoing work. Third, the establishment should be both prepared and willing to have them visit. In return for their hospitality, the children are carefully prepared for what to expect and are especially primed to be well-behaved guests. Most hosts are pleasantly surprised at how manageable and appreciative the children are when they go visiting.

The primary purpose of trips to work sites is to give the children the general impression that the products they see in the environment come about in part through the ingenuity of people who work together at their jobs and who take pride in their skills. Precisely which occupations the children see is not as important as grasping the idea that adults in our society are industrious and have learned the skills of their trade.

From time to time guests are invited into the school and are asked to perform their work for the children to watch. A carpenter, for example, can be invited to construct some interesting object—perhaps a birdhouse or dollhouse at school. He can set up the equipment and materials he needs in one section of the room using school equipment as much as possible and just work, allowing the children to come and go at will and watch as long as they like. He may talk informally with them about how he constructs the objects or about the tools he uses and, finally, what color he will paint the finished project. Following such a visit the children should be allowed to work at the school workbenches, making anything they like or just nailing pieces of wood together.

Learning something about the jobs held by the older brothers and sisters of the preschoolers can give the children a special feeling of anticipation of the time when they, too, will be old enough to work. For example, in one group a local newsboy was induced to let the children each deliver a paper to a home in one block of his route under careful supervision from him and a teacher.

Some school projects focus more on the products being produced than on the job of producing them. Children are particularly curious about objects that are of major significance in the maintenance of community living, like houses, vehicles, and home conveniences such as work appliances, telephones, and television sets.

Social studies projects on these subjects need not be overly technical or extended beyond a few related activities to be meaningful and informative to the children. One project on transportation in the three-year-old group, for example, consisted of the children simply collecting all of the pictures they could find that showed ways people have of getting trans-

ported from one place to another. After several sessions in which various members of the group looked through magazines and old store catalogues, the children had filled a large section of the wall with pictures, including not only trains, airplanes, and cars but a pogo stick, a baby carriage, a wagon, a submarine, roller skates, a snowmobile, and a stagecoach.

In another transportation project about trucks, the children learned the names and distinguishing features of 10 or 12 different kinds of commercial trucks including dump trucks, pickup trucks, tow trucks, stock trucks, and flat trucks. Several local drivers of commercial trucks were asked to stop by so that the children could see the inside of trucks used for specific purposes, including a refrigerated ice cream truck, a bakery truck, a cleaners' and launderer's truck, and a long-distance moving van. The driver of the moving van told the children about some of the terms drivers use to describe their trucks and the long-distance runs they make, including the fact that they call the large tires "bolognas."

Some projects are designed to help children see the sequence of operations that go into the construction of a product. For example, one project on house building was coordinated with the construction of a building in the vicinity of the school. The children visited the site of the new building from time to time and learned what kinds of things had to be done to complete a house including excavating, pouring a foundation, putting up the walls, putting on the roof, wiring, insulating, installing the furnace and air ducts, putting in plumbing, plastering, and installing windows and doors. A well-illustrated children's book was used as an aid to the project as well as some contractors' pictures of various aspects of home building.

In some projects the children followed the changes that take place in a product as it is processed. For example, one project on "spaghetti" informed the children of the sequence of events that took place beginning with the planting of grain and including harvesting, the preparation of the grain by the manufacturer, packaging, and finally shipping the spaghetti to the supermarket for purchase by their mothers. Similar projects were done on the making of butter and ice cream.

Some projects maximize the children's skill in using products. For example, for one telephone project the children were supplied with two working telephones through the compliments of the telephone company. Over the phones they could carry on conversations with each other from one school room to another. The older children were also helped to dial their own home phone numbers or the number of a relative so that they could talk with that person on the regular school phone.

While some nursery school projects are carefully planned in advance, others are fortuitous events that the adults take advantage of as they become available, for example, the presence of workmen in the building who are replacing a broken window, removing a wall, or constructing one where one did not exist before.

Projects for the younger preschoolers are likely to be short and involve only one or two related activities, but projects for the older children can be more complicated, extending over a longer period of time. The adults in the nursery school are not too concerned about precisely what children learn about—whether it is the production of a toy, an item of clothing, food, or a building. What is important is that the children become interested in the process of acquiring new information through (1) looking at objects and watching people in the environment, (2) talking with people who have interesting information to tell, (3) looking at pictures or films, and (4) listening to books being read.

There is no attempt to formalize the social studies curriculum of the school by, for example, specifying the projects that are to be presented each year in the three- or four-year-old groups. Teachers may repeat projects done in previous years if they wish to but most also develop new projects based on the suggestions of their present teaching staff and the interests of the particular children in their group. Communication between teachers makes it possible to avoid the specific repetition of a project in successive years of a child's attendance in the nursery school, unless the repetition is deliberate on the part of the teaching staff.

Most school groups have from 20 to 30 different social studies projects distributed throughout the school year on these topics of special interest to young children. While the children do not participate actively in all projects, they typically participate in two-thirds to three-fourths of those presented in their group.

CELEBRATIONS AND HOLIDAYS

Some social studies projects help children to become more fully aware of the celebrations and holidays observed in their community. School groups typically celebrate Valentine's Day, Mother's and Father's Days, Halloween, and the Hanukkah, Christmas, and New Year holiday season. When holidays have religious significance as well as secular significance, only the secular aspects of the occasion are observed in school. The purpose of most holiday celebrations in the preschool is to increase the child's feeling of being a participant in the affairs of the community rather than to inform him of the significance and historical roots of various holidays. Holiday projects help to prepare the child for the things that will be done in the community in celebration of the day such as making valentines for one's friends and family members for Valentine's

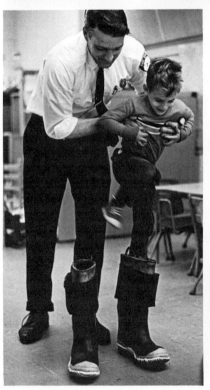

Day, carving pumpkins and dressing up in costumes for Halloween, and trimming trees and watching for the appearance of Santa Claus at Christmastime. Children are also honored on or near their birthdays with special recognition during the school snack time or at a group time.

In a university community, sports events and special days like Homecoming have a particular significance for the parents and older brothers and sisters of many of the children in school. To help the young children share some of the excitement of these activities, the school may arrange a visit from a football or hockey player to show his gear and equipment, baton twirlers or cheer leaders may be asked to come and give a demonstration or hold a practice session in the nursery school yard, and a few members of the marching band may be invited over to the school so that children can march with them. One group of children made their own "Homecoming float" in preparation for watching the Homecoming parade and viewing the campus floats. Through these experiences the children can participate in the things that interest the older members of the community.

COMMUNITY CUSTOMS AND PEOPLE
FROM OTHER LANDS

Teachers in the nursery school take advantage of opportunities to help the children become acquainted with people in the community who are from other subcultures and from ethnic backgrounds different from their own. The children themselves and their families represent different national, racial, and ethnic groups; getting acquainted with each other before the period of time when cultural biases and stereotypes distort their attitudes may help the children to be accepting of each other and to be comfortable in the presence of people from different cultural backgrounds. Young children are sometimes reticent to approach people who look, speak, or dress differently from themselves and their families. The school can work toward allaying any fears the child may have about these things. Ethnic songs or dances, distinctive costumes, and customs characteristic of particular segments of the community are presented to the children from time to time through stories, pictures, projects, guests at school, or special performances. Contributions of these kinds that can be made by parents or families are particularly valued, since the children have an added investment in their participation.

Snack time is a good time to introduce children to some of the favorite food products of another culture. In one group, the Chicano mother of one of the children spent the first part of the morning making tortillas at school with the children for a special midmorning snack. Another time a mother who was a native of France helped the children to make crepe suzettes for the snack time. Even though young children are not notoriously adventuresome in trying new foods, they seem to sense the significance of the occasions when a special snack is prepared that is a favorite of some of their schoolmates, and most participate enthusiastically. Of course, the mothers do their part too by reducing the unfamiliar seasonings or rich ingredients used.

Some of the children in school speak a language other than English or in addition to English. This, too, is presented to the children as a point of interest to be shared and enjoyed in the school group. The children who speak another language may be helped to teach the other children some of the words that they use for familiar things such as "madre" and "padre" for mother and father, "muchacha" and "muchacho" for girl and boy, and "amigo" for friend by a Spanish-speaking child. At the same time the children in the group may be helped to realize that the non-English speaking child is trying to learn their language and needs their help and patience.

Although children are surprisingly nonchalant about racial difference, comments are occasionally made about differences in skin color or other racial features of various members of the school group. When this happens, the adults comment on the differences in the racial background of the children or adults in the group as a point of general interest. While evidence suggests that even young children are aware of racial differences, our observations lead us to believe that if the adults in the school value the cultural and racial differences among the members of a group, the children, too, will learn to accept them casually without alarm or prejudice.

7
Geography

7 Geography

The preschooler's interest in geography is generally limited to the "here and now." Three- and four-year-old children are most keenly aware of characteristics of their local environment and are not likely to be curious about the characteristics of other places in the world.

We could approach the topic of geography for young learners by explaining that the surface of the earth is composed of masses of land and masses of water. We could further explain that the land masses are called continents which are, in turn, divided into countries; that the larger bodies of water are called oceans, and so forth. But young children do not ordinarily have as a part of their experience anything to make the concepts, earth, continent, or country meaningful. They may be able to understand that an ocean is "something like a lake but much, much bigger so that it takes many days to go across it in a ship." Country, continent, and earth, however, can best wait for definition at a later time in the child's concept development. A young child who has been touched directly by the geography of distant environments, of course, will have the makings of some understanding that the others lack. A child, for example, who has crossed the ocean either by plane or ship may have some idea of what an ocean is. Similarly, a child who has spent time in another country may have some impressions of how countries differ from one another. One sophisticated four-year-old, when told that a school visitor was from a "foreign country," asked, "Do people talk a different language there?" This child's concept of a foreign country as a place where the people talk a different language is not complete nor even totally accurate—but it is a beginning.

Young children clearly do not have a concept of earth as a planet in space, generally round in shape, and inhabited by us! Of course, contemporary space exploration has had a tremendous impact on our society, and even very young children are able to see photographs of earth from outer space and watch such impressive sights as men walking on the moon. Undoubtedly, these experiences will contribute to an earlier development of children's understanding of what planets are and what relation they have to each other. Children as young as three and four who are particularly interested in space can already talk with some authority about space suits and blast-offs, moon walks, the rover moon vehicle, moon craters, and moon dust. They are familiar too with the floating slow motion that characterizes the movement of astronauts on the moon and can imitate that gait. Some of the children even associate the slow movement of people and objects on the moon with the fact that the moon's gravity is different from the earth's. It is quite evident, however, that the child's understanding of gravity is restricted to this situation. He simply knows what to call it when he sees something that is effected by it in this one situation. He does not understand it as a principle that governs many different events —but he will in time.

The preschooler's interest in space exists primarily because space activities have been made a significant part of the child's personal experience —through the visual medium of television. Ironically, this is not true of many of the more mundane characteristics of the planet earth or of the little part of the earth that they inhabit. Some young children have visited other parts of the country and can recall experiences like playing in snow near the top of a mountain in the middle of summer, looking into a canyon, camping in wooded areas among bears, or seeing a waterfall. But many have not been away from their city homes enough to realize that environments can be very different from their own home ground. Listening to others talk of these things may give them some understanding, but a vital interest in these things will probably have to wait until the child has had more experiences of his own exploring new environments, or until he is better able to imagine those he has not experienced directly.

In the meantime, the preschool can make the study of geography meaningful by giving first consideration to facts and concepts that are closest to the childrens' direct experience. To this extent, geography in the preschool will vary depending upon the geographical location of a school.

Children can begin to become aware of the uses that are made of the geographical features of the areas in which they live. In one project, for example, our children identified as many different uses of the local lakes and rivers as they could think of, including recreational swimming, boating, and fishing in the summer, ice fishing, snowmobiling, and skating in the winter, and transporting people by boat. With the help of films, they also learned about other uses of the bigger lakes and rivers; for instance, their use in transporting commercial products in cargo boats on Lake Superior, and in transporting logs by floating them down a river instead of loading them on trucks or trains.

In another project children talked about "what you can do with big hills." They decided that they were good for climbing and looking far away, skiing, and bobsledding, but they were not good for roads and railroads, since cars and trains often had to go around or through them instead of over them.

Projects that help children to understand the relation between the climate of the area and the work activity of adults are meaningful. For example, children near a rural area can learn that farmers plant in the spring, let their crops grow in the summer, and harvest in the fall— before the weather gets cold enough to kill crops. Farmers must also arrange to take care of their livestock through the cold winter months. Most geography projects include visual aids such as photographs, drawings, or films as well as teacher commentary to facilitate children's learning.

UNDERSTANDING THE CONCEPT OF A MAP

One tool of the geographer that children can begin to learn about is the map. Once the child understands the notion that a map is representational, that is, a kind of "picture" of a place that gives you information about that place, some interesting map projects can be done. Children, for example, can help to map out their room in school or the entire school space. Things in the room or the rooms in the school can be placed with reasonable accuracy relative to each other without worrying about exact measurement to scale, a feature of maps that children will learn about later. Activities with maps provide another example of the interrelationship of learning in different content areas. Map projects often involve both mathematical and social studies concepts.

At first, the children may need some help in understanding that a map is representational. In one school project with older three-year-olds and young four-year-olds, a teacher constructed a maze on the floor in the shape of a "Y." The maze consisted of nine large hollow building blocks painted a bright orange. The teacher also sketched out a small map of the maze on paper using a square to represent each block. When the children were not looking she hid a small picture decal under one of the blocks on the floor. She then pointed out to the children, the square on her map that represented the block under which the decal was hidden. The children had to identify the correct maze block from that information. When the children had trouble doing this, the teacher revised her map. She made it much larger (using 18 by 24 in. easel paper) and painted large orange colored squares in the pattern of the maze. She then laid it down on the floor directly to the side of the real maze of orange blocks. With these additional cues, children were able to grasp the idea of using the map for information about the maze, and could go directly to the correct block to find the decal. After this experience, the children were able to go back to the much smaller map that lacked the color cues and use it as well.

In another map project to help children learn to "read" maps, the children had to find trinkets hidden in the room in various spots by looking at a map of the room. The location of furniture, shelves, equipment, and cupboards was marked. A small "x" was marked to indicate where each trinket could be found. The children could look at the map and know where to look for a trinket. For this project, too, the representational cues were made very obvious. A table and chair would be indicated by a small sketch of these things—or when they were indicated by a rectangle or square, they would be colored the color of the corresponding furniture in the room. At first, children used the color cues more than the spatial and relational cues of the map, but gradually some of them learned to use the map to identify the particular section of the room in which a trinket was hidden and which of several tables or shelves to look under. Some of the older children were also able to reverse their roles and to hide the trinkets, coming back to mark the map appropriately.

With a little experience in working with maps, children can learn to fill in the blanks left on maps. In one map project, children went for a walk within just a few blocks of the school, following a map all of the way, and noting significant marked features as they came to them. The things marked on the map included a stop sign, a prominent "Y" intersection, a distinctive gate at the campus entrance, and a bridge over a railroad track. Along the way children suggested still other things that should be put into the map as they came to them. When they returned to the school, they filled in the details of their map with some help from their teacher.

A large map of the city in which the children live can be helpful to the group once they have some understanding of maps. Adults can help children to locate their own homes and to see, for example, that their home is closer on the map to the home of a child who lives just down the block from them than it is to a child who lives a mile away. The older children can be helped to trace their route to school, remembering the street names and one or two significant features marked along the route such as a river crossing or a viaduct. A small section of the city map that contains the community in which many of the children live can be enlarged enough to include tiny representational pictures of buildings, bridges, railroads, and other distinctive features to help children to make the translation from the map to the real thing. One tourist map of the state of Minnesota has been particularly interesting to the children since it shows, in tiny sketch drawings, all of the things such as fishing, boating, swimming, and sightseeing that people do when they visit different parts of the state. Many of the children have been to one or another of these areas and can begin to associate what they know of the area with the information that the map conveys.

Generally, the directional concepts north, south, east, and west are not meaningful to the children, nor do they associate north with the top of the city map, south with the bottom, and east and west with right and left, respectively. The adults occasionally use these terms in talking to the children about the city map, but the children do not use them themselves nor is this information usable to them.

8
Science

8 Science

The nursery school staff attempts to accomplish two objectives by introducing children to information of a scientific kind. First the teachers hope to increase the number of accurate facts that the children know—facts about plants and animals in the environment and facts about the physical properties of the environment. Second, the teachers in the nursery school wish to interest the children in an increasingly deliberate and careful approach to the study of things around them.

While preschool children are neither capable of nor interested in the systematic mastery of scientific subject matter, they are ready for the less formal, prescientific study of things in the world that interest them. Early in the child's school experience he should learn to think of himself as a good learner and a student, without having to meet the demands of excellence that this usually implies—in much the same way that he is allowed to think of himself as a good helper or a good worker at home even though, admittedly, most household tasks can be done more efficiently without his help.

The introduction of scientific subject matter must be approached with the nursery school child's developmental level in mind and not as though he were a mature, disciplined student. The teacher of three- and four-year-olds will approach the study of animals with pragmatic questions having more to do with the child's motivation to learn than with his need for the systematic mastery of the subject matter. In planning activities, the teacher may ask herself questions such as which animals in the environment already have high interest value for the young child, which are the most fun to watch, which can the child easily handle safely, which are present and prominent in the environment and, therefore, are useful for him to know something about, which animals can be kept and cared for in the school, and which ones are available to be observed in their natural habitat.

In studying a particular animal, the older, more sophisticated student may begin with an exhaustive cataloging of the anatomical parts of the animal and may investigate each of the major body processes. By contrast, the teacher of young children focuses on selected bits and pieces of this content, posing questions or responding to the queries of children about the most interesting and distinctive features of an animal, what he eats, how he cares for his young, where he usually lives, and how he survives there.

A student's gradual mastery of a field of scientific inquiry can probably best be conceptualized as a spiraling process in which he encounters the same subject matter several times over a period of many school years. Each time he encounters a topic, he approaches it with greater sophistication, adds more bits and pieces of information, and corrects misconceptions that are left over from his previous encounters. In time, when his store of accurate information is considerable, he will need to organize his knowledge into a conceptual framework that allows him to define the field as a whole, assess the weaknesses in his knowledge, and fill in the gaps. Needless to say, this is not the level of sophistication of the preschooler. The preschooler is not a very systematic learner. His information in many areas is sketchy, limited in quantity, and contains some inaccurate generalizations.

As a toddler, the child's first exposure to the study of animals is likely to be when he learns that the four-legged creature named Rover who lives next door is a dog! He will eventually learn that other similar creatures are also called dogs at which point he may call a neighborhood cat, "dog." His mother will explain that that creature is not a dog, it is a cat. She will probably, in the course of events, find other opportunities to label cats (or pictures of cats) for him, and he will eventually learn that cats have a rather distinctive face and are similar in size and body contour, unlike dogs which come in many different sizes and shapes. When he first attempts to classify a rabbit, he may mistakenly call it a "cat" because of some of its facial features and size, or he may suspect that it is not a cat (since cats do not have such long ears and short tails) in which case he may ask: "What is it?" After the child learns that rabbits are not cats and cats are not dogs, he must learn that all of them are animals, and that other medium-sized, four-legged animals also are not dogs—such as goats, sheep, colts, and calves—and so it goes! It is this process of accumulating new knowledge and refining incomplete or faulty information that preoccupies the young child in his efforts to make sense of the world. One of the child's most formidable tasks at three and four years of age, is to learn the conventional names for living things, objects, and events and to gradually classify them according to appropriate likenesses and differences. The nursery school can help the child in this process by providing good opportunities for him to accumulate new information and to refine his present information in an atmosphere in which learning is interesting and rewarding.

We know that much of the young child's information has been learned through informal "discovery" as he interacts with the environment, encountering objects, people, and events. Relatively little of what he knows has been learned through didactic lessons. The nursery school continues to rely heavily on the learning experiences that are an informal part of the child's everyday activity, based largely on the child's own initiative in exploring an enriched environment. Nevertheless by the time the child is three and one half or four, he is aware of the fact that much of the learning of older persons is accomplished through more didactic procedures and that these procedures are associated with "school." We once asked a group of four-year-olds what they thought they would do when they went to elementary school. Their comments included things like "I'll learn to read," "I'll have a desk," and "I'll do homework." While the prospect of such a regime is a little frightening to the young child, it also inspires pride and confidence in his growing ability to work diligently at the job of learning. Adults in the nursery school reinforce the child's image of himself as someone who is getting ready to learn more formally through deliberate study. Science projects, for example, are sometimes introduced to the children as projects in which the group will "investigate" something or "observe and write down what we see."

A project about insects was described to the four-year-olds in this way: "We are going to learn all we can about insects. First we will have to find many different kinds of insects crawling around in the yard. We will collect some jars to keep them in so that we can look at them very closely. Insects are so little that we will need to use the magnifying glass to see their legs, heads, feelers, and wings if they have them. Then we will look at our books about insects to see if we can find out the names of the ones we have found." An orientation of this kind suggests to the children that when you set out to investigate or study something, you need a plan and you use a variety of resources. You look in the natural environment (in this instance, for insects in the yard and elsewhere) but you also use other resources, like a magnifying glass to improve your ability to observe and books about insects to aid in the process of identification and labeling.

The project about insects provided a number of ways for the children to approximate the attitudes and methods of the scientist. For example, in this project children were asked to confirm the identification of various insects by checking features one by one—body shape, head, eyes, wings, feelers, and number of legs—matching them to the features of an enlarged picture of the insect from an insect book. The teacher suggested that, instead of trying to remember all of the insects they were able to find, she would write down their names as they identified new ones.

Simple hypothesis testing is also a part of science projects in the nursery school. For example, the children had heard that some crawling insects do not stay in lighted areas but prefer to be in the dark. A teacher helped them to check this information by providing a shelter in one corner of a jar in which some insects were kept, waiting for the insects to come out, then shining a flashlight near the jar to send them scurrying back under the shelter.

The success of a science project such as this will be judged largely by the degree of interest and personal involvement shown by the children in the group. For the insect project, for example, children collected pictures of insects to mount on the wall, painted pictures of insects (without rigid demands for accuracy), and made "bugs" out of clay. At times, the purity of a project is sacrificed in favor of child involvement. For example, children began embellishing their clay figures with "Dr. Seuss-like" qualities that in no way resembled insects but that certainly made for interesting viewing. Some bugs were given long noses, porcupinelike quills, curly tails, and various other appendages. The possibility that the children did not always know precisely where real information about insects ended and their own fun-and-game bug fantasies began was not allowed to reduce the fun of creating bugs the likes of which never existed. The adults enjoyed the children's creations for their humor and imagination. The general impression one had was that the children, too, realized that they were creating some imaginary variations.

Science projects in the nursery school are often brief one- or two-session episodes that involve things such as the reading of a story that is accurate enough to be presented to the children for its factual content (for example, the popular story of "Tim Tadpole" and his metamorphosis from a tadpole to a frog) or the showing of interesting nature films on subjects like seasonal changes and animals in their natural habitat. Films are especially good for showing children processes that can only be observed over long periods of time in nature, like the blossoming of a flower, the spinning of a spider web, or the building of a bird's nest. Ten-to fifteen-minute films are frequently shown to the children twice or even three or more times over a period of two or three days with comments and other related activities interspersed during or between showings.

Whenever it is feasible, interesting objects for study are brought into the school as they come to the attention of the teachers or parents of the children. At one point, for example, a large stuffed owl was brought into the classroom for children to see. Another day several fossils were brought in that had been found by the brothers and sisters of one of the children while on vacation. An adult in the group took the responsibility for finding resource material on fossils so that he could provide the children with a few interesting facts and some correct labels for the specimens. During the few days that the fossils were displayed this young man took advantage of many opportunities to talk with the children individually or in groups about them.

Litters of mice, gerbels, hamsters, kittens, rabbits, or puppies are brought to school when opportunities occur so that the children can see, touch, and hold them. During a typical school week, it is not unusual for two or three of these events to come about fortuitously through the alertness of teachers and parents. Nevertheless the nursery school staff does not rely primarily on incidental learning experiences or the emergence of casual curriculum activities for their groups; all teachers plan curriculum of an informational kind for balance and variety of subject matter. Because of their familiarity with the developmental levels and interests of young children, the teachers in the nursery school are able to develop curriculum projects that are highly successful and interesting to the children. Many of these projects would never have emerged from the expressed interests of the children without the impetus of the adults.

Science projects in the nursery school can be classified under one of three general subject matter headings: information about animals, information about plants, and information about the physical properties of the world.

ANIMAL PROJECTS

Projects about animals are almost certain to be popular with young children; especially those dealing with household pets like dogs, cats, fish, and some species of birds. Pet projects sometimes focus on the physical growth and development of animals. For example, in one project a young kitten only a few weeks old was brought to school for two or three hours during which time the children held her, played with her, and let her sleep. Moving pictures were taken of the children holding the kitten on their laps. By prearrangement the kitten visited again every few weeks and again pictures were taken of her activities and play behavior. Before each visit the children in the group viewed the film from the previous visit to remind them of the kitten and to show them how much she had grown between visits. After a period of about four months and four visits, the films from each visit were spliced so the children could view them in sequence showing how big the kitten had grown, the change in her food from milk to cat food, and the development of her agility and playfulness.

Occasionally a project involves the study of an animal that undergoes gross structural change as it develops, for example, a caterpillar that develops into a butterfly or moth. These projects often involve keeping the animal at school in a seminatural habitat during the period of change so that the children can realize that the animal has not been replaced by another different one but has, indeed, changed! A movie or film strip of the process is often used as a supplementary visual aid.

Some projects call the children's attention to the gross differences among creatures of different species. In one such project the children discussed all of the ways that animals have of getting around from place to place, including walking on anywhere from two to hundreds of legs, using wings to fly, or tails and fins to swim, or moving by virtue of elegantly segmented bodies. In this project the children watched a worm crawling in a confined area directly under a magnifying glass so that they could easily see the constriction of the body segments as the animal moved. They also observed the same feature of movement in a six-foot snake named "Rachel" that was brought to school by its keeper. They were able to actually feel the movement of the snake's body as she twisted and turned under their hands.

Some animal projects focus on the care and feeding of animals and require the presence of an animal in the school for a period of many weeks or months. During most years the school is generously endowed with guinea pigs, gerbils, pet mice, and rabbits. The children share the responsibility for the care of the animals by helping with the cleaning of cages and the feeding and watering of the animals. Even if the animals are fed prepared pellets, the children are taught what natural foods the animals like so that occasional treats can be brought from home for their pets. They sometimes weigh and measure the pets at regular intervals to be sure the animals are growing.

Learning to handle animals properly and gently is one important part of pet-care activities in the nursery school. Children are generally expected to sit down on the floor when playing with animals so that the animal can be held or placed in a lap without danger of being dropped or stepped on. They must learn to hold the very small animals very gently and not grab or squeeze them even if the animal seems about to get away. The children get very skillful at corralling lively little animals so that they can keep them close without hurting them. They let them climb around on their hands, arms, shoulders, and laps or in and out of their pockets in search of pellets of food. A child who is frightened or reluctant to hold the animals can just watch or pet the animal while a teacher holds it.

Occasionally an animal is sturdy enough and the children experienced enough to carry the animal around to different play or work areas of the room or to just let it run free. These activities are always under the watchful eye of the adults, and children generally must have permission to let an animal out of a cage or box.

Learning that animals have "feelings" and can be frightened, injured, or angered is part of school pet care. One group of children had a pet rabbit named Roger who was allowed the free run of the room during a good part of each school day. Anytime Roger was chased or frightened, he immediately retreated to his cage and would not come out again for 10 or 15 minutes. The school rule was that if Roger was frightened he should be allowed to get away from the children and should not be made to come out of his cage until he came out on his own. If the children wanted him to stay out, they simply had to learn not to frighten him.

The children become especially fond of animals that can be played with, handled, and held. Solicitude and tenderness is the prevalent attitude expressed toward the animals and abuse is relatively rare. Children who do mistreat an animal by grabbing or teasing are often responding to the frustration of not being able to get the pet to stay near them. The adults can help these children learn to handle the animal appropriately so it will not be frightened.

Occasionally a child's abuse of animals is motivated by general anger or hostility, and the animal is an innocent (and relatively defenseless) victim. In these instances, the nursery school staff will view the child's behavior as part of a larger problem than simple "pet-care training," and the sources of the child's chronic anger will be explored. In the meantime the child will be closely supervised whenever he is with the animals, and he will be expected to resist abusive behavior.

Occasionally an animal does get injured or even killed in some accident or deliberate act of abuse at school. If a child has been responsible for the death of an animal, teachers try to reassure the child that such things do occasionally happen. Another animal to take the place of the missing one is often helpful as a reassurance to a guilty child; but, at the same time, procedures and precautions to be taken in the handling of the animal are clarified so a similar accident does not occur again. If the children have previously had the experience of burying a dead animal and suggest this as a means of disposing of it, teachers may help them accomplish the task. More often, however, the disposal of a dead animal is handled without undue fanfare by a procedure like wrapping it in newspaper and giving it to the janitor to be put with the refuse.

The death of living things due to age or natural causes may also be encountered in the classroom. In some instances the children can be prepared for such an event. If an animal appears to be sick, its condition may be called to the attention of the children, and they can consider possible causes and what might be done to facilitate the animal's recovery. Some members of the group may accompany the teacher or school nurse when the animal is taken to the veterinarian, and they may report the diagnosis to the class. If the animal cannot be cured, his condition is usually linked with his being very old or very sick and the doctor's being unable to cure him. Some teachers prefer to return from an animal hospital with a sick animal even if the animal must be removed shortly and done away with so that children do not associate trips to the hospital with death. Whether the death is due to natural causes or to an accident, the probable cause is discussed briefly with the children. The children are helped to understand death as one part of the total life cycle. Teachers, however, do not dwell on the topic nor moralize about the causes. Teachers also are very alert for children who may become anxious or express undue concern about the death and try to help these children deal with the situation by clearing up any misconceptions and by reassurance. Most young children are surprisingly acceptant of such things, however, and generally do not interpret the death of an animal as an indication that they, too, or members of their families might die. Most children probably do not make this association until sometime during the early school years. Nevertheless, if the issue seems to worry a child, the teachers may make the point that animals do not live as long as people and that people can usually be cured by doctors when they become ill.

Animal projects also involve the process of birth. The smaller caged animals are particularly appropriate for mating and rearing litters, since they have a short gestation period and mature in a matter of weeks. Children occasionally witness the birth of a litter of animals, but more often the litter is born at a time when the room is quiet and the children are not present. In any case, children see the young within hours or even minutes of birth, and they sometimes linger over a cage for 15 or 20 minutes watching newborn creatures for signs of movement and mobility. They wait impatiently for animals to get big enough to be handled. Consideration of the mother animal and precariousness of the newborn are the reasons usually given for having to wait until the babies have grown a little before taking them out of the cage.

Egg-hatching projects are also popular in school. Most years the school has at least one incubator set up so that baby chicks or ducklings can be hatched. In one project of this kind, the children followed a chart plotting the development of the embryo chicks and opened an egg from time to time to observe the early development of the chick. If an incubator is not available at school, eggs can be obtained from a local hatchery on the day of a hatch. Eggs that are just beginning to crack open can be selected so that the chicks will be sure to hatch in the presence of the children.

Some projects focus on the different natural habitats of creatures. While some animals live in homes or schools as pets, others live on farms, in zoos, in jungles, or in caves, some burrow under the ground or live in trees, some build nests, and others live in water.

Another popular theme of nursery school projects about animals has to do with the services rendered by animals who are trained to do a task: for example, horses and camels trained to carry riders, elephants trained for heavy lifting or pulling, and circus animals trained to perform feats of balance and agility. One particularly interesting school project involved the study of "dogs that work." The children heard stories, viewed films, and saw pictures of dogs trained to herd sheep, of sled dogs at work in Alaska, of hunting dogs, guard dogs, and Seeing Eye dogs. A Seeing Eye dog and his master visited school, and the dog's owner told the children how he attended a school to learn how to give his dog commands. He demonstrated how his dog leads him around obstacles in his path.

The fact that some animals supply food products such as fish, foul, meat, milk, and eggs is another recurring theme of school projects. Most years the children learn something about farms and farm animals, and some projects include a visit to a farm. Visits are usually made in the spring of the year when baby animals are in evidence. For one project the children observed the milking operation and then learned what happens to the milk from the time it comes from the cow to the time their mothers buy it in the supermarket. There are a number of popular children's stories about farm animals and farm families that inform the children about these animals and, incidentally, about this aspect of American life.

Other popular animal themes involve the study of wild animals or prehistoric animals. Though children are not as familiar with these animals as they are with pets and animals found in their own environments, their interest in them is often aroused through stories, television productions, and the availability of commercial animal toys. In one project about prehistoric animals, the older nursery school children were particularly intrigued by the unusual names of these beasts and learned several of them. The children also helped to assemble plastic commercial models of each variety and then constructed a diorama of dirt, rocks, and caves as a setting for their model animals.

Occasionally the study of animals touches on the issue of imaginary "monsters" versus real animals, vicious or otherwise. If there is any evidence of confusion, the children are reassured that monsters like Frankenstein or "devils" do not exist in our world and that most wild animals that could hurt people are kept in cages or live in jungles far from towns and cities.

The study of their own bodies is also a popular theme of science projects for children in the nursery school. For some projects, children chart their growth by weighing and measuring themselves. Other projects have been developed around issues of health care and cleanliness. The children may discuss the reasons for washing their hands before eating, and during most school years the school nurse shows them the proper way to brush their teeth.

The children also learn something about the care needed after an injury, since they are usually taken to the school nurse at that time. The nurse is careful to tell the injured child each thing she is doing and helps him to understand what to expect. Friends may accompany the child to the nurse's office and thus have an opportunity to observe the care given. One of the more difficult issues in the care of injuries is to provide proper care without making a child unduly aware or overly concerned with his physical state. It is usually necessary for the adult to help the children to discriminate between injuries that are serious enough to require medical attention and those that can be treated with a little sympathy and some tender loving care.

With the help of our school nurse, a series of interesting curriculum projects on human physiology have been developed over the years that help children to learn about their own body parts and functions. Through the use of pictures and plastic models, the children learn the locations and functions of their spinal columns, throats, stomachs, lungs, and hearts. Children are helped to feel their own and each other's vertebrae while this feature is pointed out on a small-scale model of the human skeleton. They can also find other bones that can be detected through the skin such as the shin bone, the knee, ankle, jaw, and rib bones.

In studying about the heart, the children listen first to a magnified recording of a heartbeat and then, using a real stethoscope, listen to their own and their companions' hearts. For one session on this subject, the children each took turns letting another listen to his heart, then jumped up and down several times to increase the beat of his heart, and allowed his friend to listen again following the exercise. A life-size plastic model of the heart was also available so that children could see the heart chambers and the blood vessel "hoses" that carry the blood to all parts of the body. The real hearts of a chicken and a full grown steer were brought in so that children could see that the heart is similar to that of a human heart and serves a similar function, but varies with the size of the animal.

The children also learn how broken bones are set and held firm by casts so that they can heal. Young children often have the frightening impression that when one breaks an arm or a leg, that appendage simply falls off! The nurse explains to them that only the bone inside of the skin is broken. She shows them x-rays of broken bones and bones that have been set to heal, and also explains the workings of a cast. A real cast is then applied to the leg of one of the doll corner dolls and allowed to harden. It can then be shown that the hard cast provides excellent protection for the leg while it heals.

Sex differences in children are handled casually as are all medical and physiological questions. Toileting in the nursery school occurs in a somewhat isolated section of the room, but it is not a cloistered, private affair for the children. Where doors are available for the toilet stalls, they are often left open or ajar, and children frequently go with each other or watch each other through the toileting operation. Boys and girls use the same toilet area. Young children who are not already familiar with sex differences in children their age, clearly use this opportunity to observe the fact that boys have penises and girls do not. Most young children, however, do not find the subject particularly engrossing except for their initial curiosity. If a child seems worried or preoccupied about the sex differences he or she observes, a teacher may bring the topic up in a conversation with him to see what, if anything, seems to concern him. The conversation is likely to include a confirmation of the sex differences that the child has noticed.

Occasionally a child expresses some embarrassment or modesty about the openness with which toileting takes place in the nursery school. In this case the child is perfectly free to toilet in privacy, and a teacher will help him to arrange this. Most young children, however, do not express much concern over this issue though, of course, they will all eventually assume the attitudes of society on the subject.

The change in a mother's body during pregnancy is one phase of human physiology that is likely to have an impact on any young child whose mother has a baby. Though young children are not quick to notice the changes in women's figures as a function of pregnancy, they generally do notice these changes in their own mothers. When children express curiosity about this in the school setting, they are told that babies grow inside of the mother's body and that when the baby is big enough, the mother will go to a hospital where the baby will be born by gradually pushing its way out of her body. Young children do not usually seek more information than this, and many do not express a spontaneous interest in the subject at all until it involves their own families or someone close to them. Additional information prepared especially for young children is made available to any parent who wishes to introduce the topic to his child or to tell the child more than he spontaneously asks about.

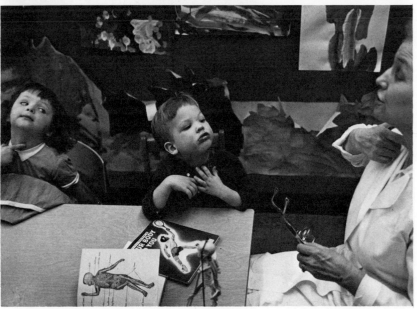

PLANTS

Planting things that grow in the ground is a common springtime activity in the nursery school. One section of the play yard is usually designated as a place to dig and plant, and children busy themselves putting seeds into the ground that will grow to be flowers or vegetables. Because the growing season is short for our school children who vacation in the summer, planting projects must be planned carefully to mature during the time that children can enjoy them. Seedlings may be started indoors in late winter or early spring to be transplanted to the yard, or plants well on the way to maturity may be purchased for the yard during the early weeks of the growing season. When it can be managed, children love to harvest snack-type vegetables to go with their juice or milk and crackers.

The children's interest in planting activities in the nursery school seems to suffer by comparison with their interest in animal projects—perhaps, because seedlings and young plants require care but offer little to sustain the children's interest as they grow compared with young animals. There are things that adults can do to help to sustain the children's interest in flowers and vegetables planted in the school garden. In one planting project, for example, the children had carrot sticks as a part of their snack on the day that they planted carrots in their garden, and about once a week thereafter until their own carrots were ready to eat. In this way the children were helped to anticipate the future payoff of their gardening.

The children share in the care of planted flowers and vegetables and may arrange a schedule for watering and weeding in which each child who wishes to participate takes some responsibility for the produce. The school garden usually is planted with many different kinds of flowers or vegetables so that the children can observe differences in the seedlings as they emerge from the ground or watch for differences in the fruit or flowers as the plants mature. Occasionally each child plants his own seedlings in individual containers and cares for his own plant until it matures.

Flower or vegetable gardens and fruit trees growing close to the school provide the children with opportunities to visit (with the consent of the owner) to see seedlings, buds, and young fruit beginning to mature. Even when children cannot observe the growth process directly (as is the case with many city-bred children) they can see from films and photographs how fruits and vegetables are grown, what they look like as they grow, and which things grow on trees, bushes, vines, or underground. One project about apples during the fall of the year began with pictures of an apple orchard and the harvesting process, and culminated in a visit to a local apple tree to pick apples for snack time. Apples in various forms were served at snack time each day of that week, including apple wedges, baked apples, apple crisp, and apple sauce. The children participated in the preparation of all of the snacks and could help themselves to an apple anytime they wanted one.

With a little planning on the part of the staff, cut flowers can be a regular part of the school scene during the spring, summer, and fall months. Children may be asked to bring flowers as they mature in their own yards, and flowers can be obtained from volunteers or from residents close to the school who have gardens. The children enjoy going with a teacher to get flowers from a local resident who has been contacted ahead of time and has agreed to cut some flowers for the children to take back to their schoolroom. Flowers usually are labeled in the classroom and referred to by their common names so that children will begin to be conversant about them as they see them growing in the community. Local flower displays or flower shows sometimes occur during the school year and can be visited by the nursery school children. Late summer produce such as corn, sweet potatoes, pears, peaches, and pumpkins can be the subject of interesting fall cooking or snack projects.

Young children can also begin to become familiar with trees that are common in their local area. Leaves can be brought in and identified from books on the subject, and particular trees in the school yard or in the immediate vicinity can be visited. Fall is an especially nice time of the year for bringing in colorful tree branches that are turning from green to red, orange, yellow, and brown.

In one interesting project on trees the children talked about all of the uses to which trees are put. They were able to recall their own uses of trees—for climbing or for shade, for tire swings, and for trimming at Christmastime. They also recalled the use of trees for birds' nests, squirrels' nests and, finally, for lumber used in building wooden toys, fences, telephone poles, and homes to live in. One child also recalled that it was part of a tree that was used to make Pinocchio's nose!

The protection of our forests and caution in the management of picnic fires is not at all beyond the understanding of young children. A visit from a forest ranger can be arranged at which he explains how he watches for fires and how care must be taken with a cooking fire.

Some planting projects have as their purpose helping children to understand what is needed for plants to grow. Inside plants may be dug up so that children can see the root system through which the plant is fed. For one project two groups of plants were started. One group was given an adequate supply of sun and water while the other group was deprived of both light and water. In this way, children were able to see for themselves what the plants needed to thrive. The children can also begin to understand how plants seed themselves with the help of air currents once they have observed seeds and seed pods. A large magnifying glass on a stand is a helpful aid to the study of plants by both children and adults. With it the intricacies of the veins in plant leaves can be seen, and the petals, sepals, pistils, and stamens of flowers can be examined in detail. Children, and adults too for that matter, seem to become more observant with the naked eye after having observed things under magnification. The magnification seems to call attention to the fact that there is much to see in nature if one looks.

In order to facilitate the effective study of both plants and animals the school maintains an excellent supply of resource books with accurate text and detailed pictures to help in the identification of specimens. In many instances teachers do not have complete and accurate information on these subjects and will make good use of resource materials in preparing and carrying out projects with the children. Even when teachers are very knowledgable, however, resource materials may be brought into the classroom to help children to begin to realize that books contain important information and that there is a real value in being able to read.

INFORMATION ABOUT THE PHYSICAL
PROPERTIES OF THE ENVIRONMENT

There are some remarkable things about the world of nature that the young child observes daily and about which he is surprisingly uncurious. He takes for granted the presence of the sun and the moon, the fact of night and day, lightness and darkness, heat and cold, and does not seek explanations of these things or wonder what controls them. He is curious about objects that have form and color but is not curious about the process of "seeing." He hears sounds and may wonder what object, person, or animal is making a particular sound, but he is not curious about the nature of sound itself. He will learn to accomodate to the pull of gravity, walking steadily and securely, balancing on climbing equipment, and taking care that objects do not fall to the floor, but he does not ask questions like "Why do things fall down instead of up?" He can quickly learn to use the mechanical advantages of pulleys, levers, wheels and axels, or wedges, but he is not curious about the underlying mechanical principles involved. What, then, if anything, should we teach the child about these things?

It would seem clear that if we take the child's own questioning and ability to comprehend into consideration, we will decide not to bother him with technical explanations of many of the common natural events he witnesses. Rather than explaining such events, the nursery school can probably be most helpful by increasing the child's awareness of the existence of these phenomena. Teachers can point them out to him as they occur in nature and can contrive demonstrations that help him to isolate the event. For example, in one wintertime project, the children talked at some length about an impressive row of icicles hanging from the roof of an equipment shed in the school yard. Their attention was called to the fact that the sun was beginning to melt the ice and that water was dripping from the tip of the icicles. The children broke some of the icicles off to look at them in detail, noticing the frozen drips of water. Later in the morning, five or six of the children took a walk to look for more icicles and brought several very large ones back to school. The children put the icicles into a tub in the school room and checked on them from time to time over a period of an hour or two as the melting process took place. The next day one of the teachers helped the children construct a setting for making icicles by allowing water to drip slowly to the edge of an inclined board placed directly outside of a school window. No attempt was made to discuss specifically what happens to water when it freezes or melts. The children's attention was called to the simple fact that water becomes ice when it gets cold enough to freeze and that dripping water gradually freezes to make icicles. The children may have been aware of the formation of icicles from their casual experiences with them, but calling their attention to them and forming icicles before their eyes gave special emphasis to a *fact* that they now know about water, cold weather, and ice. To accentuate the effect of warmth on ice, these children also made "hand prints" on the frosted school windows by holding the palms of their hands against the window until the frost under their hands melted leaving a clear print of a palm and five fingers. The adults, in this instance, asked the children why they thought the frost melted under their hands and when necessary, provided the explanation that their hands were warm enough to melt the frost. Similarly, the children can learn that when water is heated it boils and creates steam and that steam condenses on surfaces leaving deposits of water. They need not know the boiling point of water or what causes the bubbling when the water boils.

There is no magic formula to be used by the adults to indicate how much information to give children on topics like these. Teachers must use their best judgment and the responsiveness of the children to decide when enough information has been supplied or to decide which bits of information will be understandable and interesting to them. In one project about magnets, for example, the children simply played with an array of magnets and 15 to 20 different objects, some metal and some not. They learned by trial and error that magnets have the characteristic of picking up objects that are metal and do not pick up objects made of other materials. The magnets were of varying sizes and so were the objects so that the children also discovered that the larger magnets picked up heavier objects than the smaller ones. Finally the children were asked to make some guesses about which objects around the room the magnets would pick up or stick to and which they would not. The adults in this instance made no attempt whatever to explain to the children how or why magnets work as they do.

Electricity

Electricity is a phenomenon that children can experience in many different ways (some of which are painful) but cannot really understand. Consequently, explanations about electric currents can probably best be withheld until later in a child's schooling. Children can, of course, learn to be respectfully cautious around electrical wires and outlets. They can also begin to see the connection between electrical wires, a source of electrical power like a battery, and such useful respondents as buzzers, lights, and bells. The nursery school has a demonstration panel to be used with the children on which lights and buzzers can be activated when the appropriate wires are attached in the appropriate ways. The manipulation of these connections has been a source of enjoyment to the children and is well within the abilities of the older preschoolers with instruction and supervision from an adult.

In devising science projects and demonstrations for children in the nursery school, it is essential for the adults who prepare the activity to try it out in advance before they present it to the group. Teachers have discovered that, more often than not, their first idea about how to give a demonstration can be improved on by some slight—or extensive—revision of the materials or equipment used. Improvements should be made before the activity is presented to the children so that children are not bored with the trial and error fumbling of the adult or confused by temporary failures to get things to work as anticipated.

Heat and Light

Some nursery school curriculum activities involve information about sources of heat and light. In one project, for example, children did a brief experiment to confirm that a cup of water spilled on the sidewalk in the sun would dry up faster than water spilled on the walk in the shade. In the same project children were asked to guess which of several small containers of water had been left in the sun and which had been left in the shade. At first, the children were at a loss to know how to tell, but they soon discovered that they could tell with perfect accuracy simply by feeling how warm the water was in each container. A similar experiment was done in the schoolroom using a strong light bulb as the source of heat.

In another project about heat from the sun, children were blindfolded and led to different parts of the school yard. The children were asked to guess at various times whether they had just been led from the sun to the shade or from the shade to the sun by feeling the change in the amount of heat on their faces and arms.

In one project about animals, the children learned that many animals, including themselves, have warm bodies and that that is probably one reason why little puppies and kittens and other furry animals like to pile up near each other to sleep. There was also an attempt in this project to explain to the children that heavy clothing in the wintertime and covers on their beds are not themselves a source of heat but are used to keep their body heat in and keep them from cooling off. This information, however, may have been premature and not comprehensible to the children; they still tended to think of "warm clothes" and "warm covers." One astute child, however, did make the observation that when he came in from outside the outside of his jacket felt very cold but the inside, which was close to his body, felt very warm.

The use of a thermometer as a tool for determining temperature can be introduced to young children, although they need not be expected to understand the specific effect of the temperature on mercury. When the children have an outside thermometer to observe from their schoolroom, they can help to keep track of how cold it is on a particular winter day and, consequently, how long their outside playtime will be—or, in summer, how warm it is and whether or not it is a day for filling the wading pool or playing with the sprinkler. For one weather project, the children marked the temperature as they arrived in the morning and then marked it again at noon, learning that on most days the temperature gradually went up throughout the school day and was warmer at noon than early in the morning. Some of the children also checked outside thermometers at home in the afternoon and learned that the temperature usually goes down again as nighttime approaches.

Young children can begin to understand that the sun is a source of light as well as heat during the day while the moon is a source of less intense light at night. Children can sometimes watch sunlight fade as clouds move in front of the sun. A breezy day with a blue sky and vivid white clouds is an especially good one for children to simply lie on their backs in the yard and watch the comings and goings of clouds! Activities such as these must be undertaken with care, since the sun can damage eyes if one is exposed too long or looks directly into the sun without adequate protection.

Shadows are an especially interesting light phenomenon for children to observe. The shadows cast by buildings, trees, cars, and people can be pointed out to the children, and the relation of the sun to these objects can be explained. Some of the older preschoolers comprehend more detailed information about outdoor shadows, like the fact that shadows are all cast in the same direction for different objects and are longer when the sun is low in the sky and shorter, or nonexistent, when the sun is overhead.

For one project the length of shadows was systematically varied by changing the orientation of a light bulb in relation to a child or an object, and two or three shadows of the same object were cast by using two or three different sources of light. The children can also be asked to guess what object is casting a particular shadow with varying degrees of distortion. As children become familiar with this phenomenon, they may even be able to guess the approximate source of light from the direction and shape of the shadow cast by an object.

Air Currents

Projects having to do with air and air currents are also evident in the nursery school program. While generally there is no attempt to explain the composition of the earth's atmosphere or the causes of air currents, the effect that movement of air has on objects in the environment is pointed out. Children can be confronted with questions like "How can you tell whether or not the wind is blowing outside today?" The movement of the leaves of trees and bushes, tall grass, dust, or bits of paper on the ground, clothes hung up to dry, and flags and other light objects suspended in air can be used to emphasize the effect of breezes on objects.

For more controlled activities, an electric fan can be used. In one school project children placed various objects on a small platform in front of a powerful fan and noticed which things were blown away and which were heavy enough to remain in place. Some objects remained in place when the fan was on a low setting but blew off the platform when the fan was speeded up. The attitude of the children seemed to be one of "pulling for the fan"; they were especially delighted when an object was almost sturdy enough to remain in place but was gradually nudged to the edge of the platform and off! The children also produced their own air currents by blowing objects back and forth and finally off the platform, or by blowing air into a balloon and then directing the escaping air stream at an object on the platform. They learned that light objects like feathers, ping pong balls, pencils, and crayons could be blown quite easily, especially if they rolled—but that other objects, like blocks, and the toy animals could be dislodged only with the help of two or three blowers! Still other objects could not be budged at all.

The electric fan in this project was also used to keep a balloon in the air, a small flag ruffling, and a pinwheel twirling for the better part of one morning. At another time it kept a number of toy sailboats moving in a tub of water. Demonstrations such as this can help children gradually associate the use of air currents for propelling real sailboats or doing useful work like turning windmills. Children, however, do not need to make all of these associations as a part of any single demonstration.

Extremely turbulent air currents as they occur in nature can, of course, be frightening experiences for children. Shortly after a summer tornado reeked havoc in the Twin Cities area, the nursery school children talked at some length about the event and the fact that whole houses were blown off their foundations. The adults emphasized the fact that people were not hurt because they listened to their radios and learned when and where the tornado was so that they could go into their basements or leave the area. Generally, the children are encouraged to feel secure and safe in storms or in heavy rain with the one qualification that one does not stay out in an electrical storm. During warm summer rains it is not uncommon for the children to shed their shoes and clothes, put on their swim suits, and play in the rain.

Water, Wet Clay, and Mud

Activities with water, sand, clay, and mud have benefits both as pleasant, much enjoyed media and as a vehicle for teaching science concepts. Young children are almost universally attracted to water in any form— except possibly in some combinations with soap. They love to "swim" in it, walk in it, splash it, pour it from one container to another, drip it over their hands, squeeze out sponges saturated with it, or mix it with mud, dough, or clay which then can be squeezed through their fingers, stirred, or patted. A large tub or sink of water and some implements to go with it will attract two or three children at almost any time of the day.

Why so many young children are incurably attracted to water and to "messy play" with dough, clay, and mud is hard to say. Nursery school teachers express any of several rationales about why they provide these kinds of materials for children in the preschool, not the least of which is children's love of them! Some teachers feel that children learn the physical properties of materials that pour, spill, and squeeze through their play with water, clay, and mud. Others feel that children experience a primitive kind of sensory pleasure in the "wallowing" that characterizes much of their play with these materials and that no harm is done by indulging the child in this way from time to time. In fact, some child clinicians, such as Anna Freud, Melanie Klein, and Virginia Axline, feel that messy play may have therapeutic value for the young child. Children may find the easy malleability of water, clay, and mud a relaxing change from the more demanding tasks of coping with the things and the people in the environment that do not yield so readily to their manipulations.

A host of interesting projects can be carried out with water and like materials to help children understand the unusual characteristics of these substances. Learning what things dissolve in water—for instance, sugar and salt—and what things do not can be brought to the attention of the children by assembling some of each kind for testing. In one project of this kind the children's attention was called to the fact that dirt, paint, and soap leave a visible residue in the water and that sugar and salt do not—but that sugar and salt are there nonetheless and can be tasted in the water.

Demonstrations that some things float on the surface of the water and some do not can be pointed out to the children, and predictions can be made about the likelihood of common objects floating. Explanations about the displacement of water and surface tension, however, are beyond the understanding of the children and should be left for a later time in the child's exploration and experimentation with water and its properties. For preschoolers, just the simple observation that small pieces of wood, strips of Styrofoam, and rubber balls float, while other small things such as nails, keys, and spoons do not, is all that need be conveyed.

The fact that water changes its form when cooled or heated can easily be demonstrated to the children. All children have seen water that has changed to ice or to steam; as is often the case, the demonstrations of these phenomena in school are not so much to introduce them for the first time but rather to make children more deliberately conscious of the observation of such things in nature. To call attention to them and to label them "interesting" predisposes the child to notice such things on his own and to report them back to his teachers and classmates.

The use of water as a source of power can be demonstrated in many ways in school. A garden hose, for example, can be used to move objects. On one warm summer morning a teacher posed a problem to some children in the yard, asking them if they could think of some ways to move a very large rubber ball without touching it with their hands, feet, or bodies. They thought of using sticks, hitting it with other toys, throwing stones at it (which did not budge it), and whipping it with a section of rope available. Finally one child thought of the garden hose and it was turned on. The force of the stream, however, was not great enough to move the ball until the child imitated the usual adult response of putting his finger over part of the opening and directing a more forceful stream against the ball. The teacher helped each of the children to master the technique of producing a more powerful stream of water by reducing the size of the opening through which the water came. In this instance, as in some others, the teacher did not try to explain the phenomenon, but simply helped to make the children aware of it as a fact about hoses and the force of water.

The force of falling water has also been demonstrated by constructing a miniature waterfall that turns a paddle wheel. For one such project a small waterwheel was rigged to grind graham crackers that were used as topping for pudding during snack time.

The evaporation of water that is exposed to air has been demonstrated by leaving two identical containers with equal amounts of water in the room—one covered and one open—for a day or two and then comparing the water level in each.

With our present concern for pollution and the preservation of clean water, projects that call children's attention to ecologically relevant issues should be considered in developing curriculum for young children. Children can certainly talk about the need to keep lakes and streams in their communities clean so that fish and plant life can continue to thrive. Expecting the children to share the responsibility for cleaning a fish bowl or an aquarium to keep it pollution free can help to make this a relevant issue for them.

The crawling, wiggling, squirming life that exists in mud and marsh areas along river banks and lake bottoms provides the makings of interesting spring projects. A lot of the lake- or river-bottom mud and a little of the water is sometimes transported to school in a large tub to be studied over an extended period of time for whatever life it contains.

Science activities of these kinds are a regular part of the school program, but it should be pointed out that no particular bit of information, demonstration, or project is considered an essential part of the curriculum for every group of children. Topics for study are not selected as representative of things that "every five-year-old must know" before entering kindergarten; they are selected because the teachers judge that they are of interest to the children and because they supply information that the children are ready for and can grasp. As we mentioned previously in this chapter, one of the major purposes of science activities is to interest the children in an increasingly more deliberate and careful study of the things around them.

9
Art and Crafts

9 *Art and Crafts*

Art and craft materials hold a special fascination for most young children; consequently, these materials are provided in liberal amounts in the nursery school. Art activities can be seen in progress at almost any hour of the school day. During free play time children routinely have access to dough or clay, paints, crayons, paper, scissors, and paste to be used in making art and craft products, and special art projects are introduced to the group several times each week.

The purpose of most art activities in the nursery school is to help the children learn to use the materials for their own enjoyment; it is not primarily to "instruct" the children in the use of art media nor to improve their technical skill in producing artistically elegant products. The product that emerges from a child's effort does not have to be a recognizable object or figure to be considered worthy of his time, nor does it have to measure up to some external criteria of artistic merit. Nursery school teachers consider the "process" to be more important than the "product" in young children's art. Painting and sculpturing are presented to the children as avenues for self-expression instead of technical skills to be mastered.

Although it is clear that the quality of the art products they produce become more important to children as they progress through the preschool years, they generally continue to enjoy the process somewhat more than the product throughout this period. A child painting at the easel may compose an interesting pattern of bright colors and shapes only to scrub over it leaving a dreary, gray mass of color. It is not uncommon for children working with clay to squeeze interesting little figures into shape and then squash them back into a ball as soon as the figure is completed. Teachers are tempted at times to snatch things from the easels or worktables before children get a chance to "spoil" their delightful and interesting art products. It is sometimes hard to appreciate that art for young children is for the pleasure of the creator, not the viewer.

As children get older they do become more conscious of the product of their efforts. The four-year-olds in the nursery school typically work harder on a product, evaluate it more critically, and decide with more deliberation which things to keep and which to discard. If a product

121

strikes a child's fancy for some reason, he will take considerable pride in it. He may carry it around with him or return to the art area to look at it several times during the day, and he will certainly remember to show it to his mother or take it home at the end of the day.

Preschool children probably become product oriented in their artwork for several reasons. First, their art activities become more goal directed and representational as they acquire skill with the materials. When the child is capable of setting a definite goal for himself, such as drawing a picture of his house or of the helicopter he flew in at the state fair, he becomes more invested in the end product and is likely to evaluate it critically, finding it a good likeness, or a disappointment. The youngest preschoolers are, as a rule, not capable of this kind of representational art. They do not even attempt to draw or paint figures, objects, or scenes as many of the older preschoolers do. Their art activities seem to be primarily explorations in the use of color, line, and form.

The child's growing investment in the quality of his art products is also undoubtedly contributed to by the responsiveness of the adults to his better efforts. Although the teachers in the nursery school are careful not to criticize a child's less elegant art products, they do express their unqualified delight in attractive displays of color and design or unusual examples of representational art. They may talk with a child at some length about the interesting characteristics of a painting or the mood it suggests and one teacher may ask the child to show his work to another teacher or child who would especially enjoy seeing it. Parents, too, are selective in their praise of children's art objects, although they, too, tend to be careful not to be critical of the child's less mature efforts. Adults are most likely to comment on children's art products that are detailed, involve the use of bold colors, show evidence of being carefully done, and form a pleasant or attractive composition. While these characteristics are all very subjective, teachers tend to agree to a rather striking degree in their appreciation of some children's art products more than others. The ones they find the most attractive tend to have a primitive charm often lacking in the artwork of older children and adults.

As children approach five, they become capable of comparing their own art products to the products of other children. If a child at an art table or easel is producing an attractive painting using bright colors or an interesting design, another child may come over to watch or comment about the painting. Children do not often compliment each other on their artwork but, when this does happen, it is almost always one of the older preschoolers giving recognition to a companion whose work is particularly interesting. Though a child may repeat a general theme or pattern of his own over and over, as if to perfect the composition or to recapture the pleasure he found in making it, children rarely directly copy the work of other children.

Nursery school teachers have typically had some very strong biases where children's art is concerned. They place a high value on personal involvement and creativity and try not to encourage imitation and conformity. In talking with children about their paintings or sculptures teachers often use terms like "design" or "pattern" so that children will continue to appreciate their art products that are colorful and attractive without necessarily being representational even after the child has begun representational drawing and painting. Some teachers explicitly avoid asking children to name what they have made (unless the likeness to an object or figure is so obvious as to be recognizable without asking) because they feel this suggests to the child that art products are not worthy unless they are faithfully representational. The teacher may talk with the child about the bright colors he has used or the interesting pattern he has created, but she will probably not ask him, "What is it?" If adults do ask children what they have painted, most children oblige by naming something or other, but it is often quite evident that the child is simply exploring with color and design and had no particular object in mind when he created the product.

Children sometimes volunteer information about their paintings, telling a teacher what the scene is about and what each of the objects represents. Teachers usually record these comments on the child's painting. This is done, in part, to give the child recognition for his thoughtfulness in planning artwork and, in part, to have a record of his thoughts at the time the work was being done.

Because of the teachers' investment in originality and creativity, adults in the preschool do not usually provide patterns for children to follow in making art products (although there are occasional exceptions to this rule). Stencils, tracings, and outlines to be colored in, all culminate in stereotyped products only a small part of which is the result of the child's own originality. If a pattern requires instruction or help from a teacher for proper construction (such as getting the ears on the rabbit in just the right places) children often get so preoccupied with whether or not they are doing it correctly that they become impatient for their share of teacher help and direction. The prevailing atmosphere is reduced to one of trying to do it the way the teacher says it is to be done and getting it over with rather than being one of self-expression and personal enjoyment. This is not to say that children never enjoy the product of such an effort. Patterns sometimes have the advantage of helping the child to produce a product that he would not be capable of producing without "pre-fab" help. Nevertheless the process in this kind of art or craft activ-

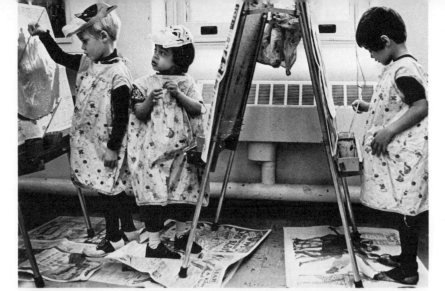

ity is not generally one in which the child has much leeway to be original and creative. For this reason, teachers use patterns sparingly. Stencils, or cutout pieces to be properly assembled, are likely to be used at times when the product, to serve its purpose, must be reasonably defined and uniform in size and style. For example, the children may be making jack-o'-lantern masks that require eye, nose, and mouth openings that are placed properly in the mask. This may be accomplished by providing a pattern for the child to copy. After that, however, each child may find some unique way to decorate or paint his particular mask.

Because nursery school teachers are generous with their praise for artwork, children sometimes come to expect teacher-recognition for minimal effort. If a child is particularly prone to seek adult approval, he may slap a few lines of paint or crayon marks on a paper and bring it to a teacher for praise. Teachers must decide how to handle situations of this kind through ways that do not discourage the child from freely using art materials but convey to him that painting for teacher approval instead of for his own enjoyment is not valued by the teacher. Some teachers handle these situations by being sparing and somewhat perfunctory in their praise of a child's artwork when it does not seem to be "special" in the eyes of the child himself. If a child seems generally inclined to seek recognition for minimal efforts, the adults may watch for opportunities to volunteer unsolicited praise at times when that child is working with unusual diligence on an art product. In fact, the teacher may specifically praise the child for "being so interested" in what he is making or for "working so hard and carefully" on his painting.

Teachers are careful never to single out children who seem advanced in their artwork, pointing out the superiority of the child's work over others, for fear that other children will retreat from art activities and stop using these media for their own enjoyment. Occasionally other children may notice and appreciate the products of more skillful children. Usually this is genuine admiration. In the nursery school atmosphere which is supportive of individuals and acceptant of differences, children also accept and appreciate differences. If a child becomes overly concerned about his relative lack of ability in comparison with a more skilled child, a teacher can reassure the concerned child and help him to appreciate his own efforts.

DEVELOPMENTAL CHANGES
IN CHILDREN'S ARTWORK

There are a number of impressions one gets from watching young children at work with paint, crayons, collage materials, or clay. Early in the child's experience with these materials, he seems to experiment with the use of the tools—brushes, paints, crayons, scissors, and paste. His earliest attempts at easel painting seem to be explorations in what happens on the paper when he uses the brush to make sweeping circular motions or vigorous scrubbing back and forth motions or staccato dotting motions. He may deliberately squeeze the brush out against the paper to let it drip. He will probably apply one color next to another or on top of another, watching the change in hue or scrubbing right through the paper. Some children are inclined to cover every inch of paper while others confine their work to a small segment of the paper or cluster their brush strokes in two or three places on the paper. Some observers have attempted to relate painting styles to personality types in children, speculating that the child whose painting covers the paper is an expansive child who takes full advantage of life, or a compulsive child who leaves nothing undone. The child who confines his painting to small segments of the paper is presumed to be constricted and withdrawn. These associations between painting and personality are not, however, founded on sound investigation and would seem, from casual observation, to be of questionable validity. Many children experiment with different styles of painting, painting more expansively one day than another.

As the child gains experience with the media of paints, he begins to compose things more deliberately, using colors and shapes in a differentiated way. For example, the child may paint a circle of one color and fill it in with a second color and, perhaps, repeat this shape two or three places on his paper varying the size and color combinations and interspersing lines or paint blobs among the circles. Patterns gradually become more elaborate. As the child incorporates a wider range of geometric shapes into his paintings and drawings, indications of symmetry appear. Only after this kind of preliminary exploration is the child likely to use lines, shapes, and colors in a more formal attempt to do representational painting, and even then he continues to be interested in shape and color for its own sake.

The child's earliest representational art often seems to be the result of accidents in that the child, in the course of applying paint, begins to produce shapes that resemble objects or figures. He notices the resemblance and adds features or characteristics that he feels are essential for the product to be valid, such as arms on a stick figure, eyes to a circle "face," or wheels on a rectangular "bus." Usually one or two prominent characteristics suffice to identify an object; however, for some children even as young as four, drawings and paintings involve a great attention to detail.

Individual differences in the complexity and maturity of children's drawings and paintings are quite marked. For one four-year-old, a head and face may be represented by a blob of paint of a circle with two dots for eyes. For another four-year-old, a head and face may include hair, ears, a hat, eyes, with eyelids or lashes, and a mouth with "character" sometimes smiling and sometimes grim or sad. While figures or objects often stand alone, out of any context, they are occasionally embedded in a scene that includes figures, objects, and general background surroundings. As children become interested in letters and numbers, these symbols too appear in their paintings, and the child may begin to print his own name on each of his pictures.

The quality of the art materials presented to children in the nursery school and the method of presentation can make a marked difference in the number of art products produced in a group. Children are more drawn to painting if paints are bright in color and thick enough to maintain their brightness on paper. For easel painting, a small quantity of each color is presented in a separate paint cup securely fitted into a paint rack attached to a stand-up easel. Each color has its own brush and the children are usually asked not to mix the paints in the cups though they may mix them on their papers. If the paints do gradually get reduced to common gray, they are replaced with fresh paint by a teacher. Easel paper is usually large (18 in. by 24 in.) newsprint. Most teachers like to have more than one easel available, since the sight of some children painting often elicits a request from others to paint too. To capitalize on this kind of "creative contagion," teachers sometimes borrow the easels from other classrooms and place as many as five or six together in a selected area of the school. Easel painting then becomes one of the main focuses of the free activity time for a particular day or two. The increase in the number and complexity of paintings that are produced on such a day is often quite impressive. Some children paint for the first time; others renew their interest in the activity, continuing to paint extensively for several days following the experience.

Paints are presented to children in many different ways in addition to easel painting. Children sometimes paint at tables, using smaller sized paper, smaller brushes and paints in bowls or muffin tins. In this case, the child may be encouraged to mix his own colors by combining the colors from two or three muffin cups into an empty cup. Painting is also sometimes done with the paper on the floor or mounted on a wall depending on the nature of the particular project.

There are many special painting projects conducted in the nursery school in the course of a school year. The purpose of some projects is simply to give children a novel experience with the medium of paints. For example, children may use small squares of sponges for blot painting, or lengths of yarn dipped in paint and drawn across the paper instead of brushes. Cork painting is done occasionally in which corks of different sizes are dipped in paints to make colorful circle designs. Spray painting can be done using spray cans or atomizers. Spatter painting can also be done using old tooth brushes. For this activity, the child is shown how to snap the brush against the palm of his hand to spatter paint on paper. The use of spatter or spray techniques are discouraged at the easel in the classroom since the child is not usually able to control the paint and needs an isolated spot in which to work—preferably outside with the ground as the backdrop.

Water painting is also a favorite outside activity. Children love to pretend to paint climbing equipment, trikes, wagons, and even the school building itself using buckets of water and inexpensive outside paint brushes.

Some special art projects involve paint-mixing experiences in which the child can learn facts about colors, such as the fact that blue and yellow, when mixed together, make green, that red and yellow make orange, and that blue and red make purple; or the fact that a color is made progressively lighter by adding white and that pastels are made by starting with white and adding small amounts of color. Children occasionally play a game in which they guess the mix of a color or attempt to match mixes that a teacher has prepared ahead of time. They also begin to learn the names of popular color mixes such as violet, fushia, pink, salmon, or mustard.

Some special art projects are designed to give the children exposure to painting as it appears in the adult culture. For example, a project might involve bringing in, over a period of several days or more, prints of famous paintings for the children to see. The paintings may be those of a particular artist, or on a particular theme; for example, famous portraits of children or paintings of animals. If children are becoming overly conscious of doing representational painting and are giving up other interesting uses of color and design, the teacher may deliberately bring in the work of one or two modern painters whose work is nonrepresentational. The children are told the name of the paintings brought in and the name of the painter. A project of this kind may be combined with a trip to a local art museum to visit four or five selected paintings—perhaps, ones that the teacher makes a special point of having among the prints available at school. Trips to galleries, museums, and other public places where art can be seen are carefully planned and generally have very specific goals. For example, if the children are looking at paintings the teacher will have visited the museum ahead of time, will have selected the pictures to be visited and will have in mind exactly where in the museum they are located so that the children can go directly to them and accomplish the purpose of their visit in a relatively short time. If the children, too, know what they are looking for, they will enjoy finding the painting on their own once they are close to where it hangs.

The laboratory school owns prints of famous paintings that have special appeal to children: prints of families, animals, colorful street scenes, still lifes, interesting landscapes or seascapes, and modern art works. The school also from time to time, borrows prints or originals from a lending museum for use with special school projects. The art objects shown at school are as likely to be ones that are a part of the art heritage of adults as they are to be pictures painted especially for children. One reason for this is that these paintings, if carefully selected, are as interesting to children as those painted especially for them. Another reason is that the child begins to become familiar with the art works that he will see in people's homes, public places, art books, and in studio windows.

"Print books" can be put together and made available for children to browse through in school along with other children's books. Prints in the book are protected from fingering by the use of plastic sleeves, and the prints can be changed from time to time. Some styles of picture frames also make it possible to change prints that hang on the school walls. These, too, can be a source of enjoyment to the children—particularly if they are changed often enough for the children to remain aware of their presence.

Another special art experience of value and great interest to children is one in which the child can actually see an artist at work. This is done at times by taking the children to a studio in which an artist is working, but it can also be a significant experience for the children to see an artist at work right in the school. A willing worker can set up his materials in one section of the classroom and simply go about his business of painting (or sculpting) throughout the school day. Children come and go from the area as they wish and often just sit to watch for a period of time. If the artist can work for several hours, a product begins to emerge and children get a feeling for the process as it is implemented by adults. Children may wish to ask questions about the picture, the materials, or the person. The children's own easel may be set up near the guest so they can paint "together." A visiting artist does not need to be an accomplished professional to make a significant contribution to the children's understanding of the creative process. It may be a student, or a teacher or parent whose hobby is painting. The guest should see his job as one in which he demonstrates to the children the seriousness and involvement he has in his work and the care with which he does it. The fast-working cartoonist or sketch artist who produces caricature and scenes for the children's entertainment has merit of his own, but he leaves something to be desired as a model of the artistic process.

At times a talented guest or teacher may work side by side with the children painting from a still life display set up near the easels. Children capture the spirit and challenge of a still life display as an impetus to painting if one is attractively set up on a table before the easels and the colors in the display are available at the easels. Good subjects for such still lifes are fruits, flowers, colorful scarfs, a basket of multicolored rubber balls, balloons, or blocks, a toy car or truck, or a dressed up doll. Occasionally a school pet, a willing (and patient) child, or a teacher may also pose for a portrait. Self-portraits are sometimes suggested by the presence of a large mirror set up near the easels so that children can paint and see themselves at the same time. Here, too, the appropriate array of colors should be made available to the child.

With the older children, teachers sometimes initiate painting sessions following field trips or special events such as a birthday party, suggesting to the children that they paint something about what they did or saw. If children seem stymied by such a suggestion, the teacher can often talk with them about what they saw until they have ideas to get them started. They may paint about something central to the point of the trip or event, or about a trivial but impressive detail, such as the bus they rode in to get to the farm. In a project of this kind, following a school "peanut butter and jelly sandwich picnic," one child painted all of the faces with deposits of peanut butter and jelly from ear to ear.

FINGER PAINTING

Finger painting is another favorite art medium of the children in the nursery school. For finger painting, the teacher usually dampens a 12 in. by 18 in. glossy surface paper with a sponge. Jars of paints are on the table so that children can select colors and spoon blobs of thick paint onto the wet paper. The child uses his fingers and hands to spread the paint, swirling it around into colorful patterns, using both hands at once if he wishes. Colors can be blended into each other or mixed completely. Different parts of the hand make different kinds of strokes as they are drawn across the paper. Children often begin finger painting by gingerly using the forefinger but in a short time they are likely to be engrossed in trying other parts of the hand. Popular techniques include using all five fingers spread out on the paper, using the outside edge of the hand when one makes a fist, or the knuckles and thumbs. Some children even use their forearm to make very broad, smooth swipes across the paper. The forefinger contin-

ues to be used by the experienced children but not as a main "paint spreader"; it is used primarily to interject geometric shapes, stick figures, and numbers or letters into their paintings. Sometimes finger painting is done on the table surfaces itself without a paper. A child is given an area in which to work and, when he finishes, the area is wiped off or smoothed out so another child can take over. Children occasionally "foot paint" in a similar manner, using much larger sheets or roles of paper on the floor instead of a table.

While most children seem to love the experience of spreading paint with their bare hands and fingers, some do not like getting sticky or messy and avoid the activity. Teachers do not insist that a child use finger paints. If a child who has refused looks tempted, the teacher may continue to invite him to try the activity and demonstrate to him that one can finger paint without getting too messy and that the paint does wash off. Cleaning up after finger painting is similar to the activity itself; children usually enjoy washing the tables or their hands and wringing out spongues saturated with paint-colored water.

Children in nursery school are expected to take responsibility for the care of their clothing during painting activities. Except under unusual circumstances the child is expected to wear an apron that covers his clothing. He will be helped to get his sleeves up and out of the way of paint and will be reminded to wash his hands when he is finished painting. Nevertheless, teachers in the nursery school must tolerate some mess if the children are to enjoy the pleasures of activities like finger painting in school. The only way to avoid occasional accidents involving dripped paint or spotted clothing is to have such a rigid set of rules and extensive teacher direction that the spontaneity of the activity is seriously impaired. Parents, too, become patient with accidents and send their children to school in playclothes so accidents do not have dire consequences for the child or his clothing.

CRAYONS AND CHALK

Young children seem to go through developmental stages in their use of crayons and chalks that are similar to the stages with paints. The younger preschoolers "scribble" across a page, try out different colors, overlap colors with each other, and incorporate rough approximations of geometric shapes into their drawings. The older children make more extensive use of geometric shapes, composing interesting designs and patterns. As the children become interested in drawing figures and objects, many prefer to work with crayons rather than paints. Crayons seem to allow better control than brushes and paints for the child who wants to add small details to his drawings. Children who are interested in copying letters and numbers also seem to prefer crayons to paints for much of their work.

As with paint, the group's attraction to crayon drawing will depend in part on how these materials are presented. There should be enough crayons available so that sharing a limited supply does not become a distracting problem for five or six children at a table. When the large sized nursery-kindergarten crayons are used, each child can have his own box of eight crayons. Large crayons have the advantage of not breaking as easily as the standard sized crayon, but they have the disadvantage of coming in only eight colors. As the children in the nursery school get older, teachers often want them to be able to use a wider range of colors, including pastels, several shades of a given color, and white and black.

Children are expected to take care of crayons in the nursery school. Although occasional accidents do happen, children are not permitted to break crayons deliberately. Some teachers regularly sharpen crayons as they wear down so that the child can always draw with a tapered point.

CUTTING, PASTING, AND COLLAGE MATERIALS

The child's earliest use of scissors and paste seems primitive and experimental compared with his eventual performance with these materials. His beginning attempts at using scissors involves about one-half cutting and one-half ripping paper to shreds. At first the child seems not to associate the cutting of the paper with the opening and closing motion of the scissors. Even after he understands this operation, he will have some difficulty in managing the cutting so that he cuts without snagging or tearing paper. Cutting with good control is still more difficult. Only the oldest preschoolers begin to master the skill of cutting along a line or around a detailed, irregular outline and even then, children lack precision. Most children in the nursery school are satisfied with the degree of accuracy they can accomplish, and few fret about having cut off the arm of a figure or the leg of an animal because of their lack of skill in cutting! While the youngest children cut paper for its own sake—seemingly to practice the operation—the older preschoolers think of their cutting as being for a purpose. After cutting a paper into small pieces, they paste the pieces on a new sheet of paper or paste them on top of each other, or carry them around as "money" in a purse. The child's first attempt at cutting out pictures usually involves cutting something that approximates an oval or a rectangle that surrounds the object or figure. Only later does the child attempt to cut more precisely around the outline of an object.

While children in the nursery school are not formally tutored in the use of scissors, occasionally a teacher shows a struggling child how to hold the scissors or how to avoid pulling paper apart in the course of cutting. Most of the learning, however, is accomplished by trying again and again and finally getting the knack of cutting. It is essential that the children have good quality school scissors that are sharp enough and do not stick or tighten as the child cuts. Most nursery school scissors are small in size with a blunt tip rather than a pointed tip for safety purposes. Scissors for left-handed children are also available.

Children also experiment with paste as a part of their initial experience with it. They seem to enjoy the feel (and taste) of it and like spreading it around on a paper, often using more of it than would be required for efficient pasting. Gradually the child learns to use it sparingly and only on the surface he wishes to paste. At a point when the child wants his pasting to be neat, the teacher may help him learn to spread the paste evenly and sparingly so it does not squeeze out onto his paper or fingers.

While teachers help children to use paste and scissors more efficiently, they do not impose high standards of neatness. Children seem to gradually assume their own standards of excellence as they mature in their use of art materials and tools. Direction from adults in this area is geared more toward helping the child to accomplish his personal goals for quality rather than imposing standards on the child or his work.

There are many special cutting and pasting projects introduced in the nursery school each month. For some of these projects children are given prepared accessories like paper strips or geometric shapes of different colors and sizes. Collage pasting is a favorite activity of the preschoolers in which the children use a variety of textured materials for pasting, such as bits of fabric, cotton, sand paper, wall paper, paper doilies, corregated paper, straws, colored sand, plant leaves, or inexpensive food products such as seeds, hard kernels of corn, rice, or dry noodles.

Some cutting and pasting projects are related to special holidays in which children make traditional holiday symbols like Valentines, Mother's Day cards, or Halloween decorations. Curriculum projects may include group products such as a picture mural of "Things to do with Snow."

Children also from time to time incorporate cutting and pasting into their make-believe play; for example, a child may wish to attach a "sign" to a block structure or some pictures of toys may be needed to mount on the wall of a "toy store." For moments of this kind, it is necessary to have a ready supply of magazines and department store catalogues for children to use on their own or with the help of a teacher.

CLAY, PLASTICINE, PLAY DOUGH,
WOODWORKING, AND
"JUNK" SCULPTURE

Clay, or some clay substitute like Plasticine, and flour-and-salt dough are also favorite art media of the children in the nursery school. These materials are usually used at tables, and each child has a section of table or a clay board on which to work. Most children like to work with a clay or dough mass at least the size of a grape fruit. They typically pound or punch the material into different shapes, pinch off pieces to roll out or pat into "cookies," and attach the pieces to each other. Appropriate implements are provided, including small rolling pins, cookie cutters, tongue-depressor "knives," wooden mallets, and small objects to press into the clay or dough.

While clay is difficult for the children to mix themselves, dough is easy and fun for them to help make. The children combine proper amounts of flour and salt, add their choice of powder paints for coloring, add water, and mix, kneading the dough as though they were making bread. Dough is sometimes mixed for use in the doll corner where children pretend to bake it in the oven, fry it in pans and serve it in doll dishes. While dough is not harmful for children to taste (and most have tasted it at some time or another), they are expected to "pretend" to eat it.

As children become interested in sculpting figures, animals, and objects, it becomes important for them to have ample amounts of good quality moist clay. Children's clay products are sometimes baked in a kiln or in a regular oven, though the brand of clay used in the nursery school dries with a minimum of crumbling so that products can be saved over a period of time without baking. Some products are painted after being dried.

The older preschoolers learn to work quite efficiently with clay. They moisten the clay to smooth out the surfaces or to blend two pieces together. They squeeze out, from the main body of clay, appendages like arms, legs, or ears and add bits of clay to simulate features of a figure or parts of an object. Sometimes the children use small accessories to be combined with clay such as thumbtacks, bottle caps, beads, or small buttons, cut up pieces of plastic straws, or used matchsticks. There is little attempt to instruct children in the management of clay. They learn by trying different things, experimenting with the materials and implements, and watching each other work.

Though most of the clay products made by preschoolers are individual clay figures or designs, some are clay "scenes" such as a zoo that includes two or three "caged animals" or a family of clay people in a living room with furniture.

Teachers or the children themselves sometimes initiate clay projects in which children make objects for some common purpose such as pastries to be placed on miniature shelves of a make-believe bakery. These products may be preserved and displayed in some section of the room for a week or two. Occasionally the children make holiday candle bases, figurines, paper-clip dishes, or pencil holders to take home as gifts for their parents.

Woodworking is also a popular activity with young children. Given tools of good quality and soft, small-sized pieces of wood, children love to saw pieces apart, nail or bolt pieces together, and embellish chunks of wood with bottle caps, corks, pieces of Styrofoam, and buttons. Working directly with a visiting amateur or professional sculptor is also an intriguing and stimulating experience for the children, and trips to art centers that display clay, wood, metal, and junk sculpture can also provide a stimulus to their activities with these materials. Junk sculpture can be produced in the nursery school by providing children with an array of three-dimensional objects to be combined into an interesting constellation of shape, color and texture using clay as an adhesive. Objects such as nuts and bolts, wood pieces, bits of roofing shingles, plastic or metal bottle caps, spools, matchboxes, used toothpaste tubes and caps, small plastic bottles, interesting stones, twigs, pine cones, acorns, and other crop products can be accumulated at school until there are enough to initiate a significant project in junk sculpture. Children may work individually on a piece of sculpture, or several may work together on one sculpture. A group product can be added to from day to day as children become interested in it and find new things to contribute.

In summary, art and craft materials are available in the nursery school for the enjoyment of the children. The child is given full freedom to use these materials without demands for competence, conventionality, or conformity in the product that emerges. The fun of the process usually takes precedence over the quality of the product.

10
Music

10 Music

Participation in music activities is well within the capabilities and interests of children of preschool age; consequently, many opportunities are provided in the school program for children to perform musically and to listen to the music of others. As with art activities, the purpose of early exposure to music is not so much to develop talent as it is to help the child think of music as an enjoyable art form and a satisfying means of self-expression. It is of primary importance that the child's early experiences with music be rewarding and pleasant rather than embarrassing or stressful. No child is urged or forced to sing or dance against his will in the nursery school—though he may be encouraged to stay near the group and listen or watch as other children participate.

Group singing is probably the most popular and regularly occurring music activity in the nursery school, but children also listen to phonograph records, play rhythm instruments, march, dance, and listen to guest musicians who visit the school. Some preschoolers enjoy music in all of the forms in which it is presented and gravitate immediately to any music group that gathers. Others enjoy music in one form or another and select and choose the music activities in which they participate.

CHILDREN'S SINGING

There is no set pattern or rigid scheduling that determines when singing will occur in the nursery school. Singing groups of four, five, or six children may be started at the request or initiation of a child or on the impulse of one of the adults. At other times a singing session may be planned ahead by a teacher, and the entire group may sit together and sing sometimes without accompaniment and sometimes accompanied by a piano. While it is important for children to have the experience of hearing instruments and singing to the accompaniment of instruments, it is not at all necessary for a teacher to be able to play the piano to provide good group singing for children. Singing without accompaniment is just as enjoyable to the children as having instrumental accompaniment; in fact, it often seems to be a more intimate and meaningful experience for the children to have their teacher sit with them on the floor as they sing together. The teacher's attention then is not divided between the children and the piano. Recorders, guitars, and autoharps are instruments that are well suited to group singing with young children. In any case, singing is an important part of the musical experiences of the children while they are in school. If a teacher does not enjoy singing with the children or does not feel capable of doing so, it is her responsibility to see to it that other adults in the program provide these experiences. Usually one or two of the adults working with any group of children do enjoy singing and if not, parents or volunteers can help to supply this important need.

In the course of a school year a group may learn a repertoire of songs that they sing together, repeating their favorites over and over again. While learning a song rarely involves tedious line-by-line memorization, teachers do usually take the time to repeat the words to children clearly and explicitly, helping them to understand the message of the song. The younger preschoolers may not realize that songs "make sense"—that they tell stories about people or events and have a message. Some are funny and some are just interesting, but they all tell a story of some kind. As the group gets used to teachers introducing songs by telling them what the song is about, the children begin to realize that one should listen to the words as well as the melody to fully enjoy the meaning of a song. In the last analysis, however, it does not seem to be necessary for a child to understand every phrase of a song to thoroughly enjoy it and sing to it with enthusiasm.

Individual differences in singing ability are clearly in evidence among the preschool children. Some of the children are amazingly accurate even at three years of age at reproducing a melody if it is not too complicated and if the song has been heard many times. While it is not the usual thing for very young children to sing with accuracy, one can observe steady improvement in the children's ability to remember and reproduce melodies with continued experience in group and individual singing.

The songs sung in the nursery school are often ones written especially for children: nursery rhymes about children, animals, or common things of significance to the child such as snow, rain, toys, or favorite occasions. These songs have the advantage of having simple lyrics and melodies and are repetitive enough for the child to learn quickly and remember from one time to the next. They have the disadvantage, however, of being isolated instances of music in the culture. They are not songs that are typically sung by the adults or outside of the nursery school. Consequently, the teachers in the nursery school make a point of introducing many other songs to the group that the child can share with the rest of the culture; songs that he will hear being sung by his parents or older brothers and sisters, songs that are sung on the radio, on television, on the street, and on records or tapes being played in the home. Folk songs, favorite camp songs, and contemporary pop songs are good choices to be introduced to the children in the nursery school provided that they have simple melodies and are interesting enough in theme for the children to enjoy. The adults in the nursery school keep alert for songs of the day that can be sung with the children. Some songs are too difficult in their entirety but can be presented in shortened form so the children can enjoy them more when they hear them elsewhere. Some of the songs from popular musicals, such as *Mary Poppins, The Wizard of Oz,* and *Peter Pan* are good examples of ones that can be taught to children in part or in their entirety. Theme songs from popular television programs that are watched by the children in their homes can be sung in school. Occasionally children may even request a favorite television or radio commercial because it is familiar and catchy.

Many folk songs are simple enough in lyrics and melody for young children to sing and are about subjects of interest to them. Several contemporary folk singers have selected folk songs or have composed folk-type music just for children. Among the contemporary vocal artists whose work is especially appropriate for children are Burl Ives, Pete Seeger, the Peter, Paul, and Mary trio, Marais and Miranda, Charity Bailey, Ella Jenkins, Susan Reed, Frank Luther, and Dorothy Olson.

Popular seasonal songs that recur year after year are also introduced to the children in school, since they are almost certain to hear them over and over in their homes and in their communities; for example, the song "White Christmas" at the holiday season, and "Take Me Out to the Ball Game" during the baseball season. The lyrics of some songs will not be fully understood by the children (though they usually get the gist of the song), but the use of songs popular in the community have the advantage of helping the child to feel he is a participant in the music of the culture and that he, too, knows the songs his family and others sing or hum. An example of such a song in the community from which our children come is the Twins baseball song. It is popular, catchy, simple, and prevalent (to a fault) during the baseball season. Learning to recognize it and to sing it in school increases the child's feeling of participation in this exciting season.

The nursery school children also enjoy the experience of helping to supply the lyrics of the songs they sing. Nursery school teachers generally have in their own repertoire a number of songs that can be suited to a particular occasion, inserting at appropriate places a child's name or some fact about him, such as the color of his shirt or the name of his friend. Children love to have jingles of this kind repeated again and again with a different child being the focal point of each verse.

With a little talent for music and some practice, teachers also become quite ingenious in guiding children in making up brief four-line rhymes to be sung to a simple tune that tells about a significant event in a child's life or some highlight of the school day. An adult who knows how to write music can record a melody in a school book of original songs about the children in the group.

Though most children become self-conscious and embarrassed at the prospects of singing alone before a group of companions, some enjoy this experience and want others to be quiet while they sing. Some children like making up their own songs which usually consist of a series of somewhat disconnected, rambling thoughts put to an equally rambling, unconventional melody.

Children in the nursery school are encouraged to sing or listen to vocal music on their own as well as in groups. Each classroom has a record player in the room that is simple enough for the children to operate without teacher help. Records are made available for the children to play in a relatively isolated part of the room, and the child is allowed to make his own selection from among the records available at a given time. In addition to numerous individual 45 RPM records of selected songs that are available on request by the children, the school maintains an extensive record collection of single records or albums of children's songs, long-playing albums of folk songs, and a miscellaneous selection of contemporary and popular songs. The more expensive records in the collection are used only with adult supervision.

Children's sing-times are sometimes recorded on tape by the teachers and played back to the children at some later time or on a special occasion. From time to time guests come to sing with the children, and their singing, too, may be recorded to be played back later. Occasionally guests who come are citizens of other countries and sing to the children in their native language, explaining the meaning of the songs they sing. Some teach the children a few lines of a song in their native language.

Singing experiences are sometimes introduced in conjunction with other curriculum activities. For example, songs about animals and their distinctive characteristics or unique antics may be introduced to help children become familiar with these particular animal behaviors.

Songs that incorporate familiar nonverbal sounds seem to have special appeal to children, for instance, songs that simulate animals sounds (such as "Old McDonald"), mechanical sounds (like the sounds in the folk song "My Favorite Toy"), or sounds of vehicle motors, sirens, squeaks, groans, and loud clashes.

Singing is an acceptable and enjoyable pastime in the nursery school. Teachers sometimes sing as they work, and children are encouraged to do the same. Singing is considered an unacceptable behavior only on those rare occasions when it interferes seriously with the group's activities of the moment.

INSTRUMENTAL MUSIC
IN THE NURSERY SCHOOL

Preschool children generally seem to be too young and immature to be given formal instruction on musical instruments. Although some carefully planned programs of instruction have met with apparent success (such as the Suzuki method of violin instruction for very young children), the degree of coordination and discipline required for mastery of a complicated musical instrument seems generally to be beyond the interest and motor skills of young children.

To give children the experience of using instruments to create sound and rhythm, nursery school teachers have capitalized on an interesting variety of rhythm instruments—some are standard instruments and some are homemade varieties. The instruments vary in the type of sounds they make and in the tones they emit, but all can be used to beat out the rhythm of a song or dance. They include bells mounted on leather straps, castanets, metal triangles, marimbas, tambourines, drums, cymbals, rhythm sticks that can be struck together or played on wooden blocks, and sand-paper-covered blocks to be rubbed together. Children love to use instruments of this kind and often impulsively get up to march or dance to the beat of the music.

As with singing, individual differences among the children in their ability to reproduce a rhythmic pattern is great. Some children as young as three can imitate subtle or unusual rhythms. Other children can match a steady beat in which the time between beats does not vary, but they cannot reproduce a more complicated pattern. Still others have trouble matching even a steady drum beat or marching rhythm. Children who have difficulty matching rhythms or beating out a steady rhythm of their own rarely seem concerned or aware of their shortcomings and enjoy the activity as much as the more musically sensitive members of the group. Though the adults in the nursery school do not call undue attention to the child's inaccuracies in matching rhythms, they do encourage the group to listen carefully to a beat and try to reproduce it. The children may be encouraged to match a rhythm produced by the teacher, or the teacher may invite a child to beat out a rhythm that she, in turn, will match.

Young children are extremely curious about all musical instruments and are eager to touch and to try them. The classroom piano is certain to attract children, and the adults must decide how to handle the children's use of it. Most teachers allow the children to play the piano at times when it will not disturb the group. The children usually go up and down the scale of keys trying each one in turn or striking them randomly. Their activity is primarily exploratory: they are not able to pick out melodies and do not usually even attempt to do so. Children at the piano are expected to use only their fingers and are not allowed to pound the keys with their fists, palms, or any other implement. Some of the children like to accompany their own singing; they typically use the fingers of both hands to simulate adult playing, look studiously at the music book on the rack, turn pages from time to time, and sing as they play. Some also like to sit next to a teacher and "play" as she does. While the procedure is not designed to enhance the quality of the teacher's performance, it can be a pleasant time of "togetherness" for the teacher and the child. If the adult is skillful enough she may capitalize on the rhythm set by the child and improvise something to fit it.

The children's handling of any expensive musical instrument in school is controlled and supervised by the adults. Teachers or guests who bring instruments into the school are usually willing to let the children touch as well as listen to them, and the children are instructed to be careful and gentle as they finger the valves, pluck the strings, or depress the keys.

A guest who brings a musical instrument to school usually accomplishes a number of things only one of which is to give the children information about the instrument such as its name and sound. Most guests accompany the children as they sing songs that are familiar to them, and most also play solo selections that particularly show off the instrument. In this way children are able to get a close look at musical expertise that few get elsewhere unless their families are very musical. The children are extremely attentive and intrigued by guest soloists and are usually as captivated by the solo selections as they are by the guest's accompaniment of their own singing.

It is also possible for a particularly musical staff of teachers and assistants to arrange to play for the children during rest times or at regular intervals in the school day, using some combination of a piano, guitar, recorder, or autoharp.

From time to time children also listen to instructional records that isolate the sounds of the various instruments of a combo, orchestra, or band. The child gradually begins to learn from these experiences which sounds come from guitars, violins, cellos, and bass fiddles, which come from woodwinds or horns, and which from the tympany.

There are also many opportunities for the children to listen to recorded instrumental music much of which is carefully selected from the classics. Records are often played during rest times, early in the morning as children are arriving, during snack time, or during a relatively quiet phase of the day's program. Teachers vary in their judgment of how and when to use records. Some feel that they should be used only when listening to the record is the main activity of the moment, since music as a background to other things tends to add to the noise and confusion of the room. Other teachers feel the children are listening and acquiring a taste for music even when they are doing other things in other parts of the room, as evidenced by their occasional looking up to attend the music, singing or humming with a record, or moving gently in time with the music. In any case, it would seem that the most valuable listening times are those in which the child is not too distracted by other things to be aware of the music.

In selecting instrumental music for the school record library an attempt is made to expose the children to some of the more familiar and famous themes or segments of symphonies, concertos, suites, and operettas. Only rarely is a young child interested enough in music of this kind to sit down and listen to an entire symphony or concerto (though it is not unheard of), but many of them seem to enjoy bits and pieces abstracted from them. Consequently, it is more likely that a single movement or selected theme from a symphony or concerto will be played at school than an entire composition. While at times the children may be told the name of the composition, at other times nothing will be said; the music is just there to be enjoyed. Some examples of classical selections that are included in the children's record library are; Tchaikovsky's *Nutcracker Suite* and *1812 Overture*, Grieg's *Peer Gynt Suites*, Grofe's *Grand Canyon Suite*, Haydn's *Surprise* Symphony and *Clock* Symphony, Rimsky-Korsakov's *Scheherazade*, and Offenbach's *Gaite Parisienne*.

A second consideration in selecting records for the library is variety. Besides music from the classics, the school record collection includes recordings of rock music, country music, jazz, and Irish, Oriental, and Israeli ethnic music. Some records feature a particular solo instrument while others feature a combo or an entire orchestra or band. Marches are available in good supply, and recordings of dance rhythms include waltzes, polkas, schottisches, cha chas, mambos, rhumbas, and tangos.

Another consideration in selecting records for school is quality. The children are exposed to good recordings of music performed by excellent musicians who are experts in whatever type of music is being played. As records or needles become worn or scratchy, they are replaced, and the record players used for presenting this music are of high quality.

A fourth consideration in selecting records for the children is the special appeal a selection is likely to have for children. While one cannot always predict the children's responses, music that is clearly suggestive of a

particular mood or event that children can understand seems to have special appeal. For example, the children can appreciate the symbolic nature of the music and understand the interpretation of selections such as "The Flight of the Bumblebee," "The Clock," The Donkey Song from Grofe's *Grand Canyon Suite,* and "The Waltz of the Flowers" from the *Nutcracker Suite.*

The adults in the nursery school are constantly alert for things they can do to enhance the experiences that the nursery school children have with music. They watch for records that they feel would be especially appropriate for school as part of the school's record collection. They are alert to the children's responses so they can pick out favorites of the group, or of particular children in the group, and make them available more often. From time to time a teacher will ask parents for information about what is available in the child's home and which things, if any, are his favorites or the favorites of the rest of the family. These selections may then be borrowed (or taped) to be played in school. If a child does not recognize the selection as a familiar one, the teacher may point out to him that the record is one that is played a lot in his home, or one that was taped from his home.

While information and the encouragement of musical talent are important aspects of the musical experiences of the children in the nursery school, enjoyment of music is the primary goal of these activities.

DANCING AND MOVEMENT TO MUSIC

It is not unusual for very young toddlers to show some inclination to move rythmically to music. Even before the child has the coordination to dance, he may bob up and down with his feet planted squarely on the floor or may sway his head or body from side to side in response to music. The child may do this at first after an adult demonstrates movement to music and encourages the child to follow, but in time the child spontaneously claps or moves to music that stimulates him. He may jump up and run or tumble to fast, vigorous music, stalk around the room to marching music, or beat time with his hands or feet to music with a compelling rhythm.

Preschoolers vary widely in the extent to which music moves them to respond motorically; some seem hardly able to sit still in the presence of stimulating music. Teachers in the nursery school encourage the children to be responsive to music—to clap or stamp out a rhythm or to march or dance. The adults usually join in these activities, both for their own enjoyment and to serve as models for the children.

The term "dance" is used rather loosely in the nursery school and usually means any rhythmic body movement done in response to music. It is not used to mean a predetermined or carefully choreographed series of movements. Though the children enjoy learning and performing simple dance routines such as the folk dances Looby Loo, the Hokey Pokey, the Seven Jumps, Bingo, and Chicken Fat, much of their dancing is free-style and not strictly coordinated with the music. The children share the improvisation with the adults; adults are alert to pick up cues from the children of interesting things to do to the music. Props may be introduced that lend themselves well to dance movements such as brightly colored scarfs, capes, balloons, or hoops. The children may decide to skip, hop, jump, stretch their arms above their heads or out to the sides, balance momentarily on one foot, spread their feet, walk stiff-legged or tip-toed, twirl, flap their arms in the air, sway back and forth, walk in a stooped position, or bend their bodies sideward or backward. One gets the impression at times that, while music provides the impetus for getting up to move, the fun of movement for its own sake takes over.

Some of the older preschoolers begin to simulate dancing postures and dancing routines with more accuracy. They imitate their impressions of ballet dancing, tap dancing, and modern or popular dancing as they see it on television or in the community. In fact, some young children show considerable aptitude for both imitating and improvising dance routines. Boys seem to be about as skillful in these activities as girls, though generally the boys are more reticent to perform. For this reason it is important for the school to supply male models for dancing. One can often observe an immediate tendency for the boys to imitate a male teacher who enters into the dance activities of the group. When a male teacher is not regularly available, a male volunteer can sometimes be talked into helping out during some of the group's dancing sessions.

While some children like the attention of the group and enjoy dancing for an audience, others are easily embarrassed by undue attention to their dancing. Some are reticent to join the group but finally do after considerable watching on the sidelines, or watching from a distance while they are seemingly occupied with other activities. Some children never join active dancing or rhythm sessions of this kind. There is no pressure exerted to get children to perform to music. The child is allowed to do other things or to watch as long as he wishes and to join when and if he wishes. Teachers may invite a child to join who is just watching, but the child is not made to feel that he is being stubborn or rebellious in refusing. Teachers generally try to time their invitation for a moment when the child is sorely tempted and needs only a word of encouragement to join. Some children will accept an invitation to dance with the teacher and then finally will initiate dancing on their own. When a reticent child dances with the group, he is likely to participate briefly and then sit again to watch for a while. Finally his participation gets less self-conscious, less inhibited, and more spontaneous.

It is difficult to say why children who have moved spontaneously to music as toddlers become so easily embarrassed at this activity as preschoolers. Perhaps the child too rarely sees adults and older children dancing so that he does not consider this a proper activity for sensible people! In any case, the children are inclined to imitate the rhythmic dancing or marching of adults whenever demonstrations are provided. Because of this, teachers in the nursery school regularly arrange opportunities for the children to see others dancing or moving rhythmically to music.

Special Dance Activities

An expert dancer or dance instructor may be invited to dance with the children. Before the visit the nursery school teacher will prepare the guest for the children's possible reticence and reassure her or him that getting all of the children to join is not necessary, since some of the children will prefer to watch and some who do not dance at the time, will do so at a later time. Two or three school-age children who are members of a dance class may be invited to come to the nursery school to dance for the children. They may be asked to demonstrate certain steps or routines and let the children imitate them if they wish. One advantage of a visit from children who dance is that the nursery school children see this activity as appropriate for children like themselves, not just for teen-agers. Also young dancers may have some simple dance routines that the younger children can more easily imitate or learn. If the dance has an interpretation the children can understand, this can be explained to them so that they can see the meaning of various parts of the dance. The group may also be taken to a dance studio in which children are being taught new dance routines or are practicing ones they already know.

Occasionally older teen-age brothers and sisters of the preschoolers are invited to the nursery school to hold a rock or rock-folk session for the children to watch. They may be invited to bring their favorite records or tapes to be played at the school, and their favorite dance partners as well. Invitations to the school-age boys and girls must, of course, be coordinated with their particular school schedules. There are usually a limited number of days each year when the local schools for older children are closed while the nursery school is open. These days are anticipated and used for special visits of this kind. College students are also willing to come to demonstrate currently popular dances (and typically have more flexible schedules than school children). Visiting groups of this kind often include one or two guests who are particularly effective in putting the children at ease and in encouraging them to participate. The teachers too can help to get children involved and participating with the older children or adults.

Folk dance groups make particularly good guests for school since they are often used to performing and dancing together. They may be dressed in their native costumes. Most visiting groups are willing to teach the children some of the simpler parts of a dance, or they may simplify an entire dance so that the children can perform it with them. They may also be taught one of the children's dances and dance it with them.

Even if children do not participate at the time that guests visit, they are often completely absorbed in watching and do imitate the movements of the dance at some later time. It is important for the teachers to provide the setting for latent imitation by having appropriate music available to be played at school during the days following the visit from the guests. In this way the children are stimulated to recall the visit and to reenact it on their own. Having a movie camera available to take movies of the guests and the children dancing together is another way to recapture the mood of the occasion at a later time.

In summary, music and dance activities in the nursery school, like art activities, are for the enjoyment of the children. The nursery school provides opportunities for the child to observe other children and adults enjoying music, and it also supports the child's efforts to give expression to his own musical impulses at his own level of skill.

11
Play Activities and Social Skills

11 *Play Activities and Social Skills*

Participation in play with companions is considered an important aspect of the young child's school activity, since it serves both the cognitive and social goals of the program. Through play experiences and the use of play materials, a number of important goals of early education are realized. First, play contributes to the child's feelings of competence and mastery in the use of his body. Second, through play, the child can acquire new information about the physical properties of objects around him and integrate information he already has. Third, the child can develop his capacity to use his imagination. And fourth, play provides opportunities to develop the social sophistication required for interacting constructively with companions.

Several general types of materials are used in play—natural elements, construction materials, large muscle equipment, toys, and games. Dirt, stones, sand, water, leaves, snow, ice and other natural elements of the environment are incorporated into the play of children both in and out of school settings. With the help of digging implements and containers, children spend many hours using these materials. Nursery schools also provide many other materials and equipment for play. Construction materials such as building blocks, large and small boxes, boards, barrels, ropes, tape, clay, dough, and paint are available. Swings, climbing bars, trikes, wagons, and other equipment are supplied for large muscle activities. Many of the toys provided are child-sized replicas of things in the environment. Toys such as cars, trains, animals, work tools, and housekeeping equipment are some of these replicas found in most nursery schools.

Other materials are provided in the nursery school to foster the development of small muscle coordination and cooperation and cognitive skills. These include puzzles, beads, games, and other learning activities.

Most nursery school days have two scheduled free-play or free-activity times, each 30 to 45 minutes long. One usually occurs early in the school day, and the other occurs near the end of the day, depending on scheduling problems and teacher preference. Generally one playtime is for outside play and one is for inside play. During these periods children are allowed to select what they wish to play with from a range of play materials. Adults do not assign activities to children during free activity

157

times. Thus children are encouraged to develop their own interests and are free to come and go from materials as they wish. Most children divide their playtime between activities that are physically vigorous and quieter table activities. While social play is encouraged, the child is permitted to play alone when he does not wish to be with companions.

COMPETENCE AND MASTERY THROUGH PLAY

Young children are eager to test the capacities of their bodies. They take great satisfaction in accomplishments that involve coordination, strength, and endurance. In the nursery school they become absorbed for long periods of time in the mastery of physical feats such as climbing above the ground, jumping from packing boxes, balancing on one foot, hopping, skipping, riding trikes, or throwing and catching balls. They struggle to conquer the sometimes frightening sensations that come from swinging on swings, riding a seesaw, sliding down slides, or hanging upside down from a trapeze bar. As the child gains skill, one can literally see the pleasure and pride he takes in moving his body with confidence to perform feats of coordination. Once a feat is accomplished, the child may practice it over and over again, thoroughly enjoying it each time and gradually perfecting his performance. At a time when his confidence is high, he may reject help that he needed before, or he may ask for an audience, inviting a teacher or some friends to watch him.

Children in the nursery school are not all alike in their approach to large motor activities. Some children confidently clamber over the equipment from the first day of school while others approach climbing and jumping with caution. Children seem intuitively to set goals for themselves that are appropriate for their levels of skill. The younger children, or the less skillful ones, practice climbing in and around the lower bars of the jungle gym, for example, while the older children head for the top bars. As the child improves in skill, he ventures further off the ground and climbs faster and with more assurance. Seeing the other children performing more daring feats spurs the child on to try something a little harder and more challenging. Young children do not seem to become as embarrassed at their lack of skill as older children and adults do. With a little encouragement, they come back to try things day after day until they gain mastery. Occasionally a child will be chided by his companions for not being able to perform some trick, but generally the more skillful children are too absorbed in their own performances to comment on the abilities of others.

Regardless of a child's level of skill, the performance of vigorous physical activity and the mastery of feats of coordination seem to bring pleasure and self-confidence to the preschooler. It is not uncommon for a child who was fearful and cautious early in the school year to finally show a degree of skill, coordination, and daring in physical activity that matches the more confident children. Only in rare instances does a child remain blatantly fearful or avoidant of these activities throughout the school year.

While vigorous physical play is somewhat more characteristic of boys than girls, many girls are skillful in these activities and are encouraged by the teachers to enjoy running, jumping, and climbing.

Teachers in the nursery school help the children in several ways to develop confidence and physical prowess. They may offer to stand near a piece of climbing equipment or give physical support until a child feels secure enough to perform on his own. They show appreciation for the child's courage or persistence in perfecting skills of jumping, climbing, and balancing and compliment him on his growing competence.

Adults in the nursery school also expect the children to learn to take responsibility for their own safety on equipment and for the safety of the people around them. The children are taught to look before they jump to be sure that they do not jump too close to an obstacle or do not collide with another child. A child who is climbing may be instructed to "hold tight" so that if his foot slips he still has a firm handhold. He is taught not to push others while on high places and is helped to check whether or not ladders and boards are stable and secure before climbing onto them or walking across them. He is taught how to carry big items in such a way that his vision is not blocked, and he is helped to remember that he must watch both ends of a long object like a board or ladder so that it does not hit someone as he maneuvers it. He is expected to manage trikes and wagons without bumping into people or objects.

Some play materials in the nursery school require the children to keep large motor activity at a minimum while they concentrate on fine motor activity involving the hands and eyes. Construction toys such as Lego, Tinker Toys, Lincoln Logs, and Bilofix, for example, require the child to attach nuts to bolts, insert small rods into holes, or link pieces firmly together in order to build. Materials such as peg-boards, Montessori cylinders, beads, and puzzles also require the child to make fine motor adjustments to maneuver pieces into place. The use of scissors, crayons, and paint brushes require the child to combine a number of motoric actions into a composite for successful handling of the materials. The younger children are often extremely awkward with materials that require refined eye-hand coordination, but improvement comes steadily with age and experience. The adults in the nursery school do not fuss with children over tasks such as coloring within an outline or cutting along a line, since only the older children begin to show a fair degree of precision in these functions.

Here, as with large motor activity, preschool children seem to find intrinsic satisfaction in mastery. It is not uncommon to see children in the nursery school concentrating so intensely on fine motor tasks that their bodies are rigid and their tongues are tightly clenched between their teeth against what seems, at times, to be endless frustration with the tools and the materials. Still they persist and take considerable satisfaction in the product that emerges.

PLAY AS A SOURCE
OF NEW INFORMATION

Much of the young child's learning comes from the informal exploration of objects in the environment while he is at play. From the time children are barely able to move about, most have a strong inclination to approach novel things and examine them in an effort to satisfy their curiosity about them. They look at what there is to see, listen to what there is to hear, and touch what there is within range to touch. Although psychologists and educators cannot evaluate precisely what a child learns from each informal encounter with his environment, there are some general characteristics of the environment during the early years that contribute to the child's learning of basic concepts in the course of his play. One is the availability of direct physical contact with many different objects in the environment so that the child can experience for himself what different things feel and look like. It is assumed that children learn more from these encounters if the adults around them take an interest in their activities and talk with them from time to time about their experiences, identifying things by name and pointing out their more interesting or distinctive features.

Free use and manipulation of objects in the environment gives the child a chance to notice that things come in different sizes, colors, and shapes, are made of different materials, and have different textures and different uses. The child gradually learns the meaning of words that describe the physical characteristics of things—words such as heavy, fuzzy, pointed, square, tiny, and strong. He learns that some things are solid and some are hollow, some things are wet and others dry, some are soft and others hard, and that some have rough surfaces and sharp edges while others are smooth and rounded. He learns that some things are alive and some are not and that some objects change over time and some remain essentially unchanged. He learns the meaning of action words such as moving, growing, running, turning, wiggling, shining, and blowing. He will learn some useful bits of information, like the fact that hot things burn, that round things can roll away, things that are off balance or unsupported fall, and that delicate things break easily.

Some play materials in the nursery school are designed to call the child's attention to one isolated physical property at a time. For example, the child's attention may be focused on color through the use of color pegs or color tablets that can be matched by the child or ordered from light to dark shades of a single color. Dimensions of size may be emphasized through things such as unit building blocks, nesting boxes, or Montessori cylinders that can be ordered by the child from smallest to largest or from shortest to tallest. Two children may discover, through their own manipulations of a balance scale, that two blocks weigh more than one and less than three. Measuring rods are available so that children can match for length or order from shortest to longest. Swatches of materials of different textures are available for children to compare and to identify —perhaps without looking first. Table materials of this kind are available throughout the free playtime, and the children are encouraged to experiment with them to discover on their own what things they can learn from them. At other times the same materials may be used for more formal instruction in teacher-directed projects or game situations using number concepts or classification and matching skills.

ROLE PLAYING AND MAKE-BELIEVE

"Pretending" is a striking characteristic of much of the play of young children. Children in the nursery school can be observed pretending to be mothers, babies, ferocious animals, storekeepers, cowboys, or anything else that occurs to them. Even without props (for instance, doll furniture, toy cash registers, and cowboy hats) to suggest this kind of activity, it emerges as one of the most common forms of play in the preschool. Considering the prevalence of role playing in the lives of young children, it is astonishing how little systematic study has been made of this behavior. We are gradually learning more about children's make-believe play, but at this point we can only speculate about the child's own reasons for playing in this way and guess at the function it has in his development.

One interesting feature of the role play of children in the nursery school is that it involves a kind of synthesis of actions, comments, and emotional responses that are generally appropriate to the role being played. A child pretending to be a dock worker, for example, will not only lift heavy blocks into a wagon so that they can be transported from one place on the dock to another, but his whole manner will suggest a "dock-worker" role. He may use a very gruff, authoritative voice as he shouts suggestions or commands to a companion working with him. He is likely to call his companion by some name other than the given name of the child involved—like "Joe," for example,—as if to recognize that his co-worker at the moment is *not* three-year-old Teddy Larson, but "Joe the dock worker." Often the child's emotional behavior as well as his comments and actions fit the role. A "mother" tending her baby will vacillate between nurturant tender care of her infant and impatient irritation at his crying or fussing. In the reciprocal role, another child playing the part of the infant will at times be peacefully curled up in the doll bed sucking his thumb and at other times will mischievously dump his cereal or fuss and cry to be attended. Two children in cowboy roles may stalk about the room boldly and then fight fearlessly when they confront the "bad guys." A child pretending to be a lost kitten will cringe in the corner and whine pitifully waiting for the mother cat to come and find it.

It is not at all uncommon for young children to assume both masculine and feminine roles from time to time in their play. Boys can be observed tending the house, caring for babies, and wearing the girls' dress-up clothes, and girls sometimes take the roles of cowboy, train conductor, or Superman. The vacillation between masculine and feminine roles for play purposes does not seem to indicate confusion on the part of the children as to their sex identity. Most children of three and four are well aware of the identity of their sex and know that they will grow up to be "fathers" rather than "mothers" or vice versa. Role playing the opposite sex seems more motivated by an interest in the activities being performed than by any confusion in the child's mind as to his own sex. Occasionally a child does show extreme preoccupation with roles of the opposite sex and may even insist that he is a girl or she is a boy. Brief excursions into this kind of fantasy are not considered ominous by the adults in the nursery school, but a child who seems genuinely rejecting of his sex identity over a period of many months will give cause for alarm. The adults will then talk with the parents of the child to determine how consistent the pattern is in the child's behavior and to see what light can be shed on the child's motivation to resist his appropriate sex identity. If the situation persists, consultation may be sought with medical, clinical, or other personnel if the parents agree to such a plan.

While the role-playing themes and sequences of the younger preschoolers are somewhat underdeveloped and fleeting, the story themes of the older children often involve very elaborate sequences of play that are maintained for 30 minutes or longer. The same theme may be taken up by the children on successive days, each day's play being more elaborate than the day before. Teachers may help to sustain this kind of play by providing additional interesting props that can be incorporated into the play and by generally protecting the play group from distraction or interference from others.

Teachers have typically valued role-playing experiences for children in the nursery school on the assumption that this kind of play is an important source of new facts and information for the children. Evidence on this point is sparse. Observation of this form of play, however, would suggest that role playing may not be so much a source of *new* information for the child as an opportunity for the child to *integrate* information that he already has. Much of the child's role-playing seems to involve the organization of bits and pieces of information into whole units of activity in which the child must recall the full sequence of things done and attitudes conveyed, for example, by a mother attending her family, or by a mechanic repairing a car. What one child overlooks, another puts into the play, and both children may, from then on, incorporate the new act or attitude into their play sequences. The child seems to practice using the vocabulary appropriate to the role (occasionally to the chagrin of the model).

Adults in the nursery school try to increase the learning potential of this kind of play by bringing in story or picture books that are relevant to the more popular play themes used by the children. Field trips, films, objects of interest, or guests are also used to improve the quality of role playing by supplying new information and ideas for play themes. Teachers often observe an almost immediate incorporation of new objects, new information, or new ideas into the play activities of the group.

While teachers do enter into the imaginative play of the children from time to time, generally their job is to facilitate the play of the children, not to participate in it, or to "show" the children how to play. Teachers provide the play props and arrange the room in a way that invites extended imaginative play; the children do the playing. The adults often watch and listen to children as they play, since much can be learned about the social techniques and the thinking of the children through unobtrusive observation of this kind.

Role-Playing Themes

Several themes recur again and again in the role playing of children in the nursery school. One common theme involves roles of *competence and mastery*. In this type of play the child imagines himself to be an adult who has complete control of the situation, performs tasks with great skill, and has power and influence over others. Work roles are of this kind where the child pretends to be a parent caring for children, a worker building a road, a pilot flying an airplane, a service station attendant fixing a car, or a nurse giving shots. The child often spends a brief time setting the stage for such play by building whatever structure he needs or by accumulating the toys and materials he requires. He then proceeds to act out the behavior he imagines to be appropriate to the setting. Much occupational role play goes on in the housekeeping corner of the nursery school and in the block area where the children have ready access to many toys that are replicas of objects used by the adults in the environment. Often the presence of a single prop, such as a fireman's hat or a stuffed animal, will set play in motion for a small group of children who then develop a theme around the toy.

It is difficult to know what motivates this kind of role playing in young children. Since so many of the roles children play do involve mastery and competence (and since children vie for the more masterful roles), one suspects that the child gets a special feeling of improved status from his pretending. In his day-to-day life, the preschooler is low on the totem pole of competent persons in the family and in the community since most of the people he knows are older and more mature. The child may get a special satisfaction from pretending to be one of these more competent persons. Whether or not his make-believe serves an important function in his development toward maturity is hard to say. It seems probable that playing at being responsible, competent, and conscientious in the performance of a job may help to prepare the child psychologically for the time when he will be expected to assume some responsibility and perform a difficult or important task. His play may serve as a kind of "rehearsal" of the attitudes and behaviors that are required in situations that demand effort and responsibility. This kind of play may also facilitate the child's general identification with adults by increasing his tendencies to imitate adults and other older more competent persons. While the imitative behavior is, in these instances, a part of play, it may actually predispose the child to imitate in nonplay situations as well.

Some of the role playing by children in the nursery school depicts themes of *dominance and control* over others. Children may pretend to be fearful monsters who descend on their victims and tie them up, run them off the premises, or devour them. Superman and Batman are popular characters to emulate, presumably because of their special powers and superhuman strength. This play, too, would seem to reflect the satisfaction that the child finds in pretending to be more powerful than he is in real life. Through this avenue he can control his companions or any of the adults who will play a reciprocal role for him. Some of this play seems quite clearly motivated by a desire to "do mischief" without really misbehaving. If the child is careful to keep his behavior within the bounds of "play," he is often allowed to be quite aggressive or wicked in the context of make-believe. The child may pretend to be a hurricane that knocks down block buildings, a puppy that chews up clothing, or a robber who steals other's belongings.

There are two opposing positions taken by psychologists and teachers concerning the wisdom of allowing aggressive play of this kind in the nursery school, and both are supported to some extent by clinical evidence or research. One position is based on the assumption that the child's fantasy aggression compensates him for the fact that much of the time in real-life situations he must control his temper and repress aggressive impulses directed toward companions and adults. According to this theory, fantasy aggression provides a form of "release" for the child, reducing tension and making it possible for him to tolerate the real-life restraints that otherwise might become unbearable. Allowing or encouraging the child to "act out" in this way, or even to observe others doing so, presumably reduces the need for the child to act out against peers and adults in nonplay situations.

According to the opposing theoretical position, fantasy aggression serves as a disinhibitor of the child's rather tenuous self-control. Being allowed to "pretend" to be aggressive gives him practice in performing aggressive acts that at some other time he may use in real-life situations. According to this position, observing the aggression of other children at play may also help a child to "learn" new aggressive responses which he may then use in nonplay situations.

Since both of these positions seem to have some validity, the adults in the nursery school are faced with the dilemma of deciding how to handle fantasy aggression. If opportunities to let off steam through make-believe aggression are helpful to the child, one would be reluctant to discourage them. On the other hand, if make-believe aggression leads to real aggression, permitting the children to continue in such play would be somewhat questionable. The position of teachers in the nursery school is a compromise one that has evolved with new research findings and the evaluation of classroom experience. Fantasy aggression is usually permitted in school on the assumption that it does fill a psychological need for the child, but the adults do take precautions against the child's vacillating back and forth between fantasy and real aggression or destruction as he plays. In other words, the child is expected to make a clear distinction between "play" and "real" aggression or destruction, and play aggression must not turn into real aggression as the child gets absorbed in the role. If a child is pretending to be a vicious lion who claws its victims, he will be expected to keep his "clawing" well within the bounds of play. If, in the course of his enthusiasm for the role, he actually begins to hurt another child, he will be stopped. Even though he does not physically hurt another child but in the course of the play causes excessive fear, he will be asked to stop or to find another companion who will enjoy the suspense and excitement of being "attacked" by a lion. Actually children often do find this kind of play fear-arousing, yet fun and exciting, and they seek it out for brief periods of time, enjoying both the role of the victim and the role of the attacker.

Aggressive or destructive fantasies may be motivated partly by the child's growing awareness that there does exist in the world frightening, fearful things and that people are at times exposed to terrifying experiences. While the child himself may have had few such experiences, he is impressed as he hears about them, sees evidence of them in the community (a wrecked car, for example), or sees them on television. Reconstructing them in his play may be a way for the child to practice coping with them. One does get the feeling of the child's struggling to keep his fear in check during fear-arousing play situations in the nursery school. If at some point his fear gets the upper hand, the child will promptly leave the play or appeal to his companions to stop.

Occasionally a child reenacts, through play, some recent traumatic experience in his own life, such as a hospitalization or a fire in his home. This play, too, seems to come about from a need to control the situation and to master intense feelings of fear or anger. The child often accentuates the fearful aspects of the situation and usually puts himself in the role of the authority figure who can do something about the situation. He seems to be "fighting back" through his play. If the event caused pain or discomfort, for example, the child is often the character who imposes the pain or discomfort on someone else, and he may perform his role with considerable gusto. Occasionally the doll corner "babies" are the victims of resentment or abuse coincident with a hospital trip or a new baby on the scene at home. Teachers in the nursery school generally do not take on the role of therapist by interpreting such incidences to the children involved or suggesting that the incident is drawn directly from the child's own life. Even if the adult's hunch is correct, and a play theme is a reconstruction of the child's experience, interpretation from an adult may cause unnecessary guilt or self-consciousness on the part of the child for having displayed his fear or his hostility.

Many of the aggressive or destructive play themes enacted by the children seem to have no direct counterpart in their real lives. For example, children playing in the doll corner may portray parents who are excessively punitive or downright monstrous even though their own parents are perfectly normal and appropriate in behavior—punitive at times, perhaps, but never monstrous.

Allowing the child to express aggression through fantasy may have a number of advantages besides letting him get things off his chest. By helping the child observe the fine line between real aggression and play aggression, the adults reaffirm their restrictions on unchecked real aggression. Expecting children to resist the temptation to get carried away by their own fantasy aggression or the aggressive behavior of others may help the child learn to resist becoming impulsively aggressive at the slightest invitation to do so. Children are frequently exposed to aggressive acts and aggressive models in real life and through television or stories. They must gradually learn to evaluate the context within which aggression occurs and must anticipate the consequences of such acts. While it is at times acceptable for them to imitate aggressive models, at other times it is totally unacceptable. The very young child will have to take his cues from the adults responsible for him as to which aggressive acts he may imitate and which he may not; but he will certainly be expected to learn *not* to indiscriminately imitate all of the aggression he sees.

If a child shows an unusual passion for aggressive play themes, repeating them again and again and preferring them to all other forms of play, the adults in the nursery school will almost certainly raise questions concerning the child's motivation. Occasionally a child who is preoccupied with aggressive fantasies is having a difficult time getting along with his companions on any terms other than dominance and control. It is also not uncommon for such a child to be experiencing more than an average amount of difficulty at home, including excessive frustration or inconsistent handling of real aggression by his parents. In any case, teachers will observe the child's school behavior, will consult with his parents in an effort to understand the causes of his preoccupation with aggressive play, and will work out a plan to help him. If the situation seems to warrant it, a clinical consultant will be asked to help.

Another common play theme observed in the nursery school is one involving *regression*. In play of this kind the child usually acts out themes of dependence or immaturity. He may become a helpless infant, a baby animal, or a sick or wounded person in need of constant care and attention. These roles are sometimes distributed among the children just to round out the characters needed for play, but if a child seems to gravitate regularly to the role of an infant in doll-corner play, the teacher will consider the possibility that the child feels conflicted about demands for independence and competence and may be looking back nostalgically at his dependent babyhood. If the child seems generally to lack self-confidence, teachers may become watchful of opportunities to bolster the child's opinion of his own ability, rewarding him with recognition and approval for even small steps toward independence and maturity.

DRAMATIC PRODUCTIONS

From time to time some of the older children in the nursery school put on simple dramatic productions for the enjoyment of each other, a guest audience of parents, or another school group. The activity may involve the development of an original episode or familiar theme, like "getting ready for school in the morning" or "opening birthday presents," or the group may recreate the events in a favorite storybook. Episodes are short, and children usually trade off roles, repeating the general theme several times with whatever individual variations the children introduce.

If the production involves recreating a story, the group will need to recall what sequence of events took place and what the characters said. If the production is an original one, the children must improvise to a greater extent, creating characters that fit the occasion. The use of props like puppets, stuffed animals, or miniature dolls and doll furniture are excellent for the encouragement of dramatic activities, since the children are often less self-conscious using a prop figure than performing without one.

Sometimes children create pantomimes in which a character or activity is presented without words or interpretation and the others must guess what the child is or what he is doing. Since the success of this activity depends on the appropriateness of the cues given the audience, teachers often take an active role in helping the children to think of subjects that have distinctive features, postures, walks, or vocalizations. The older children seem to catch on to the task and are often able to be very creative in their selections. One child, for example, became a house with a peaked roof by extending her elbows out to the sides and bringing the fingers of both hands together above her head.

"Performing" in the nursery school is an activity that is met with mixed emotions by the children and, consequently, must be handled with care and sensitivity by the adults. Elaborate group productions involving stage direction, costumes, and the learning of lines can be a source of delight for some children participating but may be a source of frustration and embarrassment for others. The group of children taking part in such an activity at any one time is kept small enough so that the demands of the situation can be adapted to the individual children involved. An important measure of the success of dramatic productions in the nursery school is the extent to which each child resonates to the group effort and enjoys his part in the activity, whether as a performer or as a member of the audience.

THE DEVELOPMENT OF SOCIAL SKILLS
THROUGH PLAY

The years from two to five are a time when children begin to establish true friendships and cooperative relations with peers. The 18-month-old toddler is strongly attracted to other children, but he tends to treat them all alike and does not develop individual friendships in which he has a great investment. By three or four years of age, the child may be expressing decided preferences for a few selected companions. He may at times be willing to share, collaborate, and compromise if he must to stay on good terms with his special friends. The intensity of some nursery school friendships is surprising; rejection or neglect from a favorite companion can cause anger, hurt feelings, or jealousy. Some of the most hostile social insults between children in the nursery school are in the name of friendships; a small group of children may reject an outsider with comments such as "He's not our friend, is he?" or "This place is just for us!" in order to reaffirm their friendship for each other.

Though it is not uncommon for pairs or threesomes of children in a group to maintain a close friendship throughout the school year, most nursery school friendships are neither that stable nor that exclusive. Many preschoolers play regularly or intermittently with at least one half of the children in their group, and changes in the composition of play groups can be observed over any period of two or three months.

Nursery school children vary widely in the intensity of their friendships with peers. Some seem to seek out and nurture companionship much more vigorously than others, adapting in any way that they can to keep a companion with them. Other children seem to be rather blasé about companionship, going their own way, accepting the companionship of another child when it is offered, but not necessarily seeking it out. Parents, too, differ in their concern over their children's peer relations in school. Some are eager to have their child be popular in the peer group; others are more concerned that their child be able to resist peer influence for fear of his learning unacceptable social behaviors. Some parents prefer to have their children become interested in the intellectual activities at school rather than the social activities on the assumption that this will best prepare them for later school success. In discussions with parents, teachers emphasize the importance of *both* social and nonsocial aspects of the child's development; the school attempts to help each child work out a comfortable balance of social and nonsocial activity to suit his or her personality and level of development.

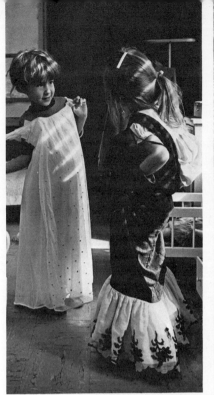

Though the adults respect the right of a child to take or leave peer companionship at any given moment, teachers will be concerned about any child whose interactions with his classmates are either so minimal in amount or inadequate in quality as to make the development of friendships impossible. More will be said on this point later.

Two of the most common forms of social play in the nursery school are *parallel play* and *cooperative play*. In parallel play, children play side by side using essentially the same kinds of play materials, but they are not actually sharing materials and each goes about his own activity independent of the others. For example, two children may be digging in the sandbox but each is working on his own sand building, or two children may be playing in the doll corner, but each is caring for a baby or preparing a "dinner." The children may talk to each other, notice what the other child is doing, and imitate each other, but each is pursuing his own activity. This form of social play is more characteristic of the three-year-olds in the nursery school than of the four-year-olds and requires a minimum of sharing of play space and materials.

In contrast to parallel play, cooperative play involves a more complicated sharing of materials and roles. In this form of play the children work toward a single goal; each child makes his particular contribution to the play, and each must consider the opinions and desires of the others. For example, two or more children may be building the same block structure. To accomplish this without trouble, the children must agree on the characteristics of the building, the division of labor among them, and the sharing of play props. Generally, they must show enough confidence in their companions to work cooperatively from a common pool of play materials, and each must let the others play with a minimum of interference. If a child does not like the way the play is going, he must appeal to his companions to proceed in some other way, for example, by changing the building they are working on from a garage for trucks to a hangar for airplanes or a cage for animals. If his companions do not agree with his suggestion, he must either convince them, leave the play and build on his own, or compromise in some way. If the cooperative play is to be maintained, the group must manage to resolve conflicts to the satisfaction of the children involved. No one can make all of the decisions or always be favored without the others protesting and demanding some consideration.

The most elaborate form of cooperative play in the nursery school is play that involves the assignment of reciprocal roles. In the doll corner, for example, one child may play the role of the mother, tending the babies and preparing the meal, while another is the baby and a third is the father who goes to work and comes home to dinner. Or one child may be a storekeeper and another a customer. Because each child is so dependent on the others for a successful play experience, this form of imaginative play is more challenging than other forms and is more subject to conflicts and disagreements.

Cooperative play activities involving two or more children do not by any means proceed smoothly just because of the presence of adults in the nursery school. The teachers take a middle-of-the-road position with regard to intervention in the management of children's difficulties during play. While they believe that well-timed suggestions guide children toward reasonable and fair solutions to problems and teach them acceptable standards of behavior, they also feel that children benefit from struggling on their own toward solutions to interpersonal problems. Teachers do not generally intervene when difficulties arise during play if they feel the children involved stand a good chance of resolving a conflict in a fair and equitable way.

There is some observational research evidence to suggest that children in the nursery school approve and disapprove of many of the same social behaviors that are approved of or disapproved of by adults. They express their approval of friendly, sympathetic behavior and their disapproval of bullying tactics, interference, and excessive aggression. Observations of this kind lead one to believe that, given some freedom of expression, children can help teach each other which social behaviors are unacceptable in the play group and which are acceptable.

A nursery school group is, in some ways, like a miniature society in which individuals have rights to be protected but in which each must, in turn, observe the rights of the other members of the group. It is the responsibility of the adults in the school to convey to the children a reasonable set of ground rules for getting along with each other.

Many of the rules in the nursery school are related to problems of sharing equipment, materials, and space. While some rules are simple and straightforward, others require qualification and allowance for exceptions. One common school rule is that a child is permitted to use a toy or piece of equipment that he has chosen for as long as he wishes to use it—until he decides he is finished with it. An exception to this rule may be made if the toy or equipment is new or novel to the group. In this instance the child may be asked to give it up after a reasonable turn. If a child brings a personal belonging from home he need not share it if he wants to just show it to others and then put it in his locker for the day. If he chooses to keep it out in the playroom, he is expected to be generous with it.

Another rule has to do with the sharing of materials such as clay, blocks, or crayons. Though the child is expected to share materials of this kind when he has an abundance, he is not expected to share beyond the point where the utility of the material is impaired. If too many children are making demands at one time on blocks, table materials, or other resources, some may be asked to play or work elsewhere until others have finished.

Although the general expectation at school is that children will allow others to join their play, a child is not specifically required to accept all comers. The right of a single child or a group of two or three children to use a part of the room or a piece of equipment for a period of time without interruption is respected. Other children may be diverted to a different area or asked to come back at another time.

The adults in the nursery school occasionally approach the teaching of social protocol through dramatic media such as stories about children who become good friends, or puppets who fight with each other and then finally learn to get along and to share. Most of the teacher's teaching, however, will be done directly in response to social situations that arise as the children play and work together. Teachers spend a considerable amount of time observing pairs or small groups of children interacting. The social techniques used by different children are noted, and an informal assessment is made of the extent to which a child's approaches and reactions are acceptable and constructive rather than destructive to the children involved, or to the child himself. Some of the bahaviors commonly shown by young children that seem to interfere with successful peer relations are the inability to share materials or equipment, a lack of consideration for other's belongings or feelings, excessive or impulsive aggression in the face of frustration, forcing peer compliance past a point of reasonable persuasion, pitting one member of the group against another to get one's own way, demanding leadership, and an excessive compliance or passivity with peers.

Teachers do not try to erase all of the individual differences in children's styles of adapting to the peer group. One gets the distinct impression from observing even very young children at play that some will continue to be more active, persuasive, and assertive in the peer group while others will be more passive, easygoing, and conciliatory. The teacher's goal is to help children gradually modify behaviors that compromise the child's own rights, or that impose unduly on the other children. At the same time, the child is supported in the development of his personal style of peer participation.

It is characteristic of the young child to think primarily of himself and not to consider how the world looks from the vantage point of another child with whom he is interacting—or if he considers it, he does not believe it is important. The young child's social blunders and lack of consideration for his peers is as often due to egocentrism and social naivete as to malice or ill will toward others. Consequently, the teacher's suggestions and comments are frequently straightforward attempts to call a child's attention to the motives of others or to the effect his behavior has had on another. Some teacher comments label or identify a responding child's anger and his attempt at retaliation, like "Carlos is upset because you knocked his building down." Or, in the case of a young three-year-old girl who drove her companions away because she confiscated all of the doll-corner toys, an adult explained, "The other children left because you didn't want them to touch any of the toys and it just wasn't much fun for them." Some comments interpret or support a child's attempt to resist interference. For example, in one instance, a three-year-old boy grabbed a toy boat from another child. The child in possession was holding onto the boat but his resolve was weakening. The adult supported his effort by stating to the maverick child, "Henry is going to hold onto the boat because he isn't finished using it—he will give it to you when he is finished." In another instance, a four-year-old girl named Mary was trying to resist the persistent block-building suggestions of another child playing nearby. The adult supported Mary's attempts at independence by explaining, "Mary really wants to try it her way. She has a good idea that she wants to try." At another time, four-year-old Rich was pulling at the sleeve of another child trying to get the child to join him in an area of the play yard. The adult explained, "Rich, Tom really wants to do something else now. Maybe another time he will join you."

Some adult comments call attention to a child's attempts to establish contact, like "Bill would like to play with you—that's why he came over and stood there," or "Jim was trying to figure out how to be friendly so he teased you." The child is never deliberately given false information, like "Joe didn't mean to hurt you," when it was perfectly evident that Joe did mean to hurt.

Some teachers comments are attempts to reflect the child's own intense feelings and to distinguish between feelings and actions. For example, a teacher might say, "I know Ted made you very angry but you still can't throw stones at him. You will have to find some other way to let him know." The child is not denied his right to become angry or to express his anger, but he is expected to keep his reactions within the limits of safety. More will be said later about the handling of aggressive behavior in the nursery school.

Friendliness in the Peer Group

Observations suggest that in spite of a considerable degree of social freedom in the nursery school, the number of friendly child-to-child social interactions far outnumber the negative interactions: that is, children are much more likely to express friendliness toward each other than hostility. As the children get older and the complexity of their social interaction increases, *both* quarrels and friendliness during play increase. Some observations show, however, that friendly interactions increase at a faster rate than quarrels; consequently, friendly interactions comprise an even larger proportion of the social interactions of the older preschoolers than of the younger ones. Among the more frequent friendly behaviors shown by the children are smiles, initiations of conversation, moving close to another child, and imitating another child. Somewhat less frequent are the giving of help, the giving of nurturance and affection (such as hugs and kisses), and the giving of tokens of friendship (such as candy or a toy).

One of the most important things teachers do in helping children develop skill in social situations is to indicate their approval of friendly, positive social behavior when the children show it. Adults in the nursery school are as alert in watching for behavior worthy of approval as in guarding against troublesome behavior. They may reinforce the child's use of friendly, constructive social behavior with comments like "That was a very nice thing you just did for Danny—he needed someone to help him," "You were a good friend of Rita's today," "You two did a good job of getting along together even though you didn't always agree with each other," "I know you were angry but you were patient too," or "You people got a hard job done by working together." A child may sometimes be asked specifically to help a companion who needs help. Though it does not often occur to young children to initiate such acts, they are very responsive to invitations to help one another. Asking a child to do something especially nice for a companion gives the child a sense of mastery and a feeling of good will that may be a powerful motivator for future sociable acts. Through incidences like these the child begins to see friendly, constructive social behavior as worthy of adult approval as well as effective with peers.

Occasionally a child seems to be fearful and totally avoidant of social overtures from peers, friendly or otherwise. The teacher's first goal with such a child may be to facilitate the development of a satisfying relationship with, at least, one other child in the group. The relationship may at first be expressed through brief encounters in which the two children sit together, help set up snacks together, or talk briefly with each other as they play in the same area of the room. If the relationship develops, the children will soon begin to seek each other out and spend some time together on successive school days. It is a rare three- or four-year old who does not desire friendly interaction of, at least, this magnitude with other children. The child who does establish a friendship after a period of cautious reticence or self-imposed social isolation is often extremely pleased with his new friend and becomes more confident in his ability to befriend others in the group.

Nursery School teachers are in an excellent position to help children develop techniques for initiating, responding to, and successfully maintaining good peer relations. Performing this function is one important aspect of the teacher's role in the school.

Aggression in the Peer Group

Arguments and fights between children do occur in the nursery school even though friendly interactions are more frequent. The three most common issues over which children fight are property rights (the sharing of materials or respecting a child's right to the use of a toy or piece of equipment), homesteading rights (the right to occupy a space in a play area or at a table without interference from another), and threats to personal well-being (including coercion, threats of physical harm, or social insults). The most common aggressive behaviors expressed by children are grabbing, pushing, chasing away, hitting, scolding, and name-calling. Although there is some variability from group to group in precisely what limits are placed on peer aggression, no teacher permits the more harmful forms of aggression like kicking, biting, or hitting with blocks, sticks, or other hard objects. These behaviors do occasionally occur, but they are never sanctioned by the adults in the group even when the aggressor is the victim of some injustice. These forms of aggression are identified as things that "hurt too much," and the child who uses them will be stopped or, if necessary, removed temporarily from the group. It is also recognized by the adults that, at times, children can hurt their companions too much with blatant taunts, insults, or rejection, in which case these behaviors, too, will be stopped.

Though there are clear and explicit limits to the amount of aggression children can show in the nursery school, they are allowed to express their disapproval and anger at their companions. It can be tempting for the adults in the nursery school to simply institute a school social order in which they themselves handle all interpersonal conflicts and the rule for the children is "if you can't say or do something nice, then don't say or do anything at all." There are, however, two serious problems with a policy of this kind. One is that children do not get a realistic picture of what reactions to expect from their companions when they behave in irritating or offensive ways unless their companions can protest on the spot. Second, the children come to rely on adults for solving their problems. Some children even feel immune from any restraint unless the

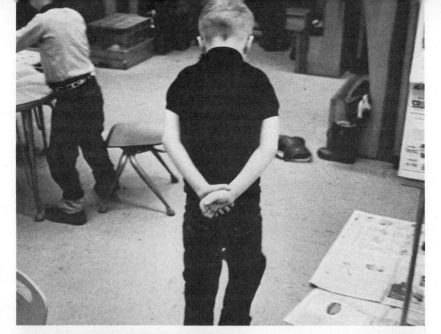

teacher is right there supervising. Others learn to tattle and fuss for teacher attention and help when difficulties arise that they could easily handle themselves.

When children are allowed reasonable freedom to protest social injustices to each other, the teacher is more often free to play the role of interpreter rather than discipliner. Because the child is angry at another child, not the teacher, she can more effectively talk with the offender about what made his companions angry and what to do about it. The teacher can even give the child some sympathetic encouragement without undermining the lesson to be learned. For example, she can say to a child who has just been rejected from a play group by his companions, "I think you can probably join Ron and Jack again later if you are careful not to break things up," or "Sue is pretty angry right now—let her calm down a little and then maybe she will be friendly again." Comments of this kind convey to the child that there are consequences to be reckoned with if one is too irritating to companions but, on the other hand, he will get a second chance. They also convey the teachers's confidence in the child's ability to learn from experience.

Adults in the nursery school are careful not to display a vindictive "you finally got what you deserved" attitude toward children who are in trouble with their companions. If the adult's attitude is one of sincerely trying to help the child cope with the problem at hand there is a better chance of the child's working *with* the teachers rather than *against* them in solving problems of social adjustment.

Besides helping children to handle disagreements when they occur, the adults in the nursery school are watchful of opportunities to alleviate the causes of conflicts between children. Teachers try to anticipate explosive situations and, if possible, prevent them from getting out of hand. Resources are provided in ample enough quantities so that the sharing of space, toys, and materials does not become excessively burdensome. Teachers watching children at block play may remind them of the close quarters and the need to watch out for fingers or for other people's buildings. A teacher who judges a child to be sorely tempted to grab something from another child can offer to help him find what he needs before the temptation becomes too great. If a child is obviously getting upset about something, a suggestion from a teacher may bring about an adjustment before things get to the explosive stage.

It sometimes becomes evident that time and time again trouble revolves around a particular child in a group whose social techniques are irritating to the other children and who does not seem to be responding to peer or teacher influence. In this instance the adults may observe the child carefully over a period of several days in an attempt to pinpoint the trouble; they will then be in a better position to help the child with suggestions, requests, and approval for his better attempts. Occasionally a group of children will play together often and seek each other out—but bicker constantly. In this instance, too, teachers will observe the group to identify the trouble and then talk with the children about some of the things that might help the members of the group get along with each other. With older pre-schoolers, the children themselves often offer suggestions about what causes their constant bickering and what they can do to reduce it.

Occasionally one child in a group becomes a scapegoat for others and is the focal point of excessive teasing or rejection. The teacher will intervene in a situation of this kind on the assumption that every child in the group has a right to a satisfying social environment while he is in school. How the situation is managed, however, will depend on the teacher's assessment of it. Frequently the child who is the victim of constant abuse from others is helping to maintain his low status by reacting to the abuse in overly babyish ways and by failing to stick up for his right not to be abused. A teacher may help him to understand the relation between the teasing and his reactions. She may bolster his confidence in his ability to cope successfully with the abuse either by ignoring it completely or by effectively fighting back. She may also appeal to the other children indicating to them their obligation to treat each other with consideration, since the school belongs to all.

Occasionally a small group of children will decide to taunt or torment another group by interfering with their play activities or by being generally disruptive. In this instance, too, the adults will have to assess the situation and make a judgement about what to do. If the taunted group is managing the situation successfully by ignoring the culprits, protesting effectively or, as is sometimes the case, enjoying the taunts, the situation may be allowed to persist. On the other hand, if the behavior threatens the constructiveness of the group or is generally creating a chaotic atmosphere, the adults may intervene. Behavior of this kind sometimes disinhibits children and seems to spread to the rest of the group through a kind of behavior contagion. If this happens, the adults may appeal to children on the basis of the effect that they are having on the group and simply ask them to stop or find another way to interact.

Children vary widely in the amount of social power and influence they seem to have over their companions. Generally the most influential children are friendly, energetic, resourceful, and confident of their ability to compete with the other children. The other children may respond by being somewhat subservient to the more influential child. If a child finds it consistently possible to take unfair advantage of his companions without protest from them, the adults may be particularly watchful for opportunities to encourage the other children to stick up for their rights against the persuasive one. At other times the teacher may intervene, indicating her expectation that the socially powerful child will be fair and just in his treatment of companions even if they do not demand this of him.

The job of the adults in the nursery school is the difficult one of maintaining a delicate balance between freedom and responsibility. The ability to express one's feelings vigorously but in socially acceptable ways is an important skill that children as young as three or four can begin to master. The adults in the nursery school must be prepared for the fact that in the course of learning to manage social freedom, children will at times be overly disruptive, rebellious, and inconsiderate of each other. On the other hand, an atmosphere of complete license to act out in a rage or ignore the rights of others creates chaos and is a threat to a group of young children that can produce the withdrawal from social participation of many of the children in the group. The adults try to maintain a sensible balance between social freedom and consideration for others.

As children in the nursery school become more experienced in managing interpersonal conflicts, the adults will help them to handle these episodes more and more through verbal exchanges rather than through physical retaliation or coercion. A teacher may remind a child to "*Tell* him what you are angry about," or "*Explain* it to him," or she may say to two children, "You two need to *talk* about it." According to some nursery school observations, the older children do more often settle quarrels through persuasion, compromise, and bargaining compared with the younger preschoolers.

Teachers also help children to become more sensible about the adaptations that they expect others to make on their behalf. The younger preschoolers are often quite unrealistic about this. They may, for example, be genuinely startled at another child's angry reaction when they move in and take over his play space. A child may complain to the teacher because "Chad hit me back," or because another child won't "share," meaning he won't give up a toy he has just begun to use. In time the children learn what concessions they can reasonably expect from others and what they can justifiably become indignant about. They gradually become skillful in avoiding rejection and hostility from peers by predicting the behavior of others from social cues like smiles, frowns, and signs of growing irritation.

Fortunately, young children are tolerant of the ineptitudes of each other. Occasionally a child in the nursery school is angered or frightened enough by a companion to remember a disagreement for a long time and to hold a grudge, but generally conflicts and injustices are forgiven and forgotten in a short time and do not seriously interfere with ongoing friendly relations between children.

12
Discipline and Influence Techniques

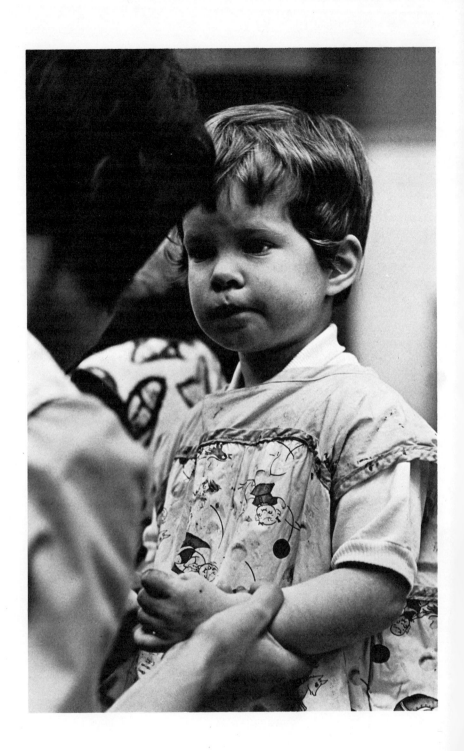

12 Discipline and Influence Techniques

Although discipline and techniques for influencing children's behavior are important and ever-present in the nursery school, adults become more conscious of them when dealing with undesirable behavior. The objectives of discipline in the preschool setting are to establish appropriate constructive behaviors and to help children develop the control over their actions that will enable them to function effectively in society.

As with the curriculum areas and other social behaviors discussed in this book, teachers first must decide which behaviors they wish to foster and which ones they wish to discourage. A number of factors are considered in making these decisions: knowledge of how children develop, their age, their cultural backgrounds, the individual characteristics of the children and their families, and the preferences and the tolerances of the adults in the school for different kinds of behavior. Although rules are generally applicable to all of the children in a classroom or group, the adults do tailor expectations and techniques to the characteristics and capabilities of the individual children in the group.

Once the teachers in the nursery school decide which behaviors they want to encourage in children and which ones they want to discourage, the job becomes one of affecting the behavior of the children. Both parents and teachers do this in part through the use of praise, approval, and rewards. Most children (and adults) are persuaded toward behaviors that bring them either material rewards, such as money or prizes, or social rewards, such as pleasant attention, compliments, or approval. By the same token, most avoid behaviors that arouse anxiety, or that bring disapproval or punishment.

A child having his first nursery school experience or adapting to a new teacher or new companions needs time to assimilate the rules and expectations of the group. Consequently, the adults in the school are patient in response to misbehavior until they are sure the child clearly understands the situation. If the child's behavior is inappropriate, teachers explain what is expected of him. They may make a special effort to approach the child in a nonpunitive, friendly manner even when the child has misbehaved in a similar way before. Children do not change their behavior patterns overnight; a child who is used to grabbing toys, responding to frustration with explosive aggression, or demanding more than a reasonable share of attention is likely to continue these behaviors in school, gradually replacing them with more adaptive behaviors. Teachers start with the assumption that the child is willing and able to adapt, if he is given appropriate feedback. One of the first jobs of the adults in the school is to give the child the information he needs. Rules are explained and appropriate behaviors are suggested to the child. Wherever possible, the child is offered alternatives for something he is not allowed to do. For example, if a child wishes to climb on the fence enclosing the yard, his teacher may help him to set up an obstacle course of boxes, climbing boards, or ladders; a child who grabs another's shovel may be reminded that there are more shovels in the storage shed. And, of course, appropriate behavior is greeted with approval and praise.

Generally children respond positively to this kind of treatment. Most young children look to adults for cues concerning the appropriateness or inappropriateness of their behavior, and most expect to have to conform to adult requests. They may protest a little , and may persist in misbehaving over a period of a few weeks, but most misbehaviors drop out of the child's repertoire—or, at least, become infrequent—by the third or fourth week of school. In any group of 15 or 20 children, however, there are one or two children who do not respond readily to the "gentle persuasion" of the adults. For these children, misbehavior continues long after the child knows what is expected of him, and in spite of constant reminders from his teachers. Children who persist in misbehavior in spite of feedback and mild persuasion from the adults usually have a history of either bullying adults into submission or of outlasting them by sheer perseverance! Teachers faced with this situation must decide on a deliberate course of action that is more carefully planned and implemented than is necessary for most of the children in the group, and which may involve regular consultation with the family.

The use of praise, compliments, or material rewards in the nursery school is, of course, dependent on the teacher's ability to get a child to perform the behavior to be rewarded; until the child performs it, it cannot be rewarded. Teachers accomplish this at times by giving instruction: simply *telling* the child what is expected of him. At other times, adults reason with the child, appealing to his sense of justice or obligation. Still other times, they depend on the child's learning things by example through imitating adults or companions. When the child shows the desirable behavior, adults indicate their pleasure by such things as smiles, compliments, praise, or a material reward. Although nothing works all of the time, generally this process increases the performance of rewarded behaviors.

Another way adults control the behavior of children is through punishment: a deliberate attempt to cause the child some form of distress either for failing to perform desirable behaviors or for performing undesirable ones. Some forms of punishment cause the child physical discomfort, like spanking or slapping; others cause him psychological distress, like rejection, shaming, disapproval, isolation from others, or withdrawal of privileges.

The adults in the nursery school prefer some forms of control over others. Rewards, for example, are used far more often than punishment. Teachers sometimes reward behaviors by directly telling a child that they liked what he did, but very often rewards are smiles or brief indicators of interest and approval given casually as adults direct their attention to the child's behavior or activity. Teachers are particularly alert in watching for behaviors that do not occur often but that they especially want to try to increase, such as generosity, responsibility, creativity, and ingenuity in problem-solving situations. Punishment may be used as a last resort, or when a behavior is potentially dangerous and a change in the child's response must occur promptly for his own safety or the safety of the other children.

Virtually no physical punishment is used in the nursery school and only mild forms of psychological punishment are used. The punishment techniques most preferred are withdrawal of privilege and social isolation. Some of the more humiliating techniques that involve ridicule, shaming through public criticism, or identification of the child as bad or inadequate compared with the other children are not used in the nursery school. While punishments of this kind may be effective in repressing children's misbehavior, there is evidence that they may also damage the child's self-confidence and may arouse excessive fear or hostility.

Wherever possible, teachers in the nursery school use punishments that have some reasonable connection with a misbehavior or that seem to be a logical consequence of a misbehavior. Most instances of misbehavior in the nursery school involve either the misuse of materials or equipment (like hammering a table or deliberately dumping something on the floor), or interference with the other children (like grabbing toys, taunting, or forcing compliance). Consequently, teachers generally prefer punishments that involve the withholding of the privilege of using the relevant materials or playing with the children involved. The rational connection between the punishment and the offense has several advantages for the child and the teacher; one is that it may seem to be less arbitrary on the teacher's part, since she can present it to the child as a necessary step she must take in order to protect the materials or the other children (which, indeed, it is). She may even say something like, "I *can't* let you do that," rather than, "I *won't* let you do that," implying that the issue is bigger than both of them. Her resolve is no less firm but her purpose goes beyond just badgering him; she has an obligation to protect the children and the school property, and he must behave accordingly.

Another advantage to a rational connection between the misbehavior and the punishment is that it seems to focus the child's attention on the behavior to be changed. Not being allowed to go for a walk following some teasing episodes of running away from the group while on a walk is likely to impress the child with his "walk behavior" more than would a punishment that is unrelated (such as being deprived of a snack for that day). Also the child may be more likely to interpret the misbehavior as the "cause" of the punishment. If he feels he has caused the punishment, he may feel that he can also rectify the situation if he convinces his teacher, by intentions and finally by action, that he can manage the walk situation another time.

Some misbehavior in the nursery school involves the child's defiance of the adult's authority and may be expressed through ignoring adult requests, teasing, or resisting compliance. This pattern of misbehavior is referred to by teachers as "limit-testing" and seems at times to be motivated by the child's desire to see whether or not the adults will actually exert their authority. Most instances of limit-testing can be surmounted by the adult with a combination of firmness and consistency without resorting to repeated use of punishment. The teacher will usually prevail if, when the child persists in misbehaving, the teacher perseveres in stopping him before the misbehavior pays off in concessions or extra privileges.

Nursery school observations suggest that some children misbehave specifically to gain the attention of the adults. This is particularly likely to happen when negative attention in the form of disapproval from the teacher is mild and not too painful to bear—as is generally the case in the nursery school. A child may very well come to feel that mild disapproval from the teacher at a given moment is better than no attention at all. The teacher is then faced with two alternatives: she can make the attention given for the misbehavior more punitive and not worth the cost to the child; or, she can ignore the child during moments of teasing and negative attention seeking, making a point of attending to him only when his behavior is acceptable and appropriate. Generally, the second alternative is preferred, and more punitive approaches are used only if inattention does not work or if the misbehavior is decidedly noxious or harmful to the other children.

BEHAVIOR MODIFICATION
IN THE NURSERY SCHOOL

There are a number of developmental psychologists in this country who have studied techniques for the modification of persistent misbehavior of children attending nursery schools. Teachers can get some very useful tips about behavior modification from these professionals. The psychologist usually goes about his task of changing behaviors in the following way. First, he observes the child in the school setting and records the frequency of occurrence of all behaviors, including misbehaviors. He also notes the consequences of the child's behavior; that is, what happens to the child and others following the occurrence of each unit of behavior. In consultation with the teachers, the psychologist then identifies the behaviors that the teachers would like the child to show—behaviors that ideally should *replace* the misbehavior. These desirable behaviors are sometimes referred to as "incompatible" or "competing" behaviors relative to the misbehaviors, since the child cannot respond with one of these and with the misbehavior at the same time. (For example, a child cannot "refuse to share" and "share toys or materials" at the same moment.) Teachers are then instructed to be particularly watchful for the occurrence of one of these competing behaviors. When the desirable behavior occurs, the child is promptly rewarded.

Teachers sometimes have the impression that the misbehaving child never performs the competing behavior and, hence, "watching for it," is a thankless job! Observations suggest that this is generally a misconception about the problem child. Aggressive children do show some instance of nonaggressive adaptation, dependent children do show instances of independence, and nonsharers do at times share. The child's best effort may not be as adequate as the efforts of other children, but they do occur and are noticeable to the adult who is especially looking for them. Most problem children can be rewarded for a desirable competing behavior at least three or four times during a school morning by alert staff members. Adults also sometimes feel that they will not be able to attend any one child as rigorously as this procedure seems to imply. Actually, problem children are attended far more rigorously than others anyway, but in this instance the teachers are being watchful for the occurrence of good behavior rather than misbehavior. It has been our experience that teachers do pretty well at being alert for instances of the competing behaviors without having to assign an adult specifically to the child about whom they are concerned.

Along with conscientiously rewarding the child for good behavior when he shows it, the psychologist may instruct the teacher to completely ignore the child's misbehaviors, even though the usual tendency is for the adults to show disapproval or annoyance—or patience and understanding—when these behaviors occur. Since teacher attention has not discouraged these same behaviors in the past, it is reasoned that it will not do so in the future and, in fact, it is possible that the child is performing the misbehavior in part to get attention or to tease and annoy the adults. If this is true, withdrawing attention for the behaviors may help to motivate the child to find other ways to get attention.

In rewarding the child's good behavior, teachers may elect to use a tangible reward (such as a small piece of candy, or a token that the child can "turn in" for a prize at the end of the day), or they may reward the child with a compliment or other indication of social approval. Most young children place great value on approval from adults, and adults find this method of reinforcing good behavior less offensive and more adaptable to the school situation than the dispensing of material rewards. Nevertheless, there are children who seem to be "soured" on adults, and adult approval is not particularly important to them; for these children, a small food or material reward for good behavior should be given serious consideration. If the dispensing of tangible rewards is managed with discretion and without great fanfare, it need not effect the other children in any adverse way. In one instance, a child in one of our four-year-old groups was told that he would be given a cookie following any half-hour period during which he did not become aggressive or destructive. (This procedure represents a slightly different management technique based on very similar principles of behavior modification.) One of his teachers showed him what time on the school clock his next cookie was due and kept track of the time for him. The child was invited out of the room and given the cookie when the time arrived—provided that he had not committed any unjustified or excessive act of aggression. He ate the cookie out of the room and then returned to the group. He learned quickly that he got the cookie only if he had not behaved aggressively, and his behavior did change for the better. He was also complimented and shown affection by his teacher when he was able to control his aggressive tendencies.

After about two and one-half weeks his teacher told him that he could now be expected to behave for even longer periods of time, and she began giving the cookie only after an hour had gone by. By this time, the child's good behavior was being maintained as much by a newly developed "taste for approval" as by the cookies. He had been befriended by several of the children in the group who had previously avoided him, and he began showing clear evidence of pleasure when he received approval from them or from the adults in school. The cookies were no longer that important and finally dropped out of the picture altogether; he occasionally asked for one and got it, but they no longer needed to be used as a kind of "bribe." From time to time children inadvertently observed this child in the school kitchen eating his cookie and asked why he was there. They were told that Tommy got a cookie because he was "doing such a good job of not fighting or getting too angry." This explanation was accepted readily and without question. (The other child usually got a cookie too and could stay with Tommy to eat it.)

As mentioned previously, psychologists have conducted a number of research studies demonstrating the effectiveness of behavior modification techniques in changing children's nursery school behavior. They have been successful in modifying excessive adult dependence, tantram behavior and other forms of aggressiveness, and excessive reluctance to interact with friendly peers.

For research purposes, the initial observation of a child (that is, before any new plan is implemented) is used as a base line measure against which to compare change in the child's behavior. The observer notes how many times a given class of changeworthy behavior occurred per hour of observing during the initial base line period and compares that with the incidence of these same behaviors after the new regime has been in effect for a period of days. The incidents of the competing desirable behaviors may also be charted in this way. In the application of this technique to everyday school management, getting initial base line information is not crucial, nor is it necessary for the teacher to "prove" that the child's behavior has changed. A teacher may feel quite confident that there has been a change for the better in the behavior of a problem child and let it go at that. It can, however, be enlightening to do some initial base line observation so that teachers have a better picture of exactly what does happen to a problem child. Such observations may show, for example, that teachers hardly ever attend to the problem child except when he is in trouble (while the nonproblem children are presumably getting much more positive social attention from their teachers). Observations may also indicate that the teachers' handling of incidences of misbehavior are very inconsistent from one adult to another, or are inept in that the child readily ignores requests from his teachers, or that, in some instances, teacher intervention actually increases the occurrence of misbehavior instead of decreasing it. If, for example, the teacher usually attends to a child when he is misbehaving, then the child is apt to increase the frequency of misbehavior to obtain more attention from the teacher. Observations of this kind can be very useful in helping teachers to become aware of ways in which their own behaviors may interact with the behaviors of their children to produce some surprising effects.

Psychologists offering behavior modification advice to teachers have not always been well received. Classroom teachers sometimes take offense at the psychologists' "calculated" approach to behavior modification, and psychologists do not always take the time to fully appreciate the practical problems, complex goals, and manpower shortages of the classroom teacher. The psychologist, for example, may stress the need to consistently reward *every instance* of a desirable competing behavior. Unless the teacher has enough staff to assign one adult to the target child, she may see this as impossible and may feel defeated before she starts. Fortunately, complete consistency is not necessary for learning to take place. If the adults who interact with the children attend to *most* instances of a desirable behavior, a change for the better should occur.

Psychologists who have studied behavior modification also stress the importance of the teachers' ignoring instances of misbehavior while rewarding competing behaviors. This suggestion can have devastating consequences for a group of children and their teachers depending on the nature of the misbehavior under consideration. If the target behavior is aggression, for example, the teacher would not ordinarily be expected to stand by—nor to walk away—while a child threatens, attacks, or abuses another child. One can seriously question the effect of this teacher retreat on the child who is being attacked, if not on the attacker! Even if teachers are not completely effective in curbing a child's aggression, they are generally expected to keep the aggressive child from threatening the other children and from damaging materials and equipment.

Here, too, there is no reason to believe that effective behavior modification depends on the adults' ignoring misbehavior completely while working to increase the occurrence of the more acceptable competing behaviors. Even if aggression is being maintained, in part, by the teacher's negative attention (in a child who takes pleasure in annoying or teasing), one might expect a change to occur if teachers give no more attention than is necessary for aggression while they conscientiously give the child positive social attention for any nonaggressive, prosocial behaviors that he shows.

When the behaviors to be modified are the attention-getting, helpless pleas of the dependent child they can probably go unattended by the teachers without dire consequences to the group. Here, too, however, teachers often elect to change the behavior by substantially increasing the attention they give the child for *independence* whenever it occurs without withholding help and support from the child when he is behaving dependently.

The Use of Punishment
in Behavior Modification

Some behavior modification studies have been conducted in which teachers have been instructed to promptly interrupt the child's ongoing behavior when a misbehavior is being performed and to restrict the child's activity for a brief period of, perhaps, 5 to 15 minutes. The procedure has been called "time-out" and generally involves the child's being made to sit on a chair or remain isolated in a room during the time-out period. This procedure is not designed to frighten a child, but the restriction of activity is clearly designed to frustrate him, causing the child to avoid performing the behaviors that lead to the restriction.

When this method of behavior modification is used, the misbehavior is "attended" by the teacher, but it is attended consistently with the same noxious consequence (restricted activity) everytime the child performs it. Being relegated to an isolation chair on the fringe of the classroom is actually an age-old punishment used by teachers as far back as pupils can remember. It must be viewed as both a form of ridicule and humiliation —banishment for all to see—as well as a form of isolation from the group. For this reason teachers in the preschool have not been inclined to use this form of punishment and, instead, often elect to remove the disruptive child from the group as unobtrusively as possible to some quiet place where he can calm down before returning to the group. The teacher may talk with the child and stay with him during the time that he is out of the group, or she may leave him alone to "think." Nurturant, nonpunitive teachers undoubtedly run the risk of this isolation procedure being a pleasant experience for the child rather than a deterrent to misbehavior. While being taken from the group right in the middle of a star performance is frustrating, being fussed over, sat with, and talked to may offer adequate compensation.

There is, of course, no particular reason to expect a child's persistent misbehavior to change unless he becomes conflicted over whether or not he should perform the behavior. Presumably the child learned to perform it in the first place because it "worked" for him; giving it up is likely to come about either because he finds other behaviors that work better or because he finds that his usual behaviors now bring him a mixed bag of consequences—perhaps, some pleasant ones, but others that he would like to avoid. While skillful parents and teachers try to avoid endless hassles with their children (since so many of the child's misbehaviors disappear with experience in dealing with people), most feel that when a child's behavior is more than ordinarily hard for those around him to live with, he should be expected to change, to avoid punishment if necessary.

An example of the modification of the aggressive behavior of a four-year-old boy helps to illustrate the process of behavior change as it is implemented in the nursery school.

The Management of an Aggressive Child

Raymond Jones was four years and four months old when he entered the nursery school. He was the third boy in a family of three boys. He was tall for his age, well coordinated and, in some ways, very mature. He was bright, alert to what was going on around him, and stubbornly independent. Ray's concept of himself included a no-nonsense toughness in coping with people. He was used to bullying children his age and even some older ones, and he also presented an aggressive, rebellious front to most adults. His mother described him as being hard to manage because of a "vicious temper for his age." When he did not get what he wanted, he shouted, stamped around the house, slammed doors, and lashed out at everyone in sight. He had deliberately broken dishes, damaged furniture, and bruised his brothers in the course of his rages.

Ray's father was the one person in his home for whom Ray was no match; his father was loud, harsh, and strict with Ray, taking none of the back talk or rebelliousness that characterized Ray's interactions with almost everyone else. His father regularly used a strap on Ray. Punishment often became a battle between them for its own sake, with Ray showing stubbornness and defiance while his father's attitude challenged Ray to "try that just once more!" Mr. Jones expressed some amazement at how hard he could slap or strike Ray without causing the child to cry. Ray's toughness seemed to be in part, at least, a defense against the harsh punishment of his father. His father was not particularly pleased with the relationship he had with Ray. He seemed to realize that there should not be so much hostility between them, but he laid the blame squarely on others. He felt Ray's outbursts and destructiveness was a direct function of the boy's stubborn nature and of his wife's being too easy on Ray and not making him mind. Ray did mind his father, though his compliance typically was accompanied by an aloof, sullenness completely lacking in good will or cooperation.

Occasionally Ray, his father, and one or two of his brothers would do something together, like attend a baseball game, fish, or wash the car. Ray always enjoyed these occasions and behaved well during them. They were not frequent, however; Ray's father was a worried businessman who put in many hours of work and was often too preoccupied with his business to enjoy his son's company.

Ray had a kind of armed truce with his older brothers from whom he probably learned much of his aggressiveness. The play behavior of the three boys often reverted to boisterous, destructive combat, and it was not uncommon for the older boys to tease Ray until he finally broke down in tears. Ray had few friends in his neighborhood and was known for his aggressiveness and destructiveness.

When Ray first entered the nursery school he could best be described as aloof and moody. He did not immediately display his aggressiveness, but he seemed suspicious of the adults and had no more to do with them than was necessary. He blatantly ignored efforts to befriend him. He avoided becoming involved in any unnecessary conversation with the adults and seemed to view the other children with an air of distain. He would occasionally announce that some school activity was "dumb" or that some child was a "freak," or he would announce loudly that he was not going to participate in some activity. He ignored the friendly overtures of both children and adults though he did pay some attention to two or three of the bigger more mature boys whom he seemed to admire. He would move about on his own, using the construction materials and building with blocks, remaining on the fringes of the play of these children but seldom making an effort to join them in their play. Whenever the possibilities of joining them confronted him directly, he retreated, acting as though he simply did not find them worthy of his attention. Teachers' attempts to help him join in the activities of the other children were usually ignored or resisted. By the end of the first month of school, teachers had become somewhat reticent about initiating friendly approaches to Ray, since they had so often been rebuffed. Ray was not, at this point, causing any particular trouble—except perhaps to himself —and the adults found the friendliness of the other children more rewarding.

Gradually as Ray became familiar with the school situation he became bolder and bolder in expressing his seemingly pervasive hostility and frustration. He began making many more overtures to other children but most were playful teasing overtures, underhanded acts of aggression, or angry demands. He would decide he wanted something another child was using and go and take it from the child, strutting away triumphantly. Often he did not even want to use the object and would drop it on the floor 30 seconds after taking it. If a child defied him, he would punch or kick or spit at his opponent, and if that didn't work he would attack with both fists flying. He was a formidable adversary and most shrunk from his onslaught.

It became clear to the adults that children could not defend themselves against this child's excessive temper and determination, and teachers found it more and more necessary, or at least advisable, to step in to try to stop him. Ray's response to this was to fight back at the adults. If the adults tried to remove him from a situation, he would kick or pull away. If they tried to talk to him, he would insist that he was not listening and sometimes would shout them down or put his hands over his ears to shut them out. Over a period of a month or two Ray's aggressiveness and destructiveness was increasing steadily rather than decreasing. He would, at times, plow through the room for seemingly no reason at all, knocking over chairs, wiping things off tables onto the floor, and kicking or hitting completely innocent and surprised victims. Some of the more timid children became quite conscious of where Ray was in the room and deliberately avoided him, which seemed to please him no end.

The adults also were inclined to avoid Ray if at all possible! Although the teachers generally agreed on the limits of aggressiveness that could be tolerated in the school, this boy was so difficult to handle that they, too, tended to renege or hope that someone else would step in when trouble was eminent. It was decided that it was time to work out a more careful plan for the management of this child in school.

In preparation for a plan, a teacher and a student volunteer made regular observations of Ray for a period of one week, including in their records the school activities he participated in, what contacts he had with either children or adults, and what characterized his behavior during the morning. Observations were made during free activity time and also during routines and group times.

It was immediately evident from the observations that Ray was not getting much attention from his teachers and that the attention he got usually occurred at a time when an adult felt compelled to step in to protect other children, materials, or equipment from his aggressiveness. It also became evident that most encounters with Ray culminated in Ray's getting the upper hand. The head teacher of the group was the only person who was generally successful in curbing Ray's impulsive outbursts; the other teachers felt helpless in the face of this child's bullying. Ray would even shout to them that they were not "teachers" and they couldn't tell him "what to do"—something he had not said to the head teacher. Ray seemed to have learned to perform his aggressive acts mostly out of direct view of the head teacher. When an assistant teacher tried to stop or restrain him, he would angrily pull away and persist in the misbehavior. Or if he left the scene, he might strut to some other part of the room and deliberately do some other aggressive thing as if to say "if I can't be aggressive there, I will be aggressive here!" He would sometimes deliberately look back at the teacher who had just chastised him, and if she seemed to be approaching him again, he would quickly move on to another part of the room or play yard. Most often the teacher was happy to be rid of him and did not follow up on her warning about his aggressiveness. Ray's hostility seemed to permeate his entire school experience; when he was not being physically destructive, he was being sullen and unpleasant with both the children and the adults. He seemed to lack other social responses, or at least find little use for them, and his way of getting attention was to misbehave.

The adults decided on a threefold plan for helping this child and for coping with his destructiveness. First, it was recognized that the adults actually were having little to do with this boy. Most of them actively disliked him. They had almost given up trying to have any friendly or pleasant social interchange with him and generally hoped that he would not join activities in their area of the room or that they were supervising. Though, at first, Ray did seem to be rejecting any kind of attention, pleasant or otherwise, from both children and teachers in the school, he now was vigorously seeking attention through his aggressiveness. Now that he seemed unwilling to be ignored, he was no longer getting attention of a pleasant kind from anyone! Teachers agreed to make a special effort to notice and pay attention to Ray at times when he was *not* giving trouble. They agreed to stay near to him instead of moving away, comment on his activities from time to time, offer to help him with something if the occasion should arise, and keep him in mind for any special kindness or favors that could be shown him. In the last category, three incidences occurred during the first week following the institution of the plan that would probably not have occurred the previous week: the head teacher approached Ray's mother to see if she would allow him to bring a football game to school that Ray often played with his brothers. The game was too complicated for the children to use properly, but with a somewhat revised set of rules and instructions it could be played by them with the help of an adult. Ray was clearly pleased to be the provider (and the star player) of the game during the period of several days that it remained at school. It was the focal point around which some pleasant experiences occurred with the children and with the adults.

Another incident occurred when one teacher took Ray and two companions, who had been selected by him, for a walk to see a 1919 model airplane that was on display in the neighborhood. The adult made a point of indicating to the two boys that Ray had asked to have them come along.

Another teacher brought a display poster of prehistoric animals—a subject that seemed to appeal to Ray. When Ray showed an interest in it, the teacher offered to let him take it home on a Friday to show his brothers and then bring it back on Monday.

Along with incidences of these kinds—contrived and deliberate—

teachers made a point of being friendly and attentive to Ray even at the risk of eliciting a hostile counter-response from him. They watched for instances in which Ray cooperated (however, reluctantly), showed the slightest friendliness, worked constructively, or held his temper. Whenever it was at all feasible to do so, they indicated their approval of these acts by complimenting him or showing an interest in what he was doing. At first the adults were careful not to be too demonstrative about their approval, since Ray tended to be suspicious of such acts. After saying something complimentary or friendly to him, they might turn away and immediately be too busy doing something else to hear him shout "Go away you dummy." Gradually over a period of several days, Ray began accepting the friendly overtures and approving responses from the adults with a kind of suppressed pleasure, as though he liked the heavy dose of friendly attention and approval he was getting, but was reluctant to let it be known! As his rejection of friendliness decreased, the adults were able to be more open and demonstrative in giving him attention.

A second point in the plan for helping Ray (and preserving the school) had to do with the handling of his aggressive episodes. It was recognized that Ray's aggression was generally too destructive to be ignored or overlooked—it had to be stopped. Since the head teacher was the only person who felt confident in restraining Ray, it was decided that she would, for a week at least, try to be available to interact with Ray when he became aggressive. During these days, she agreed to be less involved in curriculum activities with children and more available to move around at will so that she could approach him when necessary. When she was not available, the next nearest teacher was to intervene—like it or not! Intervention was to be consistent, and determined. If Ray did not heed a warning about his aggression he was promptly taken from the group to an extra teacher workroom and told to "Stay here until I decide you can come back." He was also told to leave everything in the room just as it was (which included curriculum supplies, work materials, books, and phonograph records). Teachers were warned to be alert for teacher-directed aggression from Ray when he became angry at having to leave the room. They were expected to prevent him from hitting or kicking them by holding his arm or warding off his foot if necessary. He was not to be allowed to complete acts of aggression against the adults. After about ten minutes of isolation, sometimes longer, the adult who took Ray out of the room went to get him.

In one day that first week, Ray was taken from the group three times for destructiveness or aggression. On one of these occasions while being left alone, he found some easel paint and scribbled on the doors of several cupboards. He was given material to wash off the paint marks and left to complete that task before being allowed to return to the play area. After a time, a teacher offered to help him, but walked out on him when he sat down and expected to watch her work! On the second offer of help from a different teacher, Ray and the teacher did the job together. By that time, Ray had missed snack and that was that! On another occasion he destructively pulled down a row of books from a shelf in the isolation area and had to return them before joining the group outdoors.

Ray's aggressiveness clearly did not decrease during those first few days after instituting the concerted plan; in fact, it may have increased. The vigorous, determined front from the adults seemed to frustrate and challenge him at first, but he did gradually become resigned to removal from the group following aggression and accepted it with pouting and with some threats of mischief, but with little active retaliation. He gradually became more responsive to warnings at moments when he was about to "fly off the handle" and would manage to keep his behavior within limits that could be tolerated in the group. At these times he would settle for a threatening look and verbal insults but would refrain from physically attacking people or destroying materials.

A third point in the plan to help Ray involved communication with his parents. The head teacher of Ray's group had had frequent conversations with Ray's mother—and less frequent ones with Ray's father, about the boy's behavior. Although his parents recognized that Ray's aggressiveness was extreme both at home and at school, they seemed to be disinclined to cope with the practicalities of their inconsistent treatment of him; his mother continued to be cowed by him and his father continued to use harsh, repressive punishment. Ray's father made it clear that we had his permission to physically punish his son if we saw fit, and he expressed his doubt that anything else would work!

In discussing this home situation, it was decided that the school staff would probably not have much of an impact on this family directly. Their ways of interacting with Ray were set and they seemed unwilling to consider other approaches. It was decided, therefore, to keep the family informed about our approach to Ray's behavior and hope that a change for the better from him might, in turn, influence the family to consider a change in their management behavior. This proved to be a reasonable tack. As Ray's behavior in school improved, and his mother was able to confirm this from her own observations, both the mother and father began reporting improved behavior at home as well. It is hard to say whether, in fact, Ray's behavior at home had changed, or whether his parent's anger at him was reduced as a function of his improved school behavior. In any case, the atmosphere did seem to lighten, and Ray seemed to be getting along better with both of his parents. His mother reported, however, that Ray's older brothers continued to tease and torment him beyond his tolerance. It was decided, with the consent of his parents, that the head teacher and a male assistant teacher working in the group would talk with the older boys about ways in which they could help Ray. That meeting went extremely well. The two older boys came in and talked freely about Ray's bad temper and all of the trouble he caused at home. The school plan was explained to them and they were asked (1) to avoid teasing him excessively just to get him angry, and (2) to be approving of Ray at times when his behavior around the house was helpful or cooperative. They were asked to report back in two weeks about how things were going. Both boys were very cooperative and seemed pleased to be brought in on the plan. The teachers were careful not to be critical of their parents' handling of Ray (or their's for that matter) centering the discussion exclusively on how they could help.

There is little doubt that Ray's behavior improved over a period of three or four weeks after instituting this threefold plan. The number of aggressive episodes dropped markedly, and those that occurred were more moderate and appropriate. Ray was in good spirits and became openly pleased with much of his school experience. He gradually lost his defensiveness and selfconscious avoidance of showing pleasure, and would smile and laugh with other children and adults.

While some of the more adventuresome boys actively befriended Ray, the friendliness of the more timid children was probably a function of relief at finding him to be not such a beast after all! They learned that his gruffness and occasional sullen moods would only rarely be accompanied by physical aggression.

Needless to say, Ray did not suddenly become a favorite of all, nor did his behavior become angelic; but he did gradually come to be an acceptable member of the group and a good friend of two or three of the children. His relations with the adults improved steadily, and he was finally on good terms even with the adults who had previously been the most intimidated or angered by him.

His behavior at home and in the neighborhood too seemed to have improved from the report of his family. Ray's dad continued to subscribe to the "harsh punishment" philosophy of discipline, but indicated that Ray's behavior less often required disciplining. The out-of-school improvement in Ray's behavior may have been a function of his having learned new modes of responding in school that he used at home, eliciting, in turn, more acceptance and friendliness from his family and neighbors. In any case, things were better for Ray and for those around him. He was getting along with other people at home and at school and was taking full advantage of his preschool program.

HOME-SCHOOL COOPERATION
IN WORKING WITH PROBLEMS

Getting information about home behavior and methods of control used by parents can be enlightening and helpful to teachers. Conferences with parents make it possible to plan effectively when it becomes necessary to be more than ordinarily consistent and clear in setting goals and determining procedures for working with a particular child. In fact, some teachers feel that problems that have their origins in the home cannot be managed effectively at school without the cooperation of the home. Fortunately, for many children, this is probably a more pessimistic view than is justified. Children are amazingly adaptive individuals. Just as they learn that mother and father are two different people to be responded to in different ways, so they learn that the school and home are two different places, each requiring its own set of behaviors. The overly dependent or immature child may take important new steps toward appropriate independence for the first time at school and the hyper-aggressive child may learn to curb his impulsivity at school even though aggression is overlooked, or even sanctioned, at home. In fact, improvement in home behavior often seems to follow on the heels of some adaptation the child makes to the school setting.

Needless to say, the child's adaptation is aided by consistent standards and expectations at home and at school. The school has an obligation to communicate its point of view to the parent and to work together with the home. In most instances parents and teachers see eye to eye on problem behaviors, but when they do not agree, parents have every right to know what the school is doing and teachers need to know how parents feel about the school's decisions. The school and home need not always approach a problem with identical strategies or even have identical goals, but it is usually helpful for each to know what the other is doing. Comparing procedures and goals and communicating about progress usually culminates in more understanding of the child by both the school and his parents. In the process, each is likely to move toward handling the child more constructively. In the last analysis, any parent who disapproves of the teacher's handling of problem behaviors should feel free to approach the teacher and discuss the issues frankly. If they cannot come to some reasonable meeting of the minds, the child may actually bear the brunt of the disagreement by being in conflict about complying with the adults at school. If this appears to be happening, the parent should be encouraged to consider a different placement for his child. The school, in fact, may help the parent explore alternatives that will be more satisfactory to the parent.

AN OUNCE OF PREVENTION

Considering the number of children in a nursery school group, their age, and general level of maturity, it is surprising that so little use of punishment is necessary to keep reasonable control and order.

There are several things that adults in the nursery school do that help them to avoid the use of punishment. For one thing they go to considerable lengths to establish and maintain good rapport with the children. They are considerate, friendly, and affectionate. In this atmosphere most children come to enjoy and depend on the goodwill of the teachers almost from the beginning of their enrollment in school. The children quickly sense the atmosphere that exists, and most return the goodwill and good intentions. They are generally predisposed to *want* to behave at school. Most are quick to sense what things are appropriate and what things are not, and look to the teacher for cues. When the child does misbehave, a little disapproval goes a long way, since the child has much to lose if he loses the good will of a supportive, nurturant adult. With many children just a slight show of seriousness or resolve on the part of the teacher is all that is necessary to discourage excessive misbehavior. For these children, punitiveness from the teacher would be devastating.

Another characteristic of adult-child interactions at school that reduces the need for punishment is the fact that limits are applied consistently from day to day and from one adult to another. In this way the child learns what is expected of him and what he can expect from the adults.

Also, teachers are alert and vigilant enough to frequently prevent misbehavior from occurring, or to interrupt it at its outset, in effect, stopping the child from misbehaving and averting the need for punishment. Vigilance is particularly useful if a child's misbehavior in certain situations is very predictable. One can watch for these situations and warn the child to stop virtually before he gets started. Usually within a few days the tendency for the child to lose control or yield to temptation in those situations is weakened or disappears.

There are a number of advantages to a pattern of adult-child interaction that emphasizes approval and rewards for good behavior and avoids the use of punishment as much as possible. Control by approval and rewards has the advantage of arousing in the child pleasant rather than unpleasant feelings toward school while control by punishment is likely to arouse negative emotions in the child. Even when punishment is an effective deterrent at a given moment, a child may, on reflection, become angry, resistant, and counter-aggressive. If he is angry but afraid of the adult's wrath, he may take his anger out on the other children and tease or torment them when adults are not present. If his anger is directed toward the teachers, he may develop a general tendency to resist their influence or to avoid their presence. Needless to say this can reduce the effectiveness of the adults in school at times when they want the child to participate in curriculum experiences under their direction or guidance.

A final disadvantage to the use of punishment is the risk of the children in a group modeling punitive adult behavior and learning to use force and coercion in handling persons less powerful than themselves.

On the other hand, a child who takes teacher-administered punishment very seriously may become withdrawn and anxious about his status in the presence of punitive adults in school. He may behave so cautiously that he inhibits some of the spontaneous social behaviors (such as hugging a companion) or intellectual behaviors (such as calling out an answer to a question) that his teachers would like him to show, for fear of getting into trouble. A sensitive child may respond with extreme caution even if he himself has not been punished, if he knows that his teacher is quick to punish other children when they misbehave.

Punishment in the nursery school seems to be effective without having severe limitations or ominous consequences if it is mild rather than severe, and if it is resorted to infrequently after attempts have been made to control behavior with rewards, instruction, and warnings. Psychologists and preschool educators are in general agreement in not recommending the use of physical punishment (spanking or slapping, for example) as ways of controlling behavior in the nursery school; these techniques are generally considered to be the prerogative of parents.

The gentleness and tolerance of competent preschool teachers predisposes them to give children every break, using punishment only when all else fails. Sanctioning the use of punishment of any kind at any time in school should never become a license for hostile teachers who don't believe in patience and tolerance anyway! A preschool teacher who finds it necessary to scold or isolate many different children in the course of a school day, some of them two or three times a day, is simply not using the other techniques available to her. It is worth repeating here that the continued effectiveness of mild punishment from teachers probably depends on its being used sparingly (albeit consistently). Teachers who slip into the habit of continually nagging their children, or complaining about their behavior, are likely to find their children—particularly those with the severest problems—becoming progressively more immune to their efforts. Teachers try to avoid creating an atmosphere in which adults indiscriminately scold or threaten children. Rules that govern the children's behavior in the nursery school are decided on after careful consideration by the full staff and are reassessed from time to time. Teachers save their disapproval for the times when they really have a point to make, and the child is then not given the option of ignoring or attending the issue at will. He is expected to comply.

REASONS AND EXPLANATIONS

Although teachers avoid long, tedious arguments with preschoolers about why they should or should not be allowed to do something, they do listen to children's complaints or appeals about rules and regulations. Children in the nursery school are routinely given reasons and explanations for demands and restrictions placed on their behavior. In this way the child has a better chance to eventually learn the rules adults use in judging behavior to be acceptable or unacceptable. He can then apply these rules to his own behavior in similar situations, even when an adult is not present. There is evidence to suggest that giving children reasons and explanations may facilitate the early attainment of self-control in young children which, of course, is the ultimate goal of discipline.

13
Independence, Self-Confidence, and Achievement Behavior

13 Independence, Self-Confidence, and Achievement Behavior

One of the major developmental tasks of the young child is to give up his overwhelming dependence on others in favor of self-reliance and independence. This task is begun earlier than the time that the child comes to preschool and it goes on well beyond the preschool years, but it clearly is one of the major emphases in the child's orientation to adults during these early years.

The child has had a long history of feeling secure in the knowledge that adults will care for him, keep him safe from harm, and satisfy his needs. He does not necessarily accomplish the transition to independence smoothly, or to the complete satisfaction of the adults responsible for him. The child often will be torn between maintaining his comfortable dependence or pleasing his parents and teachers by displaying self-reliance and independence. The preschooler's tendency to vacillate between dependence and independence can be exasperating. The child may approach the brink of a new and somewhat frightening experience, like coming to nursery school, only to back off at the last moment; he may promise and then renege, boast and then dissolve when the time comes to take a critical step.

Observations suggest that dependence is very difficult to discourage with punishment. Unlike some behaviors (aggression, for example) that have hardly ever been encouraged by adults, dependence is readily tolerated by adults while children are very young and becomes a source of concern only as the child gets older. Consequently, the child has a history of having his dependence not only accepted but rewarded by adults. Under these circumstances the child may be expected to persist in trying to maintain his dependent status in spite of some disapproval for these behaviors as he gets older. Research supports this notion. Punishment for dependence, unless it is very severe or persists over a long time, may not appreciably reduce dependent behaviors and may, in some cases, actually intensify the child's resistance to independence. Young children sometimes defend themselves against what seems to them to be unreasonable demands for independence by exaggerating their own incompetencies. A child may learn to plead "I can't" or "I don't know how" even before he knows what is expected of him.

There is evidence to suggest that progress toward self-reliance and self-help is facilitated more by instilling in the child a sense of pride in his growing independence rather than by conveying the shortcomings of his lingering dependent behaviors; that is, independence is facilitated more by rewarding independence than by punishing dependence. If independence is rewarded without the unnecessary frustration of the child's dependent needs, the child is likely to gradually replace dependence with independence without having to fight his parents or teachers at every turn. With this rationale in mind, dependence in the nursery school is generally handled (1) by a willingness on the part of adults to satisfy the child's needs for nurturance, help, and support, and (2) by giving adult approval generously for independence and self-reliance when the child shows these behaviors.

Teachers in the nursery school are careful not to deliberately foster over-dependence in the children or to imply to them that teachers like them more when they are dependent than when they are independent. There is a tendency for adults to offer more nurturance to the less mature children, particularly if they are charming or cuddly and affectionate. Care is taken to make sure that friendly teacher-affection is not given only when children are behaving dependently since this would discourage independence and penalize the more mature, self-reliant children who also like affectionate hugs or pats.

ENCOURAGING INDEPENDENCE

The adults in the nursery school can do many things to encourage independence in preschoolers besides just rewarding it when it occurs. The school environment is carefully planned so that children can manage many things easily without help. Lockers, toilets, and sinks are low enough for self-help. Materials and supplies are frequently located on open, low shelves so that children can get things for themselves. Containers for crayons, paste, beads, and paints are carefully selected so that children can manage them easily with a minimum of spilling or breakage. Climbing and jumping equipment is designed to be safe enough for children to use without constant help. Since time is often a factor working against self-help in young children, enough time is allowed for the completion of tasks at which the child is likely to be pokey and clumsy, like dressing and washing. Adults are particularly sensitive to the child's need to be unhurried when he is engrossed in a task that he is determined to accomplish on his own, even though it is difficult for him.

Fear of failure is a frequent deterrent to a young child's steps toward independence. Adults in the nursery school can do much to prevent failure from having a serious negative effect on children's motivation to try new things and to rely on their own resources. Care is taken not to shame or humiliate children who fail in things they attempt even if their failure is the result of poor judgment or cockiness. When a child oversteps his capacities in his enthusiasm for trying something difficult, he is helped to retreat without losing face. Rather than using such incidents as object lessons to teach the child modesty or humility, the adults can perform the more useful function of helping the child to recover his equilibrium and to set a more reasonable goal for himself. In one instance, a very young three-year-old quickly climbed all the way to the top of a high set of climbing bars, then panicked, and could not climb down. A teacher lifted her down and said, "That was pretty high wasn't it? Try climbing up to here (indicating the third bar up from the ground), and see if you can get down from there. I'll stay in case you need help."

THE OVERLY DEPENDENT CHILD

Some preschoolers come to school with strong tendencies to be overly dependent for their age and ability. When a child consistently makes excessive demands for support or help, the adults in the school test out the child's response to a combination of supportive encouragement and mild withholding of help. If this culminates in independence and self-reliance that can, in turn, be praised by the adult, this policy is usually followed. If the child shows resistance or anxiety at having help withheld, help will be given, but the child is gradually weaned of the need for excessive help by vigilant attention to opportunities to praise independence whenever the child does show it. At first the overdependent child is praised for the slightest indication of independence; his ability to manage on his own or to try something new is applauded and even exaggerated. Gradually, as independence comes more naturally to him, he is rewarded the most conscientiously for instances of self-help that are truly noteworthy and appropriate for his age and ability. Approval for the easier tasks is gradually reduced as both the child and the adult take their accomplishment for granted.

It is important that the child's independence be intrinsically satisfying to him—not just a performance to avoid adult disapproval. If independence is motivated by shame, fear, or disapproval, one would expect the child to long to be dependent again and to revert back to dependence at the first opportunity.

Overdependence in preschoolers often seems to be a function of a child's family having a lingering perception of the child as more helpless than he actually is. School can help parents to modify their view of their

child's ability and to compare their child's self-reliance with that of his age-mates.

Most overdependent children learn to have more confidence in their abilities and to take real pride in their independence in a relatively short time in school. Independence carries with it many of its own rewards, since the independent child is able to get his needs met and to carry out tasks like dressing, toileting, and handwashing with much more dispatch if he does not need to wait for adult help. Independence also contributes to the child's status with his companions and generally bolsters his image of himself as a capable person. Although the nudge toward self-reliance may be initiated by the adult, the resulting independence is usually a source of considerable pride and pleasure to the child as well.

In summary, the child is helped to establish his independence by doing the following.

1. Teaching him to take pride in his growing ability to do things on his own and to strive for mastery of new skills.

2. Allowing him to vacillate back and forth between dependence and independence as he gradually moves toward independence.

3. Keeping the risks of independence at a minimum by helping him to cope with the occasional failures he experiences in attaining the goals he sets for himself.

COMPETITIVENESS AND ACHIEVEMENT BEHAVIOR

The preschool years are a time when the child is gradually increasing his social milieu to include the peer group. As a toddler, his social world was confined to the family, occasional family friends or relatives, and a baby-sitter or two. As a preschooler, the child begins to make friends on his own with children his own age. For the first time he will have a reference group for comparing his own abilities to the abilities of others his age. The preschool is a particularly potent environment for these comparisons, since the child is exposed to a group of children close to his age who are performing many different kinds of tasks. Unlike the family group, the child is not given any special consideration because of his youth; he is among age-mates. If he is capable and confident for his age, he will find himself more often at an advantage in the peer group than if he is immature compared with his peers.

Having the peer group against which to judge his own abilities has some important advantages for the young child. Children are very inclined to imitate the behavior of the more capable, confident children in the group just as they try to imitate their more mature brothers and sisters in the family group. Watching another child do something that they have been afraid or reluctant to try, sometimes spurs them on to try it themselves.

One can often see children following the lead of companions in situations that require high task concentration, persistence, and sometimes courage. They not only imitate the task strategies of their peers but their attitudes of confidence as well. Accomplishments that come about through the influence of peers are not only intrinsically rewarding to the child for the sense of accomplishment he gets, but new behaviors are sometimes rewarded directly by his companions who show their approval through smiles and other forms of social recognition. Of course, the child's companions can also cause him embarrassment by their criticism or teasing if they find him excessively immature and lacking in skill.

Teachers have sometimes been guilty of pitting children competitively against each other in order to motivate them to achieve. Aroused feelings of competitiveness undoubtedly do motivate many children (and adults) to work hard to perfect their performances in order to maintain or to improve their status relative to others. But competitiveness can have some crippling effects too. Since there are only a few places near the top of any status hierarchy, children can readily learn to resent the accomplishments of others for fear that the improved status of others will be at the expense of their own status.

Children do not all respond alike to competition. The spirited, confident child may feel certain that with a little more effort he can be at the top! If his efforts in competitive situations generally pay off, he may, indeed, accomplish more in a competitive environment than in a noncompetitive one. There are children, however, who do not seem to respond constructively to competition. Some children become so concerned about their status that any test situation arouses intense anxiety. The performance of these children may actually be impaired rather than enhanced by their desire to do well in school. Some children become highly defensive in response to competition and will cheat or lie to achieve status. Some are so fearful of failure, particularly "public" failure, that they simply withdraw from competition and refuse even to try to achieve in school.

Preschool teachers have typically found it easier to guard against the hazards of an academically competitive school environment than elementary school teachers, since there is not as much emphasis in the preschool on specific academic accomplishments, and there is almost no use of tests and grades. Even when the adults in the nursery school wish to know

whether or not their children understand a concept or have a particular skill, their testing procedures are likely to be informal observations or individualized test situations or games in which the child is not conscious of being "tested."

Competitiveness between children in school seems to be a fact of life that teachers and children must learn to live with, since it enters the picture of any peer group. Even children as young as three or four constantly seek status and vie for positions of importance such as being "first" or "biggest" relative to their peers. The teacher's job is not one of doing away with all competition but, instead, is one of seeing that competition has beneficial rather than debilitating effects on the motivations of the children. Children show individual differences in both their abilities and in their forwardness in seeking recognition. Consequently, some children will get more recognition than others in the peer group regardless of how the teacher uses competition or handles competitiveness when it emerges. No child, however, should suffer by comparison with the others to the extent that this dampens his motivation to participate enthusiastically in the school program. If a child remains forever on the fringes of school activities over a period of many months, he misses out on the opportunities that the school offers to develop skill and competence, and he also misses the gratification that comes from accomplishing. It is up to the adults in the preschool to see to it that each child in the group has an adequate measure of positive recognition for his accomplishments at his particular level of maturity. This requires deliberate attention and planning, but it is essential to the welfare of the children. The occasional child in the group who lacks confidence and remains uninvolved in the school program should be identified and helped by the adult. In one research project conducted by the University of Minnesota low-involved day care children were identified and given individualized training in self-confidence. They were given an increased number of success experiences while participating in school-type activities, and they were specifically reinforced for their willingness to try new tasks and for taking initiative. Throughout the training sessions each child was exposed to positive image-building comments from his teachers which identified him as a "good worker" and as a person with "good ideas." The data indicated that children participating in these sessions showed increased interest and involvement in their regular day care programs compared with similar children who had not participated in this training. Hopefully these teacher interventions will have a snowballing effect on the children. The more confident they are, whatever their level of skill, the more chance they have of developing important skills that will, in turn, give them more confidence.

There are things that preschool teachers do to guard against, or to lessen the invidiousness of competition and social comparison in their groups. Teachers are careful to avoid situations in which the status of one child is enhanced at the expense of the status of another. An award or privilege, for example, is never taken away from one child and given to another on the basis of superior behavior. The good behavior of one child is never presented as an "example" to a misbehaving child for fear of arousing resentment against the favored child or competition among the others for teacher recognition. A child may well be complimented for his behavior in the presence of other children, but contrasting shortcomings of others will not be pointed out. Also young children are not generally rewarded by being selected to be *first*, or by being identified as *best* in comparison with their classmates.

Competitive game-type situations in the preschool are generally managed in such a way as to avoid having "scores" that identify winners and losers. When success and failure are a natural part of the game activity (as in some "think games" when a child's response may be correct or incorrect), the adult ensures that each child has a good measure of success compared with the number of his failures by regulating the level of difficulty of the specific tasks each is given. In this way, individual differences in competence are accommodated.

Some preschool educators feel that a child should never be "corrected" by his teacher in school-type tasks on the assumption that having his errors pointed out to him will arouse fear of failure. For this reason self-corrective learning materials in which the child can tell immediately when he has made an error are very popular, since errors need not be identified by his teacher. An example of self-corrective materials would be a number-matching puzzle in which the child must match a number symbol, like the symbol "4," with four dots. The materials can be constructed in such a way that they fit together only when the numbers and the dots are properly matched. The child knows immediately that he has the correct combination—or he does not! Children can learn on their own from these materials, without the help of an adult.

Although self-corrective materials have many advantages for the young school child, it is probably an exaggeration to assume that being corrected by an adult is a traumatic, discomforting experience that will undermine the child's confidence or lead to fear of failure. In fact, it may be important for the child to learn very early in his school experience to accept as perfectly natural and not at all as a sign of weakness or incompetence, the occasional errors in his knowledge that are discovered by his teacher. If the child feels generally able to measure up to the expectations held for him by his parents and teachers, and if errors are not handled in a pompous manner by the adults, there is no reason to assume that the child will become defensive or fearful about making errors. The superior knowledge of adults is a valuable source of information for young children; they should feel comfortable about using adults as both a source of new information and as a standard against which to judge the soundness of what they feel they already know. Teachers can also provide their children with examples of effective coping by admitting their own shortages of information when they find that they do not know something; they can then join the children in a quest for the needed information.

14
Home - School Relations

14 Home-School Relations

Good communication between home and school is an important ingredient of any school through the high school years. When the children attending a school are three and four years of age, adequate communication with the home is especially critical. Preschool children are still very dependent on direct support from their families for security; it is important for children to feel that their parents are acquainted with their teachers and that they approve of the things that they do at their school.

Unlike the elementary school child whose enrollment in school is dictated by law, the preschooler's enrollment in nursery school is determined by how much the child and his family feel the school is right for him. If he makes a good adjustment initially and likes his school, and if his parents feel that what is happening to him there is good, he will probably continue to attend until he is ready to go on to kindergarten. Otherwise he will drop out and wait for kindergarten.

Most of the children who come to the nursery school make prompt and easy adjustments to the separation from their families, and most participate eagerly in the school program. Typically 17 or 18 children in a group of 20 adjust to school by the second or third day that they attend, coming eagerly and no longer needing a member of the family to stay with them for more than a few minutes at the beginning of the school day. Two or three of the children in a group, however, are likely to need the support of a mother or some other familiar person who stays for all or part of the school day for several days or even beyond the first week of school. Even these children, however, gradually become secure and happy at school and generally make excellent adjustments. Most are indistinguishable from the quick adjusters by the third or fourth weeks of school. Only an occasional child—perhaps one in 80 or 90—has such a difficult time separating from his family and adjusting to school that both home and school feel the child should be withdrawn.

THE CHILD'S INTRODUCTION
TO THE NURSERY SCHOOL

Attendance at the nursery school is preceded by at least one face-to-face contact with a child and his family by the head teacher of the group he

221

will enter. The contact may be either a visit to the school by the child and his mother (and father, too, if possible) or a visit to the child's home by his teacher.

Some important purposes are served by the initial preattendance contact between the home and school. First, the child becomes acquainted with the teacher so that, at least, one adult in the school is familiar and can be identified as a friend when the child comes for his first school day. This can be a critical step in the child's introduction to school, especially if he is a little anxious about staying there without his mother. Second, the teacher can begin to get to know the child from this first visit. Even when a child is quite shy during this initial contact and responds cautiously to the teacher's friendly overtures, she can convey her friendly interest in him and his activities. Teachers are careful not to push children into making reciprocal friendly overtures to them—their main purpose is to convey *their* friendliness to the child.

The use of home visits, school visits, or a combination of both for the initial contact is a matter of personal preference, scheduling convenience, or the preference of parents. In any case, enough time is allowed for the meeting to serve its purposes, usually averaging about 45 minutes. A visit to the child's home has the advantage of meeting the child in territory that is familiar to him where he feels secure and in the position of host. On the other hand, a school visit has the advantage of acquainting the child with the school building, the toys, materials, and equipment as well as the teacher. If the visit is at the school the child is invited to play if he wishes, and a few things are usually placed out on tables or in play areas of the room to entice him to use them. The teacher may stay near the child and talk with him as he plays or works or she may come back to him from time to time from visiting close by with his mother.

The initial contact, whether at home or school, is also a critical time for teachers and parents to begin their acquaintance. Teachers do not use this time to convey routine information to parents about the school. Descriptive information about the school program, admission forms to be completed, information about tuition if the family is paying tuition, holidays, school hours, or the handling of emergencies are given to parents before the visit so that the visit can be used to talk about things of mutual interest, to answer specific questions that they may have about their child's introduction to school and to learn information about the child that will be helpful in facilitating his adjustment. Teachers attempt to convey to parents the school's philosophy of an open, informal exchange of information between the school and the home. Parents are invited to call the teacher (at home, after the child is in bed if advisable) to let her know if anything about the school environment is bothering her or her child. Parents are encouraged to observe from the school observation booth anytime they wish. Teachers indicate their intention of letting the parent know if anything of special import has happened to the child on a particular school day. Phone conversations occur frequently between parents and teachers so that both can keep the other informed of any changes in the child's behavior.

Care is taken that conversations with the mother or father that involve the child and in which the child should not be a party are conducted out of earshot. If, for example, the child has had a previous experience in attending a nursery school, day care center, or church school that was unsuccessful, or has expressed concern about staying at school without his mother, the teacher may arrange for a phone conversation with the parent at a time when both can talk freely and plan for the child's initial school days. Mothers sometimes need reassurance from teachers that the young child's reluctance to stay without his mother in an unfamiliar place, with people he hardly knows, is developmentally appropriate for a child this age and is not necessarily symptomatic of overdependence or immaturity.

It is the firm policy of the school to have the mother or some other familiar person stay with a child if he is reluctant to stay alone during his first day or two at school, and mothers are expected to comply with this policy. Every attempt is made to prevent the child's first exposure to school from being a stressful one, culminating in fearfulness, anger, or tears. Even mothers who are able to leave their children within a short time of their arrival in school the first day, usually stay close by in case their child has second thoughts about being left alone and becomes distressed after they have gone. Only when both mother and teacher feel confident that the child is secure enough to manage until his mother returns, is she free to leave the area of the school. Some mothers stay in a nearby lounge and have coffee or talk with other mothers; others observe in one of the observation booths while their child spends his first day in school.

A child's first school day is usually not more than two hours long. Even if the child wishes to stay longer, he is expected to leave after two hours—before the excitement of the occasion begins to cause fatigue. If he is reluctant to leave, he will be all the more ready to come another day!

Mothers, like the children themselves, respond to the child's initial school experience in different ways. Some are more reluctant than their children to effect the separation. Even when mothers feel confident that their child is ready for participation in a nursery school program, they may express a feeling of loss knowing that the child will now be away from them for part of his waking day. It is not uncommon for mothers to express ambivalence about their child's adjustment to school, hoping it will be easy for him but also feeling a little hurt at the thought that their child may no longer feel a need for their constant care and can manage quite well in the care of others.

Some mothers are embarrassed to have their child be one of those who clings to them and cries. Others feel angry at the child for being so dependent or manipulative in wanting them to stay. Generally, if the mother can be induced to relax and accept her child's desire to have her stay (regardless of whether the child is genuinely anxious or just being manipulative) the child, too, can relax and put his energy into getting acquainted with the teachers and the children at school. If there are going to be tears or tantrums at any time, they will come after the child has had ample time to know the people and the routines at school and has become, at least, minimally comfortable and secure in the setting. A reluctant child is generally not expected to stay alone at school for more than an hour or so at this point in his adjustment and a teacher keeps an eye on him to see that he is finding things to do. She may reassure him, if necessary, that his mother will return soon. The child's discomfort about staying is not denied by the adults. He is not told, "See, aren't you having a good time?" or "It isn't so bad, is it?" if it is clear that the child is tense and uneasy. If the teacher says anything at all about his feelings, she is more likely to indicate to him that she understands that it is hard for him to stay at school when it is so new to him but that he will soon feel more comfortable about it. She may compliment the child for getting along so well even though he is afraid of staying without his parents.

Some mothers whose children are reluctant to stay suggest that their child would adapt better if they just "slipped out" at some point when the child is not noticing. It has been the school's experience, however, that children treated in this way become very suspicious of both teacher and mother and are more reluctant than ever to stay on the following days. The child usually becomes too preoccupied with watching mother to become actively involved in school activities. While children may not be permanently harmed by this kind of adult deception, it does not seem wise to have the child's first experience with school be traumatic or painful. The child is formulating his first impressions of school during these early days. Probably even more important is the fact that he is formulating an impression of how well he can manage away from home, on his own, and what it is like to have new experiences in his life. It is important for the child's future adaptation to new experiences to feel that he has handled this one well and has measured up to his mother's and teacher's expectations of him. The day-by-day management of a reluctant child's introduction to school will help to illustrate some of the issues discussed above.

THE SCHOOL ADJUSTMENT
OF A SHY CHILD

Sue Smith was three years and five months old when she came to nursery school. From the first mention of school by her parents Sue had expressed concern and ambivalence. She had anxiously asked her mother if "mothers stayed" at school, and her mother had explained that they did not but that all of the children stayed without their mothers, and the teachers were "very nice like Mrs. Hynes," the teacher of Sue's second grade sister. The night before a home visit from her prospective teacher Sue cried at the anticipation of having to stay alone at school without her mother and stated resolutely that she would not go at all if her mother would not stay with her.

The home visit went well in spite of the fact that Sue was suspicious of her teacher and kept a safe distance both physically and psychologically. Sue's mother mentioned the crying episode to the teacher at a time when Sue was out of earshot and expressed her concern about handling the situation on the day that Sue was to begin school. Her teacher indicated that she should feel completely comfortable about staying with Sue and that other mothers would be staying as well. Sue's mother seemed quite relieved at this procedure. She did not say anything to Sue at the time, although she did explain to the child after the visit that mothers were allowed to stay with children while they are getting used to school.

During the home visit with Sue Smith and her mother, Mrs. Smith was somewhat embarrassed at her daughter's behavior. She had refused to come into the room to "meet" her new teacher and had hung back in the doorway between the kitchen and the living room peeking out from time to time looking uneasy and anxious. Since the family had recently moved into the apartment they occupied, the teacher asked how they were enjoying their new home and mentioned that another child from the street was also due to begin school. As the conversation between the mother and teacher progressed without any undue attention being given to Sue, Sue gradually worked her way out of the kitchen and into the living room—somewhat on the pretence of having to chase the family cat back into the kitchen. The teacher asked Sue what the cat's name was and Sue answered; otherwise, the teacher did not direct much attention to Sue for fear of driving her back into the kitchen. After a time, the teacher showed Mrs. Smith and Sue a book of photographs taken in the nursery school the previous year so that they could see what kinds of things the children did at school. Sue was curious about the pictures and snatched brief glances at them during the time that her mother perused them in detail. When Mrs. Smith went to prepare coffee, the teacher talked with Sue and went over to her to see a book that she had in her hand. The teacher happened to be familiar with the book and recalled parts of the story to Sue's pleasure. Throughout the remainder of the visit Sue continued her reserve, coming close enough to offer her teacher a cookie, but otherwise keeping her distance. She did, however, seem to relax and take a greater interest in the conversation between her mother and teacher. The conversation was not about the anticipated problems of this child's adjustment but was, instead, about the family's summer vacation, the ages of the siblings in the family, and how much Sue missed her special friend who lived next door to their previous home. The teacher made only one other comment about school, indicating that when Sue and her mother came to school, Sue would find other children with whom to be friends.

The teacher indicated to Mrs. Smith which day would be the first day of school for her and her child, explaining that one half of the group would come on one day and the other half would come on the next day, each group staying only about an hour and a half instead of the usual three hours. On the third day of school, all of the children would come for two hours and from then on the usual school schedule would be followed with individual exceptions. With this plan the teachers would be able to give extra attention to the children that first day and the children would not be overwhelmed by too large a group for too long a time.

When Sue arrived at school with her mother, she continued to hang back staying very close to her mother and did not let her mother out of sight. Teachers from time to time came over to talk briefly to Sue and invite her to the tables or over to the toys. She quietly refused these invitations and stayed near her mother watching the other children intently. After about 40 minutes, the teacher invited Mrs. Smith to the nursery school kitchen and lounge for coffee indicating that Sue could either stay in the room or go too. Sue elected to go but began almost immediately to coax her mother to leave the coffee room so that they could get back to the playroom. Her teacher then suggested that she would take Sue back to the playroom and her mother could follow shortly. Sue agreed and moved around the playroom this time, staying very close to her teacher until her mother returned.

On Sue's second day of school, her mother tried to leave her, but Sue immediately began to cry and cling to her mother. Both Mrs. Smith and the teacher felt it best for her to stay for a short time, taking Sue with her when she left. This day Mrs. Smith was able to spend most of the time in the coffee lounge talking with one or two other mothers who were also staying, but Sue did check her whereabouts two or three times in the 45 minutes that they spent at school. On this morning Sue moved about the room cautiously, again staying close to her teacher and getting mildly involved with a few table activities. Sue watched other children intently. Her teacher was completely permissive of Sue's staying close by and did not urge her to do anything that she did not seem to want to do. When it was time to leave, Sue tried to get her mother to stay longer but her teacher indicated that it was time to go and she could return the next day. For two more days, Sue made it clear that she did not want her mother to leave the school area, but each day she became more bold and comfortable, moving about the room, paying less attention to where the teacher was, and coyly playing nearer to other children.

On the fifth day of school, the teacher suggested that Mrs. Smith leave the school area for a short time—perhaps 30 minutes—even if Sue protested. The teacher explained to Sue that she would take care of her and that her mother would return very soon. Sue did cry and cling to her mother briefly, but allowed herself to be picked up by the teacher. She wimpered for a time, protesting that she wanted her mother to stay; her teacher assured her that she would get along just fine, since she was now getting quite used to school. After about 10 minutes of staying very close to the teacher Sue began participating in activities as she had done the previous day. She did not cry though she looked rather tense and unhappy. Her teacher this time, took the responsibility for staying in the general area where Sue was participating and commented to her about her activities two or three times in the 30 minutes. After about 20 minutes Sue asked when her mother would return and seemed on the verge of tears. Her teacher showed her the approximate time on the clock that her mother would return and suggested she find a puzzle (one of her favorite school activities) to do while she waited. When her mother returned, Sue's greeting was a mixture of pleasure at having stayed and relief at seeing her mother. When the teacher suggested that they come back the next day, Sue again urged her mother to stay longer knowing that most of the children would not be picked up until later in the morning. Her teacher again indicated that it was time to go but that she could stay longer the next day. By expecting Sue to leave when her mother returned, her teacher primed Sue for being eager to come again the next day, and also indicated by her expectations, that "staying" at school after the first few days is primarily what children do, rather than what mothers do! (Her teacher may even have interrupted her in the middle of complete involvement in an activity indicating that it is now "time for you to leave" to maximize the conflict Sue would feel between wanting to stay and protesting her mother's leaving.)

Within a few days Sue was staying at school with no more than mild attempts to get her mother to stay an extra few minutes or return from the door for a second goodbye kiss. She gradually expanded her activities to include more of the play areas and almost all of the table activities and began befriending two or three of the quieter, less threatening children.

Sue continued throughout the school year to gravitate to the less vigorous school activities, and she also continued to show a preference for the quieter children, but she did get over her excessive cautiousness and timidity in approaching school activities. She soon allowed her mother to go without a second glance and looked forward to coming to school each day. Her only relapses of not wanting to be left at school were understandable ones; once following a two-week midwinter illness and, again, in spring when her grandparents were visiting and she felt that she would miss something special at home (in which case her teacher suggested she be allowed to stay home).

In all probability, this child would have managed to adjust even if she had been left promptly at the door of the school, crying and protesting her first day of school! Handled as it was, however, Sue's eventual tears at being left were more an expression of her annoyance with her mother and teacher than fear or anxiety in saying in a strange place, as might have been true if she had been left the first day. Needless to say, this procedure requires cooperation between the home and the school, but the payoff in a less traumatic entrance to school is well worth the effort.

PARENT CONFERENCES
AND PARTICIPATION

Teachers continue to have contacts throughout the year with the parents of children enrolled in their groups. Communication may be in the form of phone conversations or brief comments in the classroom as the child is brought to school or picked up at the end of the school day. Teachers also typically have two prearranged conferences with parents during the school year, one sometime after the third month of school and another late in the spring of the year. There are no written reports of "grades" submitted to parents indicating their child's progress in school, but the child's school participation is discussed in considerable detail with the parent at the conference. Conferences usually last 45 minutes or longer to give plenty of time for discussion. Each teacher handles parent conferences according to her own plan, but all attempt to inform the parents fully about the child's school behavior. The parent is told what activities the child typically participates in or seems to especially enjoy, which children he spends most of his time with, and how he gets along with them. Any changes in the child's school behavior are discussed and a general assessment of the child's skills and abilities based on the teacher's impressions from observing him with his age-mates is given to the parent. The parent is also told of any problem behavior that has been of concern to the teachers, and the school's handling of the behavior is described in detail. Of course, if a problem is of any magnitude, the parent will more than likely have already been consulted about it before conference time through informal chats or phone calls: the conference may then be a kind of progress report to the parent.

In preparation for conferences, teachers typically write a status report on each child in their group for their own school files. In this way the teacher carefully considers all aspects of a child's school progress and current status before talking with his parents. If the teacher feels less informed than she should be concerning some aspect of the child's school participation, she will probably plan special observations of the child prior to the conference and will discuss him with the other teachers in the group to get their impressions of his participation in the school activities that they have supervised. Some teachers also ask parents to observe at least once at school before a conference so that they have a better base for communication with the teacher and can ask questions that occur to them from their observation.

While parent conferences are usually the responsibility of the head teacher, assistant teachers may, from time to time, participate in them. In special cases in which rapport is especially good between a parent and an assistant teacher, that teacher may conduct the conference without the presence of the head teacher.

Conferences are also viewed as a time for teachers to get helpful information from parents. The child's school progress as seen from the parent's standpoint is of prime interest to the teacher. She will want to know the parent's impression of the child's attitudes about school and what behavior changes, if any, the parent attributes to the child's school attendance. Most parents are pleased with their child's response to the school experience. During the first weeks of school some children come home more tired and keyed up than usual, but by the end of a few weeks most have adapted to the routine and manage it without becoming overstimulated. Parents often report that their child's home play seems more constructive and his relationships with neighborhood friends and members of his family is improved when he has his school to attend part of his day.

Most parents are eager to take advantage of the teacher's normative perspective about children, since she works with many other children about their child's age. This is especially true when the child attending is a first child in a family, but other parents seek this information as well. They may ask if the teacher feels their child is socially adequate for his age or if his interest and skill in learning activities suggests that he will be ready for kindergarten when he is old enough to go.

Some parents are concerned that their child may be bored in kindergarten, since so many of the nursery school activities provide preacademic preparation for school. Teachers can be generally reassuring to parents on this point. Many parents have asked this question, but few have reported any serious problem with boredom of their child during his kindergarten experience. It may, in fact, be helpful for the child to find that he is able to perform well in prereading tasks in kindergarten because of his previous experience with preschool materials. Repeated learning experiences seem to be appropriate and beneficial to the young child. Of course, if parents are concerned enough to convey to their child a firm expectation that he will be bored in kindergarten, we may oblige them by reporting boredom. One suspects that some reports of child-boredom begin with the independent judgment on the part of the parent that a kindergarten program is not adequately stimulating his child (which may or may not be true), and the child then responds with appropriate complaints.

Parents sometimes have specific concerns about their child's maturity or readiness for school and express their hope that the nursery school will help him to become ready. The opportunity for the parent and teacher to compare impressions of the child's readiness can be helpful and is often enlightening to both teachers and parents. Teachers recognize that while parents may be understandably biased about their own child, they also have had many excellent opportunities to compare the child with others his age or with their older children when they were his age. One thinks of the typical parental bias as being in favor of one's own child, leading to an overestimation of the child's abilities. It is the school's experience, however, that parents are just as likely to overlook some of the more salient features of their child's behavior or personality and to underestimate his ability or his appeal. There is usually, however, good agreement between parents and teachers in identifying either outstanding abilities or worrisome shortcomings in a child's behavior, and each uses the conference to check the validity of his own observations.

If parents and teachers agree that a child needs special help in promoting development in some problem area, they will discuss plans for handling the behavior in considerable detail. While occasionally a child's school and home behavior is quite different and a problem shows up one place but not in the other, most problems of any magnitude are evident both to the school and to the home. Usually both are similarly concerned about the child and are attempting to modify the problem behavior.

Parents and teachers may compare the child's responsiveness to the different handling of problem behavior by the school and by the home. Although a teacher rarely criticizes a parent for the way that he handles his child at home, she will document specifically the kinds of things the school is doing to help the child in problem areas, and she will explain the reasons for doing these things instead of other things. She may also indicate her impressions of ways in which the problem behavior may have been maintained or perpetuated at school and how the school regime is being modified to help the child learn more adaptive behaviors. She will not necessarily suggest that the parent should approach the problem in a similar way. In fact, the teacher may very well indicate that she does not know if similar tactics would work at home, since what "works" seems to depend in part, at least, on the situation and on the confidence the adults have in a given procedure for modifying a child's behavior.

Parents often seek suggestions from teachers concerning what they might do at home to cope with problem behavior, and teachers can help them to explore alternative approaches. The teacher's attitude is one of helping the parent to decide what would seem right for him and his child given their particular family scene. The teacher's suggestions are usually in the form of alternatives that the parent must feel free to reject or incorporate as he sees fit. Teachers often convey this specifically by asking a parent if he thinks a particular approach would work for them or not. In this way the parent can be reassured that rejecting an idea offered by the teacher will not be awkward for him nor detrimental to future constructive contacts with the teacher.

Teachers can sometimes help parents approach their child's behavior more analytically, focusing on questions like what *causes* the child to misbehave in the way that he does and what things in the family scene are helping to perpetuate, or even encourage the misbehavior that they are trying to discourage. This approach may lead the parents to consider alternative attacks on the problem that they had not considered before, and it can often be more helpful than specific suggestions of what to do.

Parents are surprisingly frank about their children's problem behaviors, and they usually have good hunches about what is causing a problem. They are, for example, often aware of the fact that their child's misbehavior is treated inconsistently from one time to the next or that the misbehavior is paying off for the child in some way even while they are trying to discourage it. Parents sometimes indicate that they do not always agree with each other about what to expect of their child so that no clear, consistent expectations have been conveyed to the child in the problem area.

Even when parents have a pretty good idea of how they ought to cope with a child's problems, sometimes other family duties and responsibilities distract them from a more diligent approach to the situation. Teachers cannot and should not presume to resolve issues of this kind for parents. The parent has both the right and the responsibility to decide what, if anything, he is going to do about a child's behavior at home. The teacher may help in any way that she can, and may encourage the parents to try to change things at home, but the final decision about the management of a child at home must be left to the parent.

While it is an uncommon occurrence, from time to time a child's behavior concerns the teachers when his parents see no reason to be alarmed. Differences of opinion between parents and teachers may reflect discrepancies in social values, or different management techniques in the handling of aggression, dependence, or compliance at school compared with the handling of these behaviors in the child's home. These matters should be discussed fully with the parents, and parents should feel free to express their views. The outcome of such a discussion generally is a better understanding of each other's position and may involve compromises by both parents and teachers. While parents do not always agree with the teacher that a problem exists, the teacher has a professional responsibility to indicate her concern to the parent just as the parent has a right to disagree. In such cases, time alone will determine the direction of events. If the parents of the child continue to get negative feedback about the child, they may eventually take some definitive action. If not, they were perhaps right in the first place not to worry.

Teachers working with young children occasionally encounter a child with very serious physical or psychological problems. Dealing with problems of this kind can be more difficult for both teachers and parents and must be handled with thoughtfulness and tact. Teachers should be especially well prepared with concrete information about the child's behavior and with information about possible community resources to which the parents might turn for help or assessment of the child. If, in this instance, the parents are unwilling to acknowledge the problem or seek additional assessment, the teacher may need to carefully evaluate whether or not she can continue to accommodate the child in the group and still provide adequately for the other children. If the child cannot be accommodated and the parent refuses to seek help, the parent may be asked to withdraw the child. A request for withdrawal, however, should be used as a last resort, after the school has attempted to work with the child and to help the parents obtain appropriate help.

In addition to the initial family contact, school observations, and parent-teacher conferences, the school sponsors parent meetings from time to time. Meetings having to do with the general educational program of the school usually involve the parents from all of the groups meeting together. At other times, however, individual teachers and their assistants sponsor parent meetings for the parents of the children in their groups at which time they discuss the educational goals and program for their particular group. Parent meetings have included curriculum demonstrations, slides showing school activities, and "participation night" during which the children, their brothers and sisters, and their parents are invited to come to school early in the evening and participate in school activities together. Recently parents have also been invited to participate in child-study sessions that meet weekly and are conducted by community parent educators.

Occasionally parents have also volunteered to assist in a group on a regular basis, though more often parent volunteers participate in special curriculum activities or help out on special occasions like field-trip days. The school philosophy is "permissive" with regard to parent participation. It is the impression of the staff that parent involvement that facilitates feedback about a parent's own child is welcomed by most parents and easy to maintain; rarely does a parent decline an invitation to meet with the teacher to discuss how his child is getting along in school. Attendance at other more general school activities, however, depends more on the interest of parents, time, and other commitments or obligations. Although teachers feel it is necessary to have regular communication with every family regarding his child's progress in school, parent participation in other things is invited, but left to the discretion of the parent.

15
The Montessori Method

15 The Montessori Method

No report of contemporary preschool education would be complete without a discussion of the educational system of Maria Montessori. Montessori education for preschool children is a visible and influential force on the contemporary scene, and a brief orientation to its philosophy and curriculum is in order.

In the early 1900s, an Italian physician, Dr. Maria Montessori, developed a comprehensive educational program for young children. Montessori's philosophy and materials are based on her observations and work with mentally retarded children and with young children living in a slum tenement in Rome. Montessori's conception of education was broad. Education was viewed as the preparation of children for life; for spiritual as well as intellectual maturity. She believed that early experience affected later development and that the young ghetto children with whom she worked particularly needed a prepared environment to support adequate development.

Her materials and methods reflect her beliefs in common developmental patterns with variation in rates, and in "sensitive periods." The materials are designed to be intrinsically interesting and self-correcting. The emphasis in a Montessori program is on the growth of individual children through their use of a sequence of carefully programmed lessons; learning is guided primarily through the structure of the materials. Children select their own activities from those available and work at their own pace. The general atmosphere of the classroom is suggestive of "work" rather than "play." Teachers are observers, diagnosticians, and facilitators rather than the primary source of information or disciplinarians. Self-discipline is developed through academic content. Creativity, Montessori believed, develops after mastery.

Montessori's approach to education was introduced into the United States in 1909. Interest in her philosophy continued for about five years and then subsided until the late 1950s when Nancy McCormick Rambusch reintroduced Montessori philosophy in her book, *Learning How To Learn*. Around the same time, Mrs. Rambusch also began a Montessori school in Whitby, Connecticut. Interest mounted once again. Numerous articles, publications, and comments on the Montessori method appeared. More schools were opened, and in 1960, Mrs. Rambusch founded the American Montessori Society and began a teacher training program. Currently in the United States, there are two somewhat different approaches to Maria Montessori's philosophy and materials. In addition to the American Montessori Society, there is the Association Montessori Internationale, which is headed by Dr. Montessori's son, Mario, and which has its headquarters in the Netherlands. Since membership in either of these groups is voluntary, it is difficult to estimate the number of Montessori schools currently in operation. The majority of the Montessori programs are in private or parochial schools with few classrooms in public schools. Classes are most commonly offered for preschool children, although Whitby school now extends through high school. There are a few programs for disadvantaged children in some of the larger cities of this country, but most Montessori students come from middle-class backgrounds. There are usually 20 to 30 children of mixed ages in each Montessori classroom. The preschool level of a Montessori school includes three- to six-year-olds. Each class is supervised by a directress, as persons trained in the Montessori Method are called, and an assistant.

The physical appearance of a Montessori classroom is one of orderliness. Usually there are small individual tables and chairs which may be grouped together for two to four children. Materials are arranged neatly on low shelves around a room so that the children may help themselves. Materials are grouped according to the aspect of development involved: science materials are in one area of the room, mathematical materials are in another area, and so forth.

The materials through which children learn are, indeed, one of the most distinctive aspects of the Montessori learning environment. They are attractive and generally easy for the children to handle. Nearly all of the items are wooden, simply designed, and precision constructed. The finish is clear or painted with primary colors. More important for learning, however, is that many of the items are self-correcting units that will fit together in only one way. Thus a child can discover his own errors and can correct them without teacher direction.

MONTESSORI CURRICULUM

Although Montessori developed materials and activities for children through elementary school, the discussion here focuses on the curriculum for the three- to five-year-olds. The activities described are intended to be illustrative; they do not, by any means, include the total curriculum provided in the Montessori programs for young children. For further information about Montessori curriculum and methods, the reader should refer to *The Montessori Method* and *Dr. Montessori's Handbook* by Maria Montessori.

Some of the Montessori curriculum activities for preschool children provide training in "practical life tasks." Practical life tasks include practice in pouring water and rice without spilling, learning prescribed procedures for washing hands, dishes, and tables, practicing tying, zipping, buttoning, and snapping fasteners mounted on frames, peeling vegetables, and polishing silver. The procedure for each of these exercises is clearly specified and must be mastered before a child is considered to have performed the task satisfactorily. Snack and mealtimes are used to teach courtesy and politeness. A boy may be expected, for example, to pull a chair out from the table so that a girl may sit for snack. The children wait until all have been served before eating and until everyone has finished before asking to be excused from the table. Small items necessary for a single practical life task activity (such as silver polishing, vegetable preparation, or pouring) are stored on small trays that can be carried, intact, from the shelf to a work table.

Other Montessori curriculum materials provide sensorimotor training and discrimination training for the young child. Some activities emphasize simple visual, tactile, auditory, and olfactory acuity. Two such activities are the Game of the Blind, in which the children attempt to identify objects in a cloth bag by feeling them, and the matching of the sounds made by shaking boxes or cylinders containing corn, sand, salt, or macaroni. Tactile discrimination is fostered through sorting samples of different grades of sandpaper, feeling fabric samples, tracing shapes with the finger, and ordering small pieces of different kinds of wood according to weight. Practice in visual discrimination is involved in many activities such as matching color tablets and identifying letters and numbers. The well-known "Montessori cylinders" help to provide important sensory experiences in visual discrimination and eye-hand coordination for the young children. These materials consist of solid blocks of wood into which are inserted a row of ten cylinders. In one block the cylinders decrease gradually in diameter from one end of the block to the other; in another block the cylinders decrease in height, and in still another, in *both* diameter and height. Each cylinder has a small knob on the top for easy removal from the block. The child's job is to remove the cylinders, mix them up, and replace them, systematically comparing them on the dimensions on which they vary. The cylinders are a good example of self-correcting materials, since they cannot all be replaced in a block unless each is in the correct hole.

The academic curriculum for three- and four-year-olds consists primarily of mathematics, geography, language-reading activities, and some science and music activities. The materials for teaching mathematical concepts are the most extensive of all of those designed by Montessori. They provide concrete experiences in the perception and manipulation of quantities, number recognition, and mathematical operations. For the preschool children, emphasis is placed on the correct sequencing of shapes and objects that are ordered along one or more dimensions. The children work, for example, with a "pink tower" (a series of ten solid wooden cubes that graduate in size from one centimeter to ten centimeters), the "broad stair" (a series of brown wooden prisms that graduate in size and that form a series of stairs), and the "number rods" (ten wooden rods segmented into units with each rod being one unit longer than the last). Work specifically with numerals includes tracing sandpaper numbers from a standard and practice with addition and subtraction, sometimes with the help of worksheets.

Language, prereading, and prewriting activities are also fairly extensive and a formal part of a Montessori program. The children trace sandpaper letters with their fingers, learn to recognize the letters of the alphabet, become familiar with their phonetic pronunciation, and copy letters from models. After these exercises, they are ready to begin to blend sounds and to write letters into words. A sight vocabulary is developed through the use of labels for farm animals and equipment, proper names, and the names of objects in the room. The directress writes or helps a child to write the names of objects he wishes to learn. The particular vocabulary words used in the teaching of reading are closely related to an individual child's interests. Small cards that are color coded according to the parts of speech are used in constructing grammatically correct sentences. Later the child will receive written notes from the directress that he will read and carry out as evidence of his comprehension of the message.

Science and geography activities are less closely related to the learner's immediate interests. Children learn by rote the names of leaves, parts of flowers, countries, bodies of water, and continents. They also trace representations of these objects from standard puzzle pieces, cutout shapes, and drawings.

Musical activities at the preschool level seem to be limited to the use of bells and other materials that foster tone discrimination.

Montessori schools use a more formal method of reporting on the progress of students than is used in most preschool programs. Usually, written reports are given to the child's parents and progress in the specific curriculum areas mentioned above is clearly stated. The child's general adjustment to the classroom situation is also indicated. Conferences with parents may be held for the purpose of discussing a child's progress in the program.

All of the Montessori activities carried on in the classroom are labeled "work." Nursery School materials such as blocks, art supplies, and other creative materials, if they are available, are separated from Montessori materials to help children to distinguish between work and play.

Equipment for outdoor activities may be available, but in many contemporary Montessori programs, large-muscle activity that characterizes outdoor play is not considered an important part of the program.

Generally, there is little duplication of materials in the Montessori classroom. Only one set of each item is available. This is believed to help children to learn the necessity of taking turns. Materials and equipment do not change, and the same items are available everyday of the school session. The children do, however, use different materials as their abilities improve.

Children are expected to attend to their own tasks and to take pride in their accomplishments. Since there is a single correct way for most of the materials to be used or for the concepts to be learned, the standard is clear to the child, and he can recognize when he is correct. The sequencing of materials also enables the child to predict what he will be doing after he has mastered his present task. Because the same activities are always available he can practice a previously learned task if he chooses. Specific progress in each activity can be easily observed by the directress, and can also be readily communicated to parents.

The role of directress is different from that of the conventional classroom or nursery school teacher. Emphasis is placed on her ability to observe and to assess each child; and then to stimulate the child to undertake the task for which he is ready. Maria Montessori believed that "the personality of the teacher disappears" in the classroom setting. The teacher is not supposed to be a source of either praise or punishment for the children. Rather the materials and the activities are designed to be intrinsically rewarding for the learner. Montessori defined the role of the teacher as that of an observer and diagnostician who prepares the classroom so that the children can learn. Achievement standards in the Montessori school are clearly defined for both the children and adults, and the children can readily recognize when they have mastered a task.

The use of a standard format for instruction, Montessori felt, helped to make things clearer to the children. Instruction in the use of each piece of equipment is given in brief, simple, carefully chosen words or statements and the child does not use a piece of equipment until he has been specifically instructed in its use. Initial instruction for an activity consists of teacher demonstration of the correct use of the materials with the child observing. In teaching a child how to work with the cylinders of different heights, for example, the directress will first remove each cylinder, one at a time from the block. When all of the cylinders have been removed, she will point to the highest one and say, "This is high." She will repeat this and then point to the lowest, saying "This is low." In the next step the child is asked, "Which is high?" "Which is low?" The child indicates the correct cylinder by pointing or by handing the correct cylinder to the directress. After this, instruction on the comparison of cylinders of different heights takes place in a systematic manner. The concept also will be illustrated by the child's measuring various cylinders, using the materials by himself. The child will remove them, measure them against each other, and replace them in order. When the child feels he understands the concept, he indicates this to the directress. She then tests his knowledge by asking him to indicate the highest and lowest of any remaining cylinders until all of the cylinders have been replaced in the block.

The materials used in teaching specific concepts are ordered in difficulty. They progress from the sensorimotor level to the abstract. In learning about different geometric shapes, for example, a child first might trace around the metal insets of geometric shapes with either his finger or with a pencil. Then he might color the shape being very careful to stay within the lines. He probably will also handle some solid wooden models of the same shapes. After these experiences, he will learn the correct names for the shapes, practice labeling them correctly and, perhaps, will draw them freehand.

If a child selects an activity that the directress considers too much beyond his current skills or if he does not use the materials in the prescribed fashion, he is reminded of the procedure and expected to comply either by using the materials correctly or by returning them to the storage area. If the child does not respond to the reminder, the materials may be removed by the directress. Although most directresses do give the child a warning, Montessori stated that "the teacher does not repeat and does not insist, she smiles, gives the child a friendly caress and takes away the materials." If stronger punishment is necessary, a child may be isolated from his classmates for a period of time. However, Montessori anticipated little need for punishment, since the materials and activities were designed to appeal to children.

Montessori classrooms are exceptionally quiet in comparison with traditional nursery schools, although the atmosphere may vary a little with the directress and school philosophy. Both adults and children speak only when necessary and, then, usually in very low voices or whispers. Patience, politeness, and noninterference with another's work are important behaviors that are fostered. Among the first things a child learns is to concentrate on his own work and to interact as little as possible with peers. With the exception of snacks or meals, most activities are undertaken individually. Occasionally children help each other, but Maria Montessori believed that each person must "perfect himself as an individual" before he can work with others. To teach appropriate classroom demeanor, that is, to "normalize" the children, a few children enter a Montessori classroom at a time in the beginning of the school year. This allows the teacher to teach each child how to conduct himself and how to work with the materials.

Although each child may select his own activity, movement within a Montessori classroom is orderly. A child goes to the shelf, chooses what he wishes to work with, and returns to his desk or to a small rug on the floor to work. Only one set of materials may be used at any one time by a single child. Since there is only one set of materials for each activity in a classroom and since children are not generally encouraged to work together, they learn to take turns, to wait quietly, and to make alternate selections when their first choice is not available.

Many of the materials must be removed or carried in a prescribed manner. The number rods, for example, must be carried one at a time with one hand holding each end of the rod. Montessori believed that this procedure would help children to feel the difference among the various lengths of rods. This means that in order to use the set of ten rods, the child must make ten trips to get the materials to his desk or rug and ten more trips to return the rods to the shelf. Other activities may involve fewer steps.

DISCUSSION OF MONTESSORI

Few research studies of the effects of Montessori education on later school adjustment, intellectual, or social development have been undertaken. Consequently, little can be said about the effects of this particular model of early education relative to no preschool experience or relative to other models of preschool education.

There is no doubt, however, that Maria Montessori made a significant contribution to the education of young children. Her ability to translate her observations and knowledge of young children into a comprehensive educational program was exceptional. The Montessori program is probably the most extensive curriculum following a single educational or developmental rationale in practice. Montessori capitalized on intrinsic motivation and advocated the development of each child at his own rate at a time when public education was using formal lecture methods even with very young children. She recognized the needs for activity and sensorimotor involvement of preschoolers and devised a curriculum based on materials that were attractive, colorful, and could be manipulated by the children. The standards for success were clear; a student undoubtedly felt a sense of satisfaction and mastery when he learned a Montessori task.

Many of the materials that Montessori developed, especially those for teaching mathematics, are excellent, and some have been incorporated into traditional preschool programs—with or without acknowledgment of the source. The rebirth of Montessori education in this country during the past decade has helped to stimulate the evaluation of the curriculum provided for young children in traditional nursery schools.

Despite its obvious contribution to the field of early education, however, the Montessori system of education has been criticized on several accounts. One criticism has to do with the narrow range of learning materials available to the children and with the limited number of different curriculum activities provided in each of the content areas of mathematics, science, geography, reading, and writing. In most Montessori classrooms, learning comes about through the child's use of the carefully prepared, self-correcting instructional materials, and little use is made of less formal supplementary learning materials including storybooks, books of general information for children, field trips, and special curriculum projects.

Another criticism of the Montessori system has to do with the classroom atmosphere of restraint and control over movement and social exchange. The instructional style is formal and rather solemn; informal communication, conversation, and discussion between children and adults is not generally encouraged.

Also a conspicuous omission from the Montessori curriculum is attention to social interactions with peers. While children in Montessori programs learn "social graces" in the form of manners and protocol, they have few opportunities for informal play with their peers. Few toys are present, and blocks, climbing equipment, and art and craft materials are either not available or are a tangential part of the school program.

Modern Montessori education, like all education for young children, is undergoing change. Many Montessori teachers in this country are moving in the direction of more flexibility in both style of education and curriculum. More extensive social interaction and informal educational experiences are being added to conventional Montessori programs, and the classroom atmosphere is lightening in many Montessori schools. Montessori teachers, like other educators of young children, are attempting to extract the strengths of both informal and formal educational models for young children.

16
Current Research
in Preschool Education

16 Current Research in Preschool Education

Since the advent of Head Start in 1965, there has been a marked increase in research in early childhood education. The Head Start program itself was the subject of a nationwide evaluation to test the effectiveness of the Head Start programs that sprang up all over the country. Research institutes and research units of universities began conducting controlled studies in early education. Support for this research has come primarily from federal funds administered through the United States Office of Economic Opportunity, the Office of Education, and (more recently) the Office of Child Development of the Department of Health, Education, and Welfare. Most of the research and demonstration projects conducted during the past several years have combined the expertise of psychologists and educators in program development and in the assessment of the effects of preschool education.

An effort has been made by experimental educators to define and to describe the educational philosophy espoused in their schools. They also discuss in detail the assessment techniques used to judge whether or not their programs have been effective. A brief review of this research is presented here. Rather than describing each research project individually, an overview will be presented of the kinds of curricula available in the experimental programs and of the effects these programs have on the children attending. Occasional references will be made to specific programs as examples.*

EDUCATIONAL PHILOSOPHY AND CURRICULA OF EXPERIMENTAL PRESCHOOL PROGRAMS

With hardly an exception, the experimental preschool programs that have been carried out during the past seven or eight years (since the advent of Head Start), and those presently being conducted, are attempts to enhance the cognitive functioning of the children participating. In deciding

---

*Bibliographical references citing reviews of preschool research, and references to specific experimental preschool projects are included at the end of this book.

specifically what curricular activities to emphasize in their programs, the first thing that program directors had to consider was the stated educational purposes of Head Start. Head Start was to be, among other things, a compensatory program to alleviate the learning and school-readiness deficiencies of young children from low income families through a comprehensive, multifaceted program.

These deficiencies were most evident in the areas of language skills and intellectual functioning and were considered by educators and psychologists to be the result of the discrepancies between the lower- and middle-class child's opportunities to learn, reinforcement for learning, and exposure to achievement-oriented adults. A preschool program could presumably benefit the child; however, the traditional preschool approach was not considered to be a promising model by the experimental educators for two reasons. First, nursery school teachers have traditionally relied heavily on informal learning and have tended to be suspicious of structured, didactic learning activities for young children. They stress the learning potential of play and self-directed exploration of materials and allow the curriculum of their schools to emerge out of the interests of the moment as expressed by the children. In preschool programs where teachers were not observant and responsive to the expressed interests of young children, there might, in fact, be very little curriculum of any kind other than social play.

A second reason for skepticism about the traditional nursery school model was the equivocal nature of the evidence that traditional nursery schools improved the intellectual functioning of the children attending. The results of studies conducted in this country during the 1930s and 1940s in which gains in IQ of children attending nursery schools were compared with those of children not attending, varied from study to study but were generally not very impressive. Consequently, many experimental preschool educators developed their own educational rationale and came on strong with an approach to early education that stressed didactic training in language and cognition and was in considerable contrast to the play- and discovery-oriented traditional nursery school.

In deciding precisely what should go into the training of the young child's intellect, project directors and educators turned to the psychologist. Their efforts to get help from developmental psychologists were somewhat frustrated by the paucity of comprehensive theories about language and cognitive development in young children. An adequate theory of early intellectual development should tell us not only what cognitive performances the child is capable of during the preschool years but also what are the processes by which he moves to higher levels of competence. Knowing this, a school program could presumably be devised that would be developmentally appropriate for the child and that would also support and stimulate further growth.

With the possible exception of the theory of the Swiss psychologist, Jean Piaget, we have virtually no comprehensive theories to guide us in the development of preschool curriculum. Theories are developed hand in hand with extensive observation and experimentation and, in fact, surprisingly little is known about the child's early mental development. Our theories tend to be hardly more than hunches based on bits and pieces of information about isolated aspects of the child's intellectual functioning. The bits and pieces are accumulating at a rapid rate, since early cognition and language development has been the subject of much research during the past several years, but comprehensive theories take time. In the meantime developmental psychologists have been helpful to the educator in identifying some of the relatively discrete skills and abilities that characterize the effective learner and in speculating about the processes by which these abilities develop. Clearly, Jean Piaget has been one of the most thought-provoking contributors to this endeavor. Piaget has delineated stages of early intellectual development through which the child passes beginning with the direct sensory-motor manipulation of objects in the environment and progressing to the use of symbols (such as pictures, parts of objects, or words) to represent objects. As the child learns to use symbols to represent objects he can "think" about objects that are not actually present in the environment; this is an important step toward intellectual maturity.

While the work of Piaget is rich in descriptive material about children's development, it gives less attention to the processes (other than getting older) by which the child moves from sensory-motor intelligence to conceptual intelligence and the use of symbols; that is, we know more from Piaget about what cognitive performances the child is capable of at three, four, and five than we know about how the child reached a particular stage and how the environment can support and facilitate his successful transition to the next stage of cognitive maturity. It is this last issue that is at the heart of an educational program, especially a compensatory one. Presumably, culturally disadvantaged children have been functioning in an environment that did *not* support their intellectual growth to the maximum of their potential. If this is the case, what is missing and how do we provide "catch up" education?

In spite of the fact the Piaget's contributions have been primarily descriptive rather than process oriented, his ingenious work has provided educators with rich normative observations that have led to speculations about process and have helped in the formulation of educational goals and curriculum. Two experimental preschool curricula that have been based on the observations and theorizing of Piaget are the program developed by Constance Kamii and her colleagues working at the Perry Preschool in Ypsilanti, Michigan, and the early childhood curriculum developed by Celia Stendler Lavatelli at the University of illinois.

Other psychologists have also contributed significantly to our thinking about early cognitive development and education. In *Intelligence and Experience*, published in 1961, J. McVicker Hunt attacked the notion that intelligence is predetermined and presented evidence for the modifiableness of intellectual ability as a function of experience. This view of intelligence gave impetus to the notion that the quality of the learning environment to which a child is subjected in his home and school can make a difference in his ultimate intellectual functioning. In 1964, in *Stability and Change in Human Characteristics* Benjamin Bloom emphasized the importance particularly of the early years in determining a child's ultimate intellectual functioning since the child's intellect seems to be relatively malleable up to six or seven years of age and relatively stable thereafter.

The well-known Harvard psychologist, Jerome Bruner, also has made significant contributions to our understanding of how, in fact, a child becomes "educated" through his provocative volumes *The Process of Education* (1960) and *Toward a Theory of Instruction* (1966).

With the help of the research and speculations of the psychologists, and through insights gained from classroom experience, experimental educators identified the elements of what they hoped would be a good compensatory school readiness curriculum for young children. Emphasis was given to language activities, cognitive stimulation, prereading, and premathematics activities.

Language Curriculum

In the area of language, lesson-type materials were developed for preschoolers that encouraged the child to use language extensively for both informal conversation purposes and as a tool to aid thinking and problem solving. Some materials give the child practice in "decoding" language, that is, in understanding a message delivered verbally by another person. Other tasks were designed to improve the child's ability to "encode," that is, to put his own thoughts into words that are effective in communicating a message. These functions are referred to in different terms by various experimental educators; they may, for example, be called "receptive" and "productive" language skills, but essentially they involve the processes of understanding the language of others and of using language effectively in communicating to others. No contemporary experimental preschool program that has come to our attention is without this component of the curriculum; all emphasize this aspect of the child's intellectual development.

Another aspect of language development that is a strategic part of most contemporary experimental preschool programs is training in the use of standard English dialect (in some instances, *in addition to* training in the use of the native language of the community). In a word, this simply suggests that the child should be helped to speak in complete sentences, using appropriate grammatical syntax, since this is the language of the school and of the books that he will soon be reading. Ghetto and other dialects have rich communication value for the child in his home and in his neighborhood, but they differ in some crucial ways from the standard English of the larger culture of which the child will become a part. If he develops facility with both dialects, he can presumably function effectively with either. While every contemporary intervention preschool program gives attention to this aspect of the child's language development, some programs place major emphasis on the informal opportunities for the preschool child to *hear* standard English spoken by his teachers, who serve as models as they talk and read to him. Other programs (for example, the one originally developed by Carl Bereiter and Siegfried Englemann and now being implemented by Englemann and Becker) stress pattern drill exercises in which the child reproduces simple factual statements (such as "This ball is red") using standard English speech forms.

The development of the child's vocabulary is another aspect of language behavior that is given attention in experimental programs. In most programs some carefully selected words (or "concepts" as they may be called) that the child should know and have facility in using are identified, and lesson plans are provided for teaching them. Among the words, or concepts, considered most basic to the child's school-readiness vocabulary and included in virtually all intervention programs are color names, names of geometric shapes, letter and number names, words that help the child to describe positional relations (such as over, under, in, out, or around), words that help him to describe temporal relations (such as before, after, earlier, and later) and spatial or directional relations (such as near, far, left, and right), and words that help him to describe the precise ordering of events or objects (such as first, last, biggest, and shortest).

The broader vocabulary of the child—that which reflects his store of general information—is attended to in some programs through enriched reading activities, social studies, science projects, and field trips. In many experimental programs, however, this aspect of the child's intellectual development is given little attention and is left to the ingenuity of the teacher to include as she sees fit. This could be an unfortunate omission in experimental programs, since the culturally different child appears to be at a decided disadvantage in the amount of general information he knows, at least, of a school-relevant kind, compared with his middle-class peers. The middle-class child is more likely to have been directly taught more factual information, to have been read to more often, and to have been taken to more places that contribute to his knowledge of the broader culture and the environment. This may give the middle-class child more self-confidence in his quest for school knowledge and may also arouse his interest in school when topics about which he knows something come up for discussion in the classroom.

In many of the experimental preschools, the informational content of the child's intellectual exercises is incidental to the teaching of the selected basic concepts—so that if, in the course of learning something about the concepts *under* and *over*, the child learns something about bridges and tunnels—fine; otherwise don't worry about bridges and tunnels. A more traditional nursery school approach to the child's intellectual education would be to teach him something about bridges and tunnels and to assume that, in the course of this and other similar experiences, he will gradually come to understand the meaning of the words *under* and *over*. Of course, the approaches are not incompatible. Both approaches are represented in a few experimental programs, such as the programs of the Bank Street College Preschool and the Tucson Early Education curriculum.

One aspect of language development that is *not* usually approached in a direct tutorial way with children in contemporary experimental preschool programs is the child's nonfluency with language. The speech of most preschoolers is riddled with falterings, stammerings, and hesitations. No attempt is made to make the child conscious of his nonfluency on the assumption that self-consciousness may be more interfering than facilitating. Instead, the child is given plenty of time to get out what he wishes to say, and teachers are expected to be patient, good listeners. Traditional nursery school teachers handle nonfluency in this way too.

Articulation errors are also assumed by many teachers in both traditional and experimental nursery schools to disappear with time and experience without specific speech training except in extreme cases. Certain articulation errors are very common among young children, for example, substitutions or distortions of the sounds l, r, s, st, and th. While, in some instances, a child may be asked to repeat a word after a teacher, producing the closest approximation of which he is capable, more often it is assumed that articulation errors will be reduced as a function of experience and exposure to good language models without any specific training.

If a child's speech is seriously distorted compared with that of his class-mates because of, for example, lingering "baby talk," the help of a speech therapist may be sought.

Cognitive Activities

Some aspects of the child's cognitive functioning that are closely related to language, but that presumably involve different skills and processes, have also been given attention in the experimental preschool programs. Included among them are the child's ability to pay attention and to listen carefully, to notice things in detail, and to remember what he has seen, heard, or experienced. Skills that are involved in the processing and cataloging of information are also stressed. Curricular activities may, for example, involve the classification of objects, animals, or people in ways that require attention to similarities and differences or to associational linkages of one kind or another. Activities that will presumably facilitate the child's ability to reason, think critically, and problem solve are also built into some of the experimental programs using prepared materials and activities. For the interested reader, a bibliography of curriculum guides and suggestions developed by the staffs of various experimental preschool programs is provided at the end of this book.

Prereading and Premath Activities

The child's readiness in two school-content areas, reading and arithmetic, has also been given attention in the compensatory preschool programs. In some programs, training in preparation for reading involves very general visual and auditory discrimination training. In these programs children are given opportunities to "read" pictures and other visual material, observing carefully for likenesses and differences and for details of color, form, and representational features. In the reading-specific training programs, visual discrimination includes working directly on the identification of the letters of the alphabet, simple word recognition, and word reproduction.

In the area of auditory training, the more general training programs stress listening skills, attention to the details of the spoken word, and to the "sound of things," while the reading-specific programs train the child in letter sounds and beginning phonics. The New Nursery School program developed originally by Dr. Glen Nimnicht and his colleagues in Greeley, Colorado is an example of a program in which specific training in reading is given. Children in this program spend time each day working with an electric typewriter on letter and word recognition, reproduction, and production with the help of an attending adult.

In general, the tendency is for the experimental compensatory pre-schools to include in their programs, training activities specific to reading as well as the more general training in visual and auditory discrimination. Traditional nursery schools, on the other hand, are likely to favor the more general discrimination training, leaving structured work with letters and words for the school years.

In preparation for math too, these programs vary in the specificity of their training. In programs with a more general approach to math readi-ness, the teacher will use concepts that express quantitative relations such as "less than," "more than," "first," "next," and "last" in talking with children. In programs with more specific training the child will be taught to count and to identify number symbols, to match numbers with their respective quantities (such as the symbol 3 with three dots), and to per-form simple manipulations involving addition, subtraction, and division. Here, too, the experimental preschools are likely to include specific math training in their programs while traditional nursery school teachers are more likely to stress the child's understanding and use of the more general quantitative concepts.

The Role of the Teacher

In virtually all of the experimental preschool programs, the teaching staff is carefully oriented to the educational philosophy of the school and to the specific goals of the curriculum. Teacher preparation for each school day is considered important. In programs in which the curriculum consists of "packaged" lessons, the teacher is trained to present the materi-als according to a standardized procedure. The school curriculum devel-oped originally by Bereiter and Engelmann is an example of a highly pre-scribed program of sequenced lessons in language, reading, and arithmetic in which the adult specifically instructs the child to give the appropriate verbal response. The Behavior Analysis program of Donald Bushell at the University of Kansas and the Ameliorative program developed by Merle Karnes at the University of Illinois are also examples of didactic, lesson-oriented approaches to preschool curriculum. In the program by Karnes, each child's academic deficiencies were diagnosed early in the school year through an analysis of his responses on the Illinois Test of Psycholin-guistic Abilities. Curricular activities were then tailored to meet each child's particular academic needs.

In other experimental preschool programs, teachers are given general guidelines for presenting lessons or activities but are then expected to de-velop each topic according to the cues given them by the children with whom they are working. Teacher-directed lesson-type activities are interspersed throughout the day with "supportive" self-directed activities. Examples of programs of this general description are the DARCEE program developed by Susan Gray and her colleagues in Nashville, Tennessee, the Autotelic Responsive Environment program developed by Glen Nimnicht and his colleagues at New Nursery School, and the Cognitive program of David Weikart in Ypsilanti, Michigan. In virtually all of the experimental preschool programs, the direct physical involvement of the child is sought by the teachers, and most learning materials include things to see, touch, and manipulate. In most programs, however, structured child involvement is valued more than free exploration, and children are encouraged to manipulate materials only in ways that are compatible with the teacher's academic goals for the activity. In this respect, experimental programs (with a few exceptions such as the Bank Street program) differ from the traditional preschool in which the child's own ingenuity, independence, and initiative in using toys and materials is given high status as an educational experience.

The grouping of children and the ratio of adults to children throughout the school day varies considerably from program to program in the experimental preschools. The tendency, with some exceptions, however, is to have a high ratio of adults to children so that children can be worked with individually or in small groups from time to time during the day. To insure rapport with the children and their families some, if not all, of the staff working directly with the children are selected from the same neighborhood or ethnic group as the children themselves. In integrated groups, a mix is sought for the staff as well. There is an attempt to enhance the child's pride in his identity, his family, and his community. The adults in the program who share the culture of the children present themselves as models who value their cultural heritage and who have confidence in their ability to accomplish the goals they have set for themselves.

Socialization and Play Activities

In a few experimental preschool programs, play activities and social-emotional development are given equal status with cognitive development in planning the educational environment. The Bank Street College program and the Tucson Early Education program are examples of preschool models in which considerable attention is given to each child's personal adjustment to school. Socialization and learning through play with peers and the exploration of materials within a social context is encouraged by the adults in these schools. With the exception of these programs, however, the development of interpersonal skills with peers is not a strategic part of the educational philosophy of experimental programs. Generally, the children in these programs do not have much time for options that involve "free play," and the skills involved in getting along cooperatively with one's companions are not particularly valued by the experimental educators responsible for the programs. This is an aspect of the experimental preschools that departs markedly from the traditional nursery school with its emphasis on peer relations and play.

Although the development of social skills with peers is neglected in most experimental preschools, socialization that prepares the child specifically for school is given much attention. The development of positive attitudes about "school," "teachers," and "learning" are considered to be critical ingredients of a good compensatory school situation for these young children. Helping the children to learn school-appropriate protocol and to *want* to achieve academically is stressed.

To develop traits that will help children to achieve successfully in school, the experimental preschool educators rely heavily on the principles of behavior modification and reinforcement theory. The importance of school attendance being a pleasant, satisfying experience for the child is stressed by most of the intervention programs on the assumption that only then will the child become a willing, motivated learner. An attempt is made to have demands and expectations be developmentally appropriate and reasonable so that the child experiences many successes and few failures. Whenever possible, tasks are arranged to increase gradually in difficulty so that children continue to improve in their school performances without stress or frustration. Positive reinforcement for school-appropriate behavior in the form of teacher approval, or material rewards is recognized by all programs as an important source of the young child's motivation to do well in school. Disapproval for inappropriate school behavior also enters the picture, although harsh punishment for misbehavior is not recommended or considered beneficial, and children are not punished for making errors. In fact, in Nimnicht's program at New Nursery School, teachers are explicitly instructed to refrain from correcting a child, indicating to him that he has made an error. Many of the materials used in this program are self-correcting in that they can be completed in only one way—the correct way. Therefore, it is not considered necessary for the adults to point out a child's error.

Parent Involvement

Another ingredient in experimental programs that is given considerable emphasis is communication and rapport with the parents of the children participating in the programs on the assumption that school effects will be weak and short-lived unless the child's home environment supports the school's orientation. Involvement of parents varies from participation in a PTA-type organization in some programs to the extensive involvement of the parent—usually the mother—directly in the child's education in others. In the programs developed by Weikart in Ypsilanti, Michigan and Gray in Nashville, Tennessee, workers go out to the homes of the children and train mothers to teach their children by using especially prepared curriculum materials that bolster, support, and extend the curriculum of the school. In this way the mother presumably becomes a strategic partner with the school in the education of her child. In other programs, parents function as governing board members or school staff and, thus, witness and contribute to the school's education of their children.

In summary, the experimental compensatory preschool programs, with a few notable exceptions, can be characterized as "no nonsense," didactic, preacademic training programs for young children. Tasks of a cognitive, school-readiness kind are the core of the curriculum, and playtimes and free socializing among peers is tangential to the primary goals of the programs. While a few programs encourage free exploration and discovery learning, most rely heavily on structured, teacher-directed learning activities.

The children participating in these programs are uniformly treated with respect and kindness, but every effort is made to convey to them that they are attending the preschool to learn and to prepare for school. There is a "hard sell" approach to the development of the child's concept of himself as a student, and of the school as a place for academic learning.

ASSESSING THE EFFECTS
OF EXPERIMENTAL
PRESCHOOL PROGRAMS

Though demonstration nursery schools differ in the style of education offered, there are certain features that characterize all programs that are recognized as "experimental." One such feature is that there must be an assessment component that is a strategic part of the total project. The assessment procedures must be carried out according to sound experimental principles, and the data gathered during the assessment phases of the project must be quantifiable, that is, expressed in terms of objective scores, ratings, or observations.

The most common research design used to assess preschool effects is one in which the development of children who have attended a preschool program (identified as the "experimental" group) is compared with the development of children who have not attended (the "control" group). Typically all of the children from both groups are tested on whatever assessment measures are to be used prior to or early in the school experience and, again, at the end of the experience. The development of the school children is compared with that of the nonschool children to see whether or not the school experience has enhanced the development of those children compared with the nonschool children. In some research projects, groups of children attending contrasting styles or models of preschool education have been compared with each other and with children who did not attend any preschool.

In all research of this kind it is essential that the groups of children being compared be similar on factors that effect development. They should be of the same general socioeconomic background, the educational and occupational makeup of their parents should be similar, and the children themselves should be of similar ability at the beginning of the study. Otherwise differences at the end of the study that are attributed to "school effects" in fact could be the result of home influences.

By far the most common type of assessment instrument used in investigating the effects of experimental preschool programs on children's development is the standardized test of general intelligence, or the IQ test. The most commonly used tests are the Stanford-Binet Test of Intelligence, the Illinois Test of Psycholinguistic Abilities, the Peabody Picture Vocabulary Test, and the Wechsler Intelligence Scale for Children. Other instruments that have been used to assess aspects of children's intellectual functioning and related skills include the Caldwell Preschool Inventory, the Ravens Progressive Matrices, the Goodenough Draw-a-Man Test, the Columbia Mental Maturity Scale, and the Bender-Gestalt Test.

The use of intelligence tests for assessing the effects of preschool programs has been severely criticized by project directors, teachers, and some psychologists. The criticisms have involved essentially two issues. One issue has to do with the stigma that may be attached to children who obtain low IQ scores. Unfortunately the IQ (Intelligence Quotient) and other similar indices have come to represent, in the minds of many people, the constitutionally determined potential intelligence of the child being tested. In fact, it represents not what the child *can* do in the area of intellectual performance (that is, what he is constitutionally capable of doing), but what he *did* do—on a particular occasion when asked to respond to a particular set of test questions. There is every reason to believe that an individual's performance on intelligence tests—particularly the performance of a very young child—is effected by many things other than innate intelligence. The child's mood of the moment, his rapport with the examiner, and his motivation to do well all undoubtedly can effect performance. Young children are very inexperienced test-takers. They have not yet participated in situations in which they are confronted by an unfamiliar adult who asks them questions and presents them with problems to solve that require their doing the best they can. Because the occasion may seem strange or frightening to them and because they do not understand the significance of it, they may not choose to perform with maximum attention and effort at all. The instruction to "do the best you can" may have little meaning for a three- or four-year-old in an unfamiliar situation. Finally, the child's performance may be effected by the *opportunities* he has had to learn the knowledge and to develop the skills that are being assessed. When used appropriately, tests of intellectual functioning can be very useful since they give us a rough approximation of a child's intellectual abilities as he is willing to demonstrate them in a testlike situation, but they should not be considered a precise measure of a child's native intelligence.

A second criticism of the use of intelligence tests for school assessment is the fact that the tests are not specific to the curriculum of the school; consequently, they may not be very appropriate instruments for testing school effects. This point is well taken. If an experimental educator and his staff have identified specific concepts to teach their children, let us say concepts of time and space, why not test the children's understanding of these concepts? Similarly, if the school teaches the children the visual and auditory discriminations specifically involved in reading, why not test them to see if they have improved in making these particular discriminations? While IQ tests undoubtedly incorporate some of the content of compensatory preschool programs, they sample intellectual functioning broadly and are not designed to test specifically what has been taught in the experimental preschools. In response to this criticism, some experimenters have devised their own assessments instruments based on content that has been incorporated into their particular curricula. Also standardized school readiness tests have been added to the battery of assessment instruments in a number of projects on the assumption that these tests assess the child's school-specific skills. The Metropolitan Readiness Test, for example, has been used in several projects for comparing the readiness skills of children who have attended preschool with those who have not.

It would, indeed, seem profitable to incorporate into the assessment procedures of experimental preschools, tests of the child's mastery of specifically what the school has elected to teach, but the claim that tests of general intelligence are not, by virtue of their content, appropriate instruments for assessing preschool effects is open to question. The goals of most preschools include the improvement of the general intellectual functioning of the children attending. Besides teaching the child specific concepts and something about letters, words, and numbers, preschools purport to improve the child's abilities to use language effectively, to process and organize information, and to think and reason—some of the very things that intelligence tests are designed to measure.

The use of intelligence tests as assessment instruments probably poses limitations more of omission than of commission; that is, however appropriate these tests may be, they do not include an assessment of many of the things that project directors and their staffs wish to assess. Besides omitting topics included in the school curriculum, they do not tell us anything about the child's general adjustment to the school situation, his interest and involvement in the school program, his attitudes about teachers, his concept of himself as a learner, his willingness to try new tasks, and his coping skills when faced with mild failure or with problem-solving situations that are difficult for him. All of these things would seem to be relevant to the goals of most experimental programs, yet none are directly assessed by intelligence or school readiness tests. Some progress is being made in the development of assessment instruments to supplement tests of cognitive functioning but the comprehensive studies that have been completed to date have relied heavily on the IQ test.

RESEARCH RESULTS

Given the potpourri of different educational philosophies and curricula that have been under investigation in this country since 1965, what can be concluded about the effects of experimental preschool programs on the children who attend them? First, as nearly as we can say, preschools do not uniformly have the same effect on children's intellectual functioning, (the only aspect of child behavior that has been studied extensively to date). Some programs have demonstrated significant increases in intelligence test scores or school readiness test scores of the children attending, and some have not. It is not unusual for a project using two or three different standardized measures of intelligence to demonstrate the superiority of the school children on one or two of the measures, but not on a third. In projects in which program-specific assessment instruments have been used (that is, tests to test specifically what the school purports to teach), the children may show superiority on these tests, but not on the more general tests of intelligence. When multiple classrooms or multiple schools are involved, or when replication studies have been done, a school program may produce significant change in one instance but not in another.

This pattern of results would look like chance effects (in which a few studies yield significant results by virtue of one fluke or another) except for two factors. First, more of the intervention studies do show positive effects than would be expected by chance alone and, second, the group differences that occur consistently favor the school children over the non-school control children. Results due to chance would not ordinarily be biased in this way; it does seem that many of the preschool programs investigated have had some facilitating effect on the children attending.

The next most obvious question to ask is what differentiates the programs that demonstrated positive effects from those that did not? Here, too, some educated, albeit tentative, guesses can be made from the pattern of results that is emerging. Two kinds of data can be examined. We can examine the educational philosophy and curricula of the programs in which the school children differed from their nonschool control children, and we can consider the results of the small number of studies in which contrasting school curricula have been compared with each other. From these sources of data a few generalizations can be made concerning the characteristics of programs that show positive results. First, programs that seem to enhance children's performances on cognitive tests are likely to be ones in which the school has *explicit cognitive goals* and a *planned curriculum* designed to implement these goals. The school curriculum may include projects that emerge from the idiosyncratic interests of the children themselves (depending on the school's educational philosophy and the extent to which child initiative is valued), but the successful experimental preschools do not rely solely on this "emergent" process; project directors and teachers plan the learning environment carefully and see to it that the children are, in fact, given opportunities to learn what the school purports to teach.

Given this attention to intellectual goals, it does *not* seem to be the case that any single style or model of preschool education is consistently superior to others. Among the programs that seem to have produced improved test performances in children are some that are highly didactic, lesson-oriented programs (of the Bereiter and Englemann type, for example). In these programs, children are presented materials according to prescribed lesson plans, and the child is expected to attend and to respond precisely as directed by his teacher. Children are given time to relax and socialize between the didactic sessions that are spaced throughout the school day.

But also among the successful programs are ones in which the school philosophy incorporates a more child-oriented approach to the implementation of cognitive goals. In the research projects that compare school children with nonschool children, and also in the few studies conducted to date that compare experimental models of education with each other, no one type of program emerges as consistently superior to others. An extensive federally funded research project is presently being conducted called Planned Variation to study both the overall and contrasting effects of various styles of preschool education. While the results from the Planned Variation project are tentative (since they represent only the first year of a longitudinal study), they too suggest beneficial effects from programs that differ widely on dimensions of didacticism and formality. In the apparently successful programs of Gray, Nimnicht, Weikart, the Bank Street program, the Tucson program, and others, curriculum materials are selected for their interest to the children as well as for their academic relevance. Teacher-directed learning activities are adapted along the way to capture and maintain the children's interest. Learning goals are implemented in several ways throughout the school day in these programs, sometimes through structured or teacher-directed activities, but other times through informal teacher-child communications, and still other times through the child's private use of materials and equipment. Learning activities are incorporated into play materials and games.

It is not clear from the assessment research to date that any specific kind of staff credential is necessary for success, but positive results may depend on the total level of expertise and effort expended on behalf of the program. The staffs of most of the successful programs include the services of early education consultants and psychologists. The teaching staff usually includes some combination of trained or experienced nursery school, kindergarten or primary teachers, paraprofessional assistants, parents, and interested volunteers. The ratio of adults to children is likely to be five or six children (or fewer) for each adult through much of the school day. In virtually all of the successful programs, extensive time and effort is given to in-service training of staff. The staff may meet together daily, two or three times a week or at least weekly, and many hours of time are devoted to program planning and curriculum development. Staff *expertise* and *effort* may very well be two of the crucial factors differentiating the experimental programs from their control groups in studies where a control group is a "regular" Head Start program or a traditional neighborhood nursery school or day care center. It is rare, indeed, for an unselected neighborhood nursery school—Head Start or any other kind—to be the focus of so much time and effort on behalf of its school program for the children. In generalizing from experimental programs to grass roots Head Start programs, community nursery schools and day care centers this factor should be kept in mind. It seems unlikely that we could expect to replicate the results of experimental programs in other schools or day care centers if these centers are seriously understaffed and are giving little attention to program development.

17
The State of Art

17 The State of Art

There is much we have yet to learn about young children that can help us to provide a wholesome environment for their care and education during the time they spend away from home in programs for the young. Undoubtedly, important effects of the preschool experience have not even been identified in the assessment studies conducted to date, and some of these effects may differentiate one preschool model from another. We have not even addressed ourselves to important questions such as are some models of preschool education intrinsically more rewarding and personally satisfying to children than others; that is, given a choice of program, would children prefer one model of education over another? Do some models provide learning experiences that generalize more effectively to new situations both in and out of school than others? Do some styles of education serve the child more effectively over time than others? One distressing feature of the preschool evidence is that the superiority of the nursery school children over the nonschool control children dissipates quickly unless the experience is bolstered by a continuing program of compensatory education into the school years. This certainly suggests the continued evaluation of long-term school effects as well as short-term effects.

Experimental educators are just beginning to probe for the answers to questions about the preschool experience other than whether or not it raises IQ. Unfortunately, most of the assessment studies of preschool effects are very global in design. They tell us whether or not children attending school benefit on the particular test instruments used compared with nonschool children, but they do not tell us what factors, specifically, in the school experience caused the effects. Preschool is a massive intervention in the young child's life that includes not only preacademic learning experiences but also socialization experiences with teachers and peers and experiences that probably effect the child's outgoingness and self-confidence. Beneficial school effects demonstrated in research projects of the kind conducted thus far could be due to any or all of these factors —or to still other factors that have not been identified.

To study specific aspects of a school program, research designs must be used that make it possible to isolate the effects of one aspect of the school program from other aspects. If, for example, an experimenter wishes to determine the effects of a particular prereading curriculum on children's early reading skills, he could give one half of the children attending a preschool program special prereading sessions that are incorporated into their regular school program while the other half of the children in the program do not have these sessions. The children who get the special instruction then become the experimental group, and the other children in the class become the control group. If the children are assigned to groups in an unbiased way, any extra increment in the prereading skills of the experimental group compared with their classmates can, with some confidence, be attributed to exposure to the special reading materials.*

A research strategy of this kind was used in a study conducted at the University of Minnesota in which a subgroup of children attending a day care center (the experimental group) was exposed to daily sessions of an "expansive" teaching style—a style in which the teachers made liberal use of discussion and explanations about activities being presented, encouraged questions and comments from children, and gave recognition and approval for initiative taken by the children themselves. A second group of children attending the same day care center (the control group) was given the same number of sessions and the same curriculum materials, but the teachers provided only necessary task information and, except for a show of general friendliness toward the children, interacted with them primarily on invitation. Following five weeks of these special sessions, the data indicated that the children working with the expansive teachers were themselves more expansive in their conversations and discussions with those teachers. They also performed better, compared with the children in the control group, in two test situations that required expanded verbal output. These findings suggest that children's language behavior is, in fact, affected by the communication style of the adults in the classroom. The use of expansive communication styles by the adults seems to be one way to encourage children to make more extensive use of relevant comments, questions, and discussion.

Studies of this kind will help in answering more probing questions about the effects of specific components of the educational experience for young children. The effects of prereading, premath, and language curriculum could be studied in isolation from each other and from other curricular components. The effects of such things as extensive informal story-reading sessions on children's motivation to participate in prereading

---

* A more sophisticated design of this kind would also include what is called a placebo group—a group of children who get the same amount of "special attention" as the prereading group but of some kind other than prereading instruction so that attention per se could be ruled out as a critical factor in the study.

activities could be studied. The effects of contrasting styles of teacher-child interaction could be investigated and compared with each other while other program factors are held constant. Highly didactic instructional teaching sessions, for example, could be compared with sessions in the same classroom that emphasize informal social interaction and verbal exchange between teachers and children to see if the contrasting styles have differential effects on children's acquisition of knowledge, attention to the activity, motivation to participate in the learning experience, independence, and child-initiative in the activity. It is a possibility that didactic programs oriented to raising IQ and other test scores produce a greater immediate test effect while programs that stimulate the child's motivation to participate in school and intrinsic interest in learning produce more student initiative and personal involvement in school activities. If this is the case, a young child's long-range educability may be served better in a program in which he is learning less (of a test-specific kind) but is enjoying it more! We do not know that this is so, but it is a possibility that is in accord with the intuitive hunches of many preschool teachers, developmental psychologists, and parents of young children.

Experimental educators are also working on means of assessing school effects other than the usual "test." Systematic observations of children and of teacher-child interactions directly in the school situation are badly needed. Extensive observations of this kind could be invaluable to the study of important aspects of the educational *process* as well as the *product*. Tests of intelligence and school readiness tell us something about what the child has learned and how well he functions on intellectual tasks, but they tell us nothing about how the child acquired the knowledge and skill he possesses. Observations of children actually participating in learning and play activities may give us some important leads as to how the children acquire the abilities they have. This information is crucial if we are to improve our curriculum and our teaching strategies.

Observations may also help us to describe and evaluate our teaching methods more explicitly and to differentiate among contrasting models of preschool education. The fact that we *have* different models and educational philosophies does not necessarily mean that we are implementing our respective values or reaching our respective goals. Observations can help us to identify the ways in which preschool environments actually do differ from each other, independent of the claims of their proponents.

The development of instruments to measure the impact that school is having on the families of the children attending is another high priority area in the minds of many project directors and their staffs. Long term school effects may depend upon family support of the childs educational experiences.

The next five to ten years would seem to be a critical period of time for the assimilating of new information by educators, psychologists, parents, and community representatives who are responsible for programs for young children. We have every reason to expect research in early education to provide new and important leads to program improvements. The current trend in this research is definitely in the direction of studying the educational process as well as the product, and in seeking answers to more probing questions about school effects than have been asked to date.

References for Additional Information

Adkins, Dorothy C., and Hannah Herman. *Hawaii Head Start Evaluation—1968–1969: Final Report.* Honolulu: Hawaii University, Head Start Research and Evaluation Center, 1970.   R *

Almeida, Cynthia. *A Program to Strengthen Early Childhood Education in Poverty Area Schools.* New York: Center for Urban Education, 1969.   R

Alpern, Gerald D. "The Failure of a Nursery School Enrichment Program for Culturally Disadvantaged Children." *American Journal of Orthopsychiatry,* 36 (1966):244–245.   R

Appalachia Preschool Education Program, Charleston, West Virginia. Model Programs Childhood Education, Washington, D.C.: U.S. Department of Health, Education, and Welfare, Office of Education, National Center for Educational Communication, 1970.   C

Badger, Earladeen. "A Mothers' Training Program—The Road to a Purposeful Existence." *Children,* 18 (1971):168–173.   R

Ball, Samuel, and Gerry A. Bogatz. *The First Year of "Sesame Street": An Evaluation.* Princeton, New Jersey: Educational Testing Service, 1970.   R

Barbrack, Christopher R. "The Effect of Three Home Visiting Strategies upon Measures of Children's Academic Aptitude and Maternal Teaching Behaviors." *DARCEE Papers and Reports,* Vol. 4, No. 1, 1970. Nashville, Tennessee: George Peabody College for Teachers, John F. Kennedy Center for Research on Education and Human Development.   R

Barbrack, Christopher R., and Della N. Horton. "Educational Intervention in the Home and Paraprofessional Career Development: A Second Generation Mother Study with an Emphasis on Costs and Benefits." *DARCEE Papers and Reports,* Vol. 4, No. 3, 1970. Nashville, Tennessee: George Peabody College for Teachers, John F. Kennedy Center for Research on Education and Human Development.   R

Beller, E. Kuno. "Teaching Styles and Their Effects on Problem Solving Behavior in Head Start Programs." In *Critical Issues in Research Related to Disadvantaged Children,* Edith Grotberg, ed., Princeton, New Jersey: Educational Testing Service, 1969.   R

Bereiter, Carl. "Instructional Planning in Early Compensatory Education." In *Disadvantaged Child,* Vol. 1. Jerome Hellmuth, ed., pp. 339–347. New York: Brunner/Mazel, 1968.   C

* The letters R and C after each reference indicate whether the content of that reference is primarily a research report (R) or whether it contains information about curriculum (C) activities.

Bereiter, Carl. "An Academic Preschool for Disadvantaged Children: Conclusions from Evaluation Studies." Paper presented at the Hyman Blumberg Memorial Symposium on Research in Early Childhood Education, February 1971, The Johns Hopkins University. R

Bereiter, Carl, and Siegfried Engelmann. *Teaching Disadvantaged Children in the Preschool.* Englewood Cliffs, N.J.: Prentice Hall, 1966b. C and R

Berger, Barbara. *A Longitudinal Investigation of Montessori and Traditional Prekindergarten with Inner City Children: A Comparative Assessment of Learning Outcomes.* New York: Center for Urban Education, 1969. R

Biber, Barbara, Edna Shapiro, and David Wickens. *Promoting Cognitive Growth, A Developmental-Interaction Point of View.* Washington, D.C.: National Association for the Education of Young Children, 1971. C

Bissell, Joan S. *Implementation of Planned Variation in Head Start.* Washington, D.C.: United States Department of Health, Education, and Welfare. Office of Child Development, 1971. R

Blank, Marion. "Implicit Assumptions Underlying Preschool Intervention Programs." *Journal of Social Issues, 26* (1970):15–34. R

Blank, Marion, and Frances Solomon. "A Tutorial Language Program to Develop Abstract Thinking in Socially Disadvantaged Preschool Children." *Child Development, 39* (1968):379–389. R

Blank, Marion, and Frances Solomon. "How Shall the Disadvantaged Child be Taught?" *Child Development, 40* (1969):47–61. C and R

Bloom, Benjamin S. *Stability and Change in Human Characteristics.* New York: Wiley, 1964. R

Boger, Robert P. *Parents as Primary Change Agents in an Experimental Head Start Program of Language Intervention: Experimental Program Report.* Detroit: Merrill-Palmer Institute and East Lansing Michigan State University, Head Start Evaluation and Research Center, 1969. R

Brottman, Marvin A. "Language Remediation for the Disadvantaged Preschool Child." *Monograph of the Society for Research in Child Development,* No. 124. Chicago: Society for Research in Child Development, 1968. R

Bushell, Don, Jr., and Joan M. Jacobson. "The Simultaneous Rehabilitation of Mothers and Their Children." Paper presented at the Annual Meeting of American Psychological Association, August 1968, San Francisco, California. R

Butler, Annie L. *Current Research in Early Childhood Education.* Washington, D.C.: National Education Association, American Association of Elementary-Kindergarten-Nursery Education, 1970. R

Caldwell, Bettye M., and Julius B. Richmond. "The Children's Center in Syracuse, New York." In *Early Child Care,* Laura L. Dittmann, ed., pp. 326–358. New York: Atherton Press, 1968. R

Cazden, Courtney. "The Situation: A Neglected Source of Social Class Differences in Language Use." *Journal of Social Issues, 26* (1970):35–60. R

Center for Early Development Education, Little Rock, Arkansas. Model Programs Early Childhood Education. Washington, D.C.: U.S. Department of

Health, Education, and Welfare, Office of Education, National Center for Educational Communication, 1970. R

Cicirelli, Victor, John W. Evans, and Jeffry S. Schiller. "The Impact of Head Start: A Reply to the Report Analysis." *Harvard Educational Review, 40* (1970):105–129. R

Clarizio, Harvey F. "Maternal Attitude Change Associated with Involvement in Project Head Start." *Journal of Negro Education, 37* (1968):106–113. R

Clasen, Robert, Jo Ellen Speak, and Michael P. Tomaro. "A Comparison of the Relative Effectiveness of Two Types of Preschool Compensatory Programming." *Journal of Educational Research, 62* (1969):401–405. R

Coleman, James S. *Equality of Educational Opportunity.* Washington, D.C.: U.S. Department of Health, Education and Welfare, National Center for Educational Statistics, 1966. R

Costello, Joan, with Eleanor Binstock. *Review and Summary of a National Survey of the Parent-Child Center Program.* Washington, D.C.: U.S. Department of Health, Education, and Welfare, Office of Child Development, August, 1970. R

Curtis, Carroll A., and Michael D. Berzonsky. *Preschool and Primary Education Project, 1966–1967.* Harrisburg, Pennsylvania: Annual Progress Report to the Ford Foundation, Council of Human Services, 1967. R

Datta, Lois-ellin. *A Report on Evaluation Studies of Project Head Start.* Paper read at Annual Meeting of the American Psychological Association Convention, 1969, San Francisco, California. R

Denenberg, Victor H. *Education of the Infant and Young Child.* New York: Academic Press, 1970. R

Deutsch, Cynthia P., and Martin Deutsch. "Brief Reflections on the Theory of Early Childhood Enrichment Programs." *Early Education,* Robert D. Hess and Roberta M. Bear, eds., pp. 83–90. Chicago: Aldine, 1968. R

Dickie, Joyce P. "Effectiveness of Structured-Unstructed (Traditional) Methods of Language Training." In *Language Remediation for the Disadvantaged Preschool Child,* Marvin A. Brottman, ed., pp. 62–79. Chicago: *Monograph of the Society for Research in Child Development, 33* (1968), Serial No. 124. R

DiLorenzo, Louis T., Ruth Salter, and James J. Brady. "An Evaluation Study of Pre-Kindergarten Program for Educationally Disadvantaged Children: Follow-Up and Replication." *Exceptional Child, 35* (1968):111–119. R

Disadvantaged Children and Their First School Experiences: ETS-OEO Longitudinal Study, Theoretical Considerations and Measurement Strategies. Princeton, New Jersey: Educational Testing Service, 1968. R

Early Childhood Education Learning System for Three- and Four-Year Old Migrant Children, McAllen, Texas, Evaluation Report, 1968–1969. Austin, Texas: Southwest Educational Development Laboratory, 1969. R

Early Childhood Project New York City. Preschool Program in Compensatory Education. Washington, D.C.: U.S. Department of Health, Education, and Welfare, Office of Education, Bureau of Elementary and Secondary Education, 1970. R

Education of the Disadvantaged: An Evaluation Report on Title I Elementary and Secondary Act of 1965 Fiscal Year 1968. Washington, D.C.: U.S. Department of Health, Education, and Welfare, Office of Education. OE-37013-68, 1970. R

Elkind, David. "The Case for Academic Preschool: Fact or Fiction." *Young Children, 25* (1970):132–140. R

Erickson, Edsel L., Joseph McMillan, Jane Bonnel, Louis Hofmann, and Orel D. Callahan. *Experiments in Head Start and Early Education—Curriculum Structures and Teacher Attitudes.* Final Report. Washington, D.C.: Office of Economic Opportunity, Division of Research and Evaluation, Project Head Start. Contract No. OEO-4150, November 1, 1969. R

Evaluation Report: State Compensatory Preschool Educational Program 1968–1969. Report to the Governor's Advisory Committee on Preschool Educational Programs. Mimeographed. Sacramento: California State Department of Education, Division of Compensatory Education, Bureau of Preschool Educational Programs, 1970. R

Fleege, U. H. *A Study of the Comparative Effectiveness of Montessori Preschool Education.* Mimeographed. Chicago: Midwest Montessori Teacher Training Center, 1967. R

Fowler, William. "A Developmental Learning Approach to Infant Care in a Group Setting." Paper presented at the Merrill-Palmer Conference on Research and Teaching of Infant Development, Detroit, February 1971. R

Fowler, William, Darla Gruhman, Sandra Hart, Ann Rotstein, and Sonya Ward. 1969–1970. "Demonstration Infant Day Care and Education Program." Interim Report. Toronto: Ontario Institute for Studies in Education, n.d. R

Fuschillo, Jean C. "Enriching the Preschool Experience of Children from Age 3. II. Evaluation of the Children." *Children, 15* (1968): 140–143. C

Gilmer, Barbara, James O. Miller, and Susan W. Gray. "Intervention with Mothers and Young Children: A Study of Intrafamily Effects," *DARCEE Papers and Reports, Vol. 4, No. 11, 1970.* Nashville, Tennessee: Education and Human Development. C

Glick, Joseph. "Some Problems in the Evaluation of Pre-School Intervention Programs." In *Early Education,* Robert D. Hess and Roberta Meyer Bear, eds., pp. 215–222. Chicago: Aldine, 1968. R

Goldberg, Miriam L. "Adapting Teacher Style to Pupil Differences: Teachers for Disadvantaged Children." *Merrill-Palmer Quarterly, 10* (1964):565–75. R

Gordon, Ira J. *A Parent Education Approach to Provision of Early Stimulation for the Culturally Disadvantaged.* Gainesville: University of Florida, College of Education, 1967. C

Gordon, Ira J. *Early Childhood Stimulation Through Parent Education.* Final Report. Gainesville: University of Florida, College of Education, 1969. R

Gordon, Ira J. *Parent Involvement in Compensatory Education.* Urbana, Illinois: University of Illinois Press, 1970. R

Gray, Susan W., and Rupert A. Klaus. "An Experimental Preschool Program for Culturally Deprived Children." *Child Development,* 36 (1965):887–898. R

Gray, Susan, Rupert A. Klaus, J. Miller, and B. Forrester. *Before First Grade.* New York: Teachers College, Columbia University, 1966. C

Gray, Susan W., and Rupert A. Klaus. "The Early Training Project and Its General Rationale." In *Early Education,* Robert D. Hess and Roberta Meyer Bear, Eds., pp. 63–70. Chicago: Aldine, 1968. R

Gray, Susan W., and Rupert A. Klaus, "The Early Training Project: A Seventh-Year Report." *Child Development,* 41 (1970):909–924. R

Grotberg, Edith, ed. *Critical Issues in Research Related to Disadvantaged Children.* Princeton, New Jersey: Educational Testing Service, 1969. R

Grotberg, Edith, ed. *Review of Research 1965 to 1969.* Washington, D.C.: U.S. Department of Health, Education, and Welfare, Office of Child Development, Bureau of Head Start and Early Childhood, 1969. R

Grotberg, Edith, ed. Day Care: *Resources for Decisions.* Washington, D.C.: Office of Economic Opportunity, June 1971. R

Hellmuth, Jerome, ed. *Disadvantaged Child: Head Start and Early Intervention* Vol. 2., New York: Brunner/Mazel, 1968. R

Hellmuth, Jerome, ed. *Disadvantaged Child: Compensatory Education, A National Debate.* Vol. 3., New York: Brunner/Mazel, 1970. R

Hervey, Sarah D. *Attitudes, Expectations, and Behavior of Parents of Head Start and Non-Head Start Children: Report Number One.* Detroit, Michigan: Merrill-Palmer Institute and East Lansing: Michigan State University, Head Start Evaluation and Research Center, 1968. R

Hess, Robert D. and Shipman, Virginia C. "Early Experience and the Socialization of Cognitive Modes in Children." *Child Development,* 36 (1965):869–886. R

Hodges, Walter L., and Howard H. Spicker. "The Effects of Preschool Experiences on Culturally Deprived Children." *Young Children,* 23 (1967):23–43. R

The Impact of Head Start—An Evaluation of the Effects of Head Start on Children's Cognitive and Affective Development. Vol. I and II. Westinghouse Learning Corporation/Ohio University, June 1969. Available from Clearinghouse for Scientific and Technical Information, U.S. Department of Commerce, Springfield, Va. R

Infant Education Research Project. Washington, D.C.: U.S. Department of Health, Education, and Welfare, Office of Education, Bureau of Elementary and Secondary Education, n.d. R

Karnes, Merle B. "Educational Intervention at Home by Mothers of Disadvantaged Infants." *Child Development,* 41 (1970):925–935. R

Karnes, Merle B., Audrey S. Hodgins, and James A. Teska. "Evaluation of Two Preschool Programs for Disadvantaged Children: A Traditional and a Highly Structured Experimental Preschool." *Exceptional Children,* 34 (1968):667–676. R

Karnes, Merle B., James A. Teska, and Audrey S. Hodgins. "A Longitudinal Study of Disadvantaged Children Who Participated in Three Different Preschool Programs." Paper presented at the meeting of the American Educational Research Association, 1969, Los Angeles. R

Katz, Lilian G. "Children and Teachers in Two Types of Head Start Classes." *Young Children, 24* (1969):342–349. R

Keister, Mary Elizabeth. *A Demonstration Project in Group Care of Infants. Phase II.* Narrative description of project proposal. Washington, D.C.: U.S. Department of Health, Education, and Welfare, Community Services Administration, Child Welfare Research and Demonstration Grants Program, 1970. R

Kittrell, Flemmie P. "Enriching the Preschool Experience of Children from Age 3. I. The Program." *Children, 15* (1968):135–39. C

Klaus, Rupert A., and Susan W. Gray. "The Early Training Project for Disadvantaged Children. A Report After Five Years." *Monograph of the Society for Research in Child Development*, No. 120. Chicago: University of Chicago Press, 1968. R

Klein, Jenny W. "Planned Variation in Head Start Programs" *Children, 18* (1971):8–12. R.

Kraft, Ivor, Jean Fuschilo, and Elizabeth Herzog. *Prelude to School: An Evaluation of an Inner-City Preschool Program.* Washington, D.C.: U.S. Department of Health, Education, and Welfare, Social and Rehabilitation Service, Children's Bureau, 1968. R

Kritchevsky, Sybil. "Physical Settings in Day Care Centers." In *Group Day Care as a Child-Rearing Environment. An Observational Study of Day Care Programs*, Elizabeth Prescott and Elizabeth Jones, eds., pp. 258–336. Pasadena, California:1967, Pacific Oaks College. R

Kugel, Robert B., and Mabel H. Parsons. *Children of Deprivation— Changing the Course of Familial Retardation.* Washington, D.C.: U.S. Department of Health, Education, and Welfare, Social and Rehabilitation Service, Children's Bureau, 1967. R

Levenstein, Phyllis. "Cognitive Growth in Preschoolers Through Verbal Inter-Action with Mothers." *American Journal of Orthopsychiatry, 40* (1970):426–432. R

Maccoby, Eleanor, and Miriam Zellner. *Experiments in Primary Education: Aspects of Project Follow-Through.* New York: Harcourt Brace Jovanovich, 1970. R

McDill, Edward L., Mary S. McDill, and J. Timothy Streke. *Strategies for Success in Compensatory Education: An Appraisal of Evaluation Research.* Baltimore, Maryland: Johns Hopkins, 1969. R

Meier, John H., Glen Nimnicht and Oralie McAfee. "An Autotelic Responsive Environment Nursery School for Deprived Children." In *Disadvantaged Child: Head Start and Early Intervention*, Vol. 2, Jerome Hellmuth, ed., pp. 299–398. New York: Brunner/Mazel, 1968. R and C

Miller, Louise B., and Jean L. Dyer. *Experimental Variation of Head Start Curricula: A Comparison of Current Approaches.* Louisville: University of

Louisville, Psychology Department, Child Development Laboratory, 1970. R

Montessori, Maria. *Dr. Montessori's Own Handbook*. Cambridge, Mass.: Bentley, 1964. C

Montessori, Maria. *The Montessori Method*. New York: Schocken, 1965 (originally published in 1912). C

Painter, Genevieve. *Infant Education*. San Rafael, California: Dimensions Publishing, 1968. R

Palmer, Frances. "Learning at Two." *Children*, March–April 1969, pp. 55–57. R and C

Parker, Ronald K., Sueann Ambron, Gary I. Danielson, Mary C. Halbrook, and Janet A. Levine. *An Overview of Cognitive and Language Programs for 3, 4, and 5 year Old Children*. Monograph No. 4. Atlanta: Southeastern Education Laboratory, April 1970. R and C

The Preschool Program, Oakland, California, Preschool Program in Compensatory Education. Washington, D.C.: U.S. Department of Health, Education, and Welfare, Office of Education, Bureau of Elementary and Secondary Education, 1970. R

Prescott, Elizabeth, and Elizabeth Jones. *Group Day Care in a Child-Rearing Environment: An Observational Study of Day Care Programs*. Pasadena, California: Pacific Oaks College, 1967. R

Project Head Start: Evaluation and Research Summary, 1965–1967. Washington, D.C.: Office of Economic Opportunity, 1967. R

Radin, Norma. "The Impact of a Kindergarten Home Counseling Program." *Exceptional Children*, 36 (1969):251–56. R

Rambusch, Nancy McCormick. *Learning How to Learn*. Baltimore, Maryland. Helicon, 1962. C

Robinson, Halbert L. "The Frank Porter Graham Child Development Center." In *Early Child Care*, Laura L. Dittmann, ed., pp. 302–325. New York: Atherton Press, 1968. R

Robison, Helen F., and Bernard Spodek. *New Directions in the Kindergarten*. New York: Columbia University Teachers College, 1965. C

Schaefer, Earl S. "A Home Tutoring Program." *Children*, 16 (1969):59–60. R

Sears, Pauline S., and Edith M. Dowley. "Research in Teaching the Nursery School." In *Handbook of Research on Teaching*, N. L. Gage, ed., pp. 814–864. Chicago: Rand McNally, 1963. R

Seifert, Kevin. "Comparison of Verbal Interaction in Two Preschool Programs." *Young Children*, 24 (1969):350–355. R

Smilansky, Sara. *The Effects of Sociodramatic Play on Disadvantaged Preschool Children*. New York: Wiley, 1968. R

Smothergill, Nancy L., Frances A. Olson, and Shirley G. Moore. "The Effects of Manipulation of Teacher Communication Styles in the Preschool." *Child Development*, 42 (1971):1229–1239. 1972. R

Spicker, Howard, Walter L. Hodges, and Boyd R. McCandless. "A Diagnostically Based Curriculum for Psychosocially Deprived, Preschool Mentally

Retarded Children: Interim Report." *Exceptional Children*, *33* (1966):215–220. R

Springle, Herbert A. "Can Poverty Children Live on 'Sesame Street?'." *Young Children*, 26 (1971):202–217. R

Stanley, Julian C., ed. *Preschool Programs for the Disadvantaged*. Baltimore: Johns Hopkins University. 1972. R

Swift, Joan A. "Effects of Early Group Experience: The Nursery School and Day Nursery." In *Review of Child Development Research*, Martin Hoffman and Lois Wladis Hoffman, eds., pp. 249–288. R

Thompson, George G. "The Social and Emotional Development of Pre-School Children under Two Types of Education Programs." *Psychological Monographs*, 56, No. 5, 1944. Washington, D.C. R

Van deReit, Vernon, Hani Van deReit, and Herbert Springle. "The Effectiveness of a New Sequential Learning Program With Culturally Disadvantaged Preschool Children." *Journal of School Psychology* 7 (1968–1969):5–15. R

Wann, Kenneth, Mirian Selchen Dorn, and Elizabeth Ann Liddle. *Fostering Intellectual Development in Young Children*, New York: Columbia University Teachers College, 1962. C

Weikart, David P., Dennis J. Deloria, Sara A. Lawser, and Ronald Wiegerink. *Longitudinal Results of the Perry Preschool Project*. Ypsilanti, Michigan: High/Scope Educational Research Foundation, August 1970. R

Weikart, David P., Linda Rogers, Carolyn Adcock, and Donna McClelland. *The Cognitively Oriented Curriculum*. Urbana: University of Illinois, 1971. C

Wolff, Max, and Annie Stein. "Head Start Six Months Later." *Phi Delta Kappan*, 48 (1967):349–350. R

Zigler, Edward. "The Environmental Mystique." *Childhood Education*, 46 (1970):1–14. R

Zimiles, Herbert. "An Analysis of Current Issues in the Evaluation of Educational Programs." In *Disadvantaged Child: Head Start and Early Intervention*, Vol. 2, Jerome Hellmuth, ed., pp. 545–554. New York: Brunner/Mazel, 1968. R

Zimiles, Herbert. "Has Compensatory Education Evaluation Failed?" In *Disadvantaged Child: Compensatory Education, A National Debate*, Vol. 3, Jerome Hellmuth, ed., pp. 238–245. New York: Brunner/Mazel, 1970. R

Index

277

research results, 260–262

Failure, fear of, 208–209
Field trips, 74–75
Fingerpainting, 131–134
Free-play, 157–158
Freudian theory, 17–18

Group size, 10

Head Start, 3, 20, 247, 248, 262
Health care, 16–17
Holidays and celebrations, 79–82
Human body, 104–105
  physiology, 104, 105
  pregnancy, 105
  sex differences, 105

Imitaiton, 213
Instructional methods, didactic approach,
    22–23, 96–97, 257, 267
  discovery learning, 97
  incidental learning, 20, 22–24
  Montessori, 237–244
  open-school concept, 21
Intellectual development, see Cognitive
    development
IQ test, 258–260

Language development, 250–252, 266
  nonfluency, 252–253
  standard English, 251
  understanding and usage, 250–251
  vocabulary, 251
Language experiences, 46–49, 240
  books, 49–50
  conversations, 46–47
  storytelling, 48, 50
  word games, 44–45, 48–49
Learning theory, 18–19

Maps, 89–91
Mastery, 33, 158–160, 163–164
Materials, 9, 11, 23–24
  arts and crafts, 128, 130–131, 138
  independence and, 208
  Montessori, 237, 238, 239–241, 242, 244
  music, 144, 145, 147–150
  play, 157, 161
  self-correcting, 237, 238, 241, 244, 256

small-motor activity, 159
Motivation, intrinsic, 243–244
Motor development, 9, 158–160
Music, listening, 144, 146–147
  selecting, 142–143, 147–150
  singing, 141–144
  using instruments, 145–146

Observation, 267

Parent conferences, 228–232
  preparation for, 229
Parent participation, 11, 233, 256–257
Parent-teacher communication, 28, 199–200,
    221, 222–223, 240
Peer relations, 169–172, 175–182, 256
  aggression, 177–182
  friendliness, 175–176
Physical science, 110–117
  air currents, 114–115
  electricity, 112
  heat and light, 112–114
  water, clay and mud, 115–117
Piagetian theory, 249–250
Plants, 108–110
  care, 108
  growth, 109–110
  identification, 109
  uses, 109
Play, aggression in, 164–167
  cooperative, 172–173
  free play, 157–158
  learning and, 163
  parallel, 172
  role play, 161–167, 172–173
  sex role, 162
  teacher role in, 163
Premath experiences, 55–64, 240, 254
  development of number concept, 55–58
  fractions, 59
  goals of, 64
  measurement, 61, 64
  number games, 59–60
  number recognition, 60
  object manipulation, 58–59, 60
  writing numbers, 61
Prereading experinces, 50–55, 240
  books, 49–50
  discrimination training, 253–254
  goals of, 55